THE LOW CARBON WORLD OF ALCIDAE III

Greg Soroka

ISBN-978-1-77136-953-4

To my parents, who provided a household where there could be found the opportunity for education as well as the pursuit of individualistic and adventurous interests in nature and exploration.

"I may say that this is the greatest factor: the way in which the expedition is equipped, the way in which every difficulty is foreseen, and precautions taken for meeting or avoiding it. Victory awaits him who has everything in order, luck, people call it. Defeat is certain for him who has neglected to take the necessary precautions in time, this is called bad luck."

ROALD AMUNDSEN

CONTENTS

INTRODUCTION

My interests appear to be somewhat varied, which is reflected in this book.

The average reader will be readily capable joining my level of sophistication on most of the varied subject material within this book.

I consider the nautical level of competence that I have achieved to be the highest level that I have been able to achieve regarding any of my lifelong interests.

Several nautical subjects are presented within this book; however, I have assumed that the reader's nautical level is at a similar level as mine, thus explanations of basic nautical principles will not be found.

Lifestyle and personal philosophy choices implemented at an appropriate age are probably critical to any potential nautical, as well as general knowledge levels achieved.

Such lifestyle and personal philosophy choices that are useful regarding voyaging the worlds oceans under sail would include a lifelong thirst for knowledge, frugality, simplicity, prudence, healthy diet, appropriate routine physical exercise, intellectual honesty, and integrity.

Throughout this book I tend to use pronouns such as he, himself, and his which in no way indicates that the subject matter does not equally apply to all she is, herselves, and hers of the world.

Upon arrival back in Canada after my three offshore voyages, I was repeatedly asked if I was going to write a book to which I immediately responded in the negative -my brain appears to be one of those that are hard wired in the default to the negative response-.

Quietly, I had thought that what I had accomplished was not out of the ordinary and that I had nothing to add to the body of knowledge concerning sailing single-handed within some of the world's oceans.

Four years after I sold Alcidae III I started writing voyage reminiscences as a means of preserving and recalling some of my memories.

Once this process was started, I quickly found that during the writing process my mind was reliving these experiences and in a virtual sense I could see, hear, smell, and emotionally relive the physical surroundings upon which I was writing.

These experiences often contained natural settings in many locations throughout the world and I found the experience of their reliving to be very enjoyable.

The reader will become aware throughout this book that I did indeed keep detailed notes of many of my activities, however during the writing of this book I have found that it was not necessary to refer to these notes, possibly because the matters which I wish to present remain vivid and current in my mind.

Throughout this lifestyle my carbon footprint had not been part of my thought process, however in hindsight my nautical lifestyle has produced a minimum carbon footprint.

This minimum carbon footprint is based on paying the minimum for a second vessel, personally performing all necessary vessel modifications and repairs, a lifestyle which results in negligible garbage, and an at sea philosophy which on average results in the consumption of less than three hundred litres of diesel per year.

As noted, the original impetus to write this book was as a personal vehicle for recollection, however through writing this material, I am hoping it may also be of interest to other people, possibly not dissimilar to myself who have a broad spectrum of interests and live the slogan "lifelong learning".

I am hoping also that I have come to an incorrect presumption that few young people appear interested in this type of lifestyle and thus a major goal of this book is to attempt to inspire a young person to undertake the obligatory skill and lifestyle development necessary to achieve similar exploits.

I achieved my first offshore voyage of 12,000 nautical miles when I was forty-five years old, the second offshore voyage when I was fifty years old and commenced the third nine-year duration voyage when I was fifty-five years old.

It was apparent after I had reached sixty years of age that there was a noticeable decline in both my physical abilities as well as my willingness to push or even approach my established boundaries. Approaching such boundaries required courage and daring and it became obvious that in the vicinity of sixty-five years of age, this courage and daring had noticeably waned.

I am thus recommending that anyone encouraged to undertake similar nautical activities not to wait until they are over sixty years of age.

There is a valid argument that one must prepare financially for old age, I was fortunate to have achieved such a preparation during my lengthy training phase, as well as having developed a lifestyle which did not deplete financial resources.

This book and intended inspirational nudge are intended for both young males and females, throughout my nautical travels I have had the pleasure of meeting more practising and inspired nautical females than males.

This small group of mariners is composed of four single-handed French sailors who all happen to be female, and whose nautical skills both coastal and offshore are formidable.

Whereby their nautical skills are not dissimilar to mine, their culinary skills, and their ability to create gastronomic marvels using limited and simple food ingredients as well as doing so under less than ideal physical surroundings, is far superior to what I could develop in several lifetimes.

In addition, such prowess concerning culinary abilities is often shared by male French mariners, however I have not found such a high level of nautical savoir faire in the XY contingent, although it must be admitted that my sample number is small.

Of equal importance to the nautical skills is an adventuresome spirit, which is not to be dissuaded by the likelihood of violent weather and the resulting sea conditions, rather to be viewed as the successful joining with such forces and conditions which are to be considered as an opportunity to "live life in the present" and approach one's outer boundaries.

I realize that much of this book has been written from an opinionated and possibly contrarian point of view, those may well be my views.

Any nautical achievements I have completed may well be a direct result from such a point of view.

Yachties typically spend thousands if not hundreds of thousands of dollars before going offshore, and subsequently often spend much more due to the constant apparent necessity to return to their home countries.

These annual return trips often have a duration of at least six months, as well they are constantly destroying onboard equipment and often damaging the vessel itself, thus continually paying exorbitant fees to boatyard contractors around the world to repair and bottom paint their vessels.

They damage equipment and the vessel largely due to incompetence and a lack of valid experience, although they do carry extensive and expensive training course certification which they proudly exhibit to the Port Captains of the world.

Sailboats are typically not considered good investments because one puts vastly greater sums into the initial purchase, fitting out, and subsequent maintenance and repairs than will ever be realized upon the inevitable resale.

Thus, I recommend buying or constructing a vessel of modest price, learning the necessary maintenance and repair skills, accumulate the necessary tools and spare parts and develop the knowledge and attitude to live in a self-sufficient manner, weaned from the constant necessity to moor to a dock.

A small portion of the French mariners, for reasons that I do not totally understand, possess the skills about which I write, although this is a minority, the majority remain in the Yachtie category.

In the fall of 2009 I spent limited time with Christoph Auguin in Argentinian Patagonia at both Puerto Deseado and Mar Del Plata, to whom I asked, "Why do the French seem to produce more rough weather competent sailors"?

His response validated my own philosophy concerning becoming competent and comfortable in extreme weather by experiencing such weather in a progressively difficult training program, he had developed his in the English Channel.

What will follow is what has worked for me, which is not to imply that there are not other solutions to the same nautical situations.

Some readers may interpret the manual labour thrust of many of my nautical practices as possibly somewhat outdated, and therefore practices that should possibly be relegated to the past.

Sailing vessels and the nautical abilities of their crews reached their zenith during the eighteenth and nineteenth centuries.

These abilities which include mental outlook as well as skills, had been crafted and honed over the period of several centuries and included practices such as routine arduous physical labour, often performed during extremes of vessel motion, wind, cold, snow, and tropical heat.

Such arduous physical deck work was often performed within complete darkness, except when moonlight, star light, or the light emanating from the phosphorescence of breaking seas and the ship's wake, was gratuitously provided.

These mariners knew their ship, it is equipment, the location of handholds, and consciously or more likely subconsciously continuously monitored the motions of the ship and seas, which was obligatory because they, like me took the view that most of the deck work could not be effectively and safely performed while tethered to the ship.

Of course, some of these splendid mariners were lost overboard.

Are the isolated instances of man overboard a reasonable modern justification in remaining totally tethered to the modern sailing vessel?

Those mariners were the proud owners of the feeling and sense of the ship and the sea, which were in affect their tether.

I refer often to my inner voice and this is probably a metaphor for experience, however as the years went by, I suspect a minor and probably baseless metaphysical interpretation has crept into my outlook.

I have found that vessel speed and thus passage duration were not critical issues, rather the success of a passage rested on the answer to the question upon arrival.

Had I damaged the ship, any of its equipment, or myself.

PREFACE

The nautical portions of this book I have written using vocabulary directed at mariners who have attained a technical level like mine.

Other subject areas are written from an amateur's level; however, I have worked diligently to continually elevate my understanding and vocabulary within such subjects as botany, geology, and ornithology.

It is my main purpose to encourage young mariners to develop the necessary skills and experience to undertake such a potentially fulfilling and rewarding lifestyle.

This lifestyle, as well as being physically, emotionally, and spiritually sustainable, also leaves a minimal and sustainable environmental impact.

PHILOSOPHY

The Kanaga Island volcanic cone with Adak in the foreground.

I spent my formative years on the British Columbia coast, my maternal grand father was a very skilled coastal logger in the days just before steel mobile yarding spars were introduced.

The period of rigged wooden spar trees used for log

loading and yarding as well as several different skyline yarding systems, all required an intellectual capability as well as brute strength, possibly similar prerequisites are required for my version of single-handed sailing.

He rose to the rank of hooktender, which was the working supervisor on a coastal log yarding side.

This side can also be termed a log yarding site and included the services of a rigging crew made up of multiple chokermen, a rigging slinger, chaser, and yarding engineer.

The production, safety, and quality of work were all the responsibility of the side supervisor, namely the hooktender who in turn was responsible to a woods foreman who supervised multiple yarding sides.

My grandfather did not rise to exalted heights in the British Columbia coastal logging industry, again not overly dissimilar in that regard to my entire career spent enforcing, as a field inspector, British Columbia occupational health and safety standards.

The yarding sides had two stages, hand falling and bucking of timber followed by yarding.

The job of the chokerman was not dissimilar with respect to degree of physical danger than that experienced by the hand fallers, the rigging crew's main danger was from upending logs which were being yarded, and up slope material dislodged during yarding which could strike the crew.

There were often serious physical hazards to all members of the yarding crew and a major responsibility of my grandfather, the supervisor, was to ensure that this very hazardous work proceeded with maximum log production, minimum log damage during yarding and loading, and maximum safety of the crew.

The hooktenders at that time were not known for handling their charges in a gentle manner, were not concerned about verbal abuse allegations, nor of demanding hard physical work, this occurring well before the time of political correctness or bullying concerns.

My grandfather was not only knowledgeable and able to perform all the necessary skills of each of his crew, but in addition, was required to rig the wooden yarding trees, log loading spars, back line yarding lift spars, many variations of skyline systems, and rig the numerous yarding spar guy line stumps.

During my childhood and teenage years, his physically demanding lifestyle, intellectually aggressive nature, and his admiration and knowledge of limited aspects of the natural world commanded my respect and admiration.

I have had the good fortune in my early life to have met most of my immediate fore-bearers and I am confident that a major portion of what was to become my internal drive and tenacity to learn and master single-handed sailing, in the very physical and basic manner achieved, was also expressed in this grandfather.

His physical and mental aggressiveness as well as impatience, regarding natural and man-made obstacles, also appears in my demeanour and I have little doubt that these innate attributes played a significant role in my survival in both my training and execution phases of what were to become my nautical ambitions.

I have throughout my entire sailing endeavours -1978 to 2015- developed several mental outlooks which have enriched and stabilized the lifestyle.

I have made three offshore voyages, twelve months duration in 1995-1996 totalling approximately 12,000 nautical miles, fourteen months duration in 2000-2001 totalling approximately 14,000 nautical miles, and 2004-2014 totalling approximately 40,000 nautical miles.

I termed the first two voyages as training voyages whose main purpose was to provide training and experience so that my goal, the third voyage, could be achieved.

Enjoyment, fulfillment, and satisfaction from sailing some of the world's oceans is embodied by the act of being physically propelled through the water by only the energy found in the wind.

This includes sailing against strong head winds, which provides the greatest degree of personal satisfaction.

Upon reading the section concerning furling gear versus hank-on sails, the reader may forsake that there is just too much physical work.

On occasion there is indeed significant physical exertion, which is required to work the ship, whether such exertion is performed sailing the vessel in the water or repairing and maintaining the vessel in the boatyard or at sea, are all equally rich in satisfaction.

I developed the thought process that all necessary work whether performed on deck, in the water, or on dry land was to be considered working the ship, and as such was equally enjoyable and fulfilling as that experienced sailing the seas.

On deck, at sea working the ship, duties to be embraced included robust physical work associated with changing and stowing of hank-on head sails, reefing and unreefing the mainsail, rigging, lowering, stowing, and gybing the telescoping whisker pole, rowing out and retrieving additional anchors along with associated lengths of chain, and the attachment and removal of shorelines.

Therefore, labour saving devices such as electric sheet or halyard winches, nor any form of furling sails were to be found on any of my vessels.

I have found that two sets of related, however partially separate mariner skill sets are required, open coastal and offshore.

It turns out that the offshore skills are considerably easier to master than the necessary high latitude open coastal skills.

Thus, before embarking on my first offshore passage in 1995, I underwent my lengthy coastal skills training program, beginning with the purchase of my first sailboat in 1978.

Yachties I have met often like to speak of their training courses and other certificate documented skills, however the most important level of qualification is provided when they simply describe where they have been.

I endeavour to experience nature in a form which approaches how it is, therefore, I must also accept that my aspirations and actions must be aligned with natures forces and therefore must be modified as nature's forces dictate.

The Yachtie preference of planning a passage route and timing to align with the least challenging locations and times of the year with respect to possible wind and sea conditions, results often in simply riding downwind on the trade winds.

This common method probably explains the reason why many ocean sailors are 20/20 harbour hoppers, that majority that seem to circumnavigate and make ocean crossings only within the above noted latitude band, then traversing higher latitudes only using the practice of harbour hopping within 'weather windows', usually with the assistance of a relatively powerful motor and the latest professional weather reports.

Such an artificially constricted philosophy often results in a completion of a circumnavigation having only slightly augmented the mariner's skills, compared to when the voyage was initiated.

I am proposing that adverse weather rather than being avoided should be embraced, although this does not infer that one should ever enter or remain in a hurricane zone during its active season.

The ability to continually coast downwind in moderate winds is one criterion, whereas achieving the status of mariner is quite another.

When one embarks into the higher latitudes and well out of the trade wind belts, one is certain to encounter temporary and possibly frequent adverse conditions.

My basic definition of adverse conditions would include not being able to point at your desired goal due to wind direction as well as high wind velocities and the sea conditions that such winds generate.

Adverse currents can also become very frustrating, these currents are not always accurately fixed by pilot charts but can be rather ephemeral and are often encountered on a windward leg, thus habitually sailing downwind also removes much of this natural occurring adversity.

Venturing into higher latitudes early in the spring season will provide the maximum cruising time within these latitudes, however it is not without challenging periods which may result in contrary wind, contrary current, proximity to freezing spray, periods of calm, or seemingly nonstop passing depressions which generate wind and sea conditions which necessitate significant and sustained defensive action.

I have found that the greater the challenge encountered, the greater the ensuing sense of achievement and fulfillment when the conditions change to favourable and then again when the passage is successfully completed. Recall, that the goal during the adverse period is based on the philosophy of precluding damage to the vessel, equipment, and crew.

This goal's consistent achievement requires harmony with the ocean's forces, patience, the necessary skills, and experience.

My most difficult passage was the forty-nine-day passage from Kerguelen to Tasmania and the sense of accomplishment I am describing was experienced when I redirected the ship's heading to the north, finally putting Whale Head located at the southeast corner of Tasmania between myself and the Indian Ocean.

This passage did not provide adverse wind, current, or the proximity to freezing spray, however I did encounter seven consecutive gales which produced far more fair wind and the resulting fifteen-meter seas than I or the vessel could utilize while still maintaining some semblance of control.

Thus, throughout this passage, an inordinate amount of time was spent in the defensive posture of submission, it is important to develop a hunker down attitude which persists the duration of whatever period is dictated by the physical conditions.

Contrast this philosophy with the high-tech ocean racers who taunt nature by attempting to traverse such oceans often at or beyond the outer limits of vessel con-

trol, knowing and expecting that if disaster arrives due to such a negligent and irresponsible attitude, organizations such as the worlds navies, freighters, or commercial fishing vessels will be obligated to provide rescue.
They view an approaching intense low from the point view of which side should it be permitted to pass; the goal is the provision of fair wind rather than when should I pause and protect the ship and crew.
My route from Africa to Tasmania passed within sight of both the Crozet Islands, Kerguelen, and passed just sixty nautical miles north of Heard Island which was almost the exact route routinely sailed by the magnificent clipper ships and crews plying the 19th century wool, tea, and grain trades, however they were built, designed, and equipped with a full compliment of competent crew, the sum of which produced a ship which could utilize the strong winds and resulting seas without the requirement to stop and take defensive action.
Upon arrival at Tasmania, I had not fully achieved my goal of no injury to the crew, vessel, or equipment, although the cause was not my incompetence as a mariner, rather the insufficient initial construction standards I had accepted concerning my vessel, which must point to my limited competence concerning vessel selection.
Very soon after leaving Kerguelen, I discovered I had pulled the corrosion weakened staysail tab welded to the foredeck, as well as a similar hidden interior corrosion issue concerning the port aft lower shroud deck mounted steel anchor tab.
This structural failure rendered both stays unusable and the resulting deck openings immediately permitted sea water to enter the vessel, the openings were plugged

with epoxy putty.

As well, my stainless-steel transom arch which holds my two solar panels, wind generator, high frequency radio antennas, GPS antenna, high frequency antenna tuner, and radar dome was physically broken in three locations, however the transom arch was my fabrication and my welding portion of the fabrication had already successfully performed for a period of fifteen years and several thousand nautical miles.

It appears that construction and maintenance standards which are sufficient in other regions of the world's oceans are not passable in the Southern Oceans.

The necessary repairs which would permit me to pass through the entire length of the Tasman Sea and the remainder of the South Pacific Ocean, then onward to the Bering Sea and thus back to the west coast of Canada required only one day of my own steel repair while tied alongside in Hobart.

The tiny boatyard where I performed the repairs, was arranged by Jeanne Socrates of sv Nereida, who appears to have an almost infinite number of contacts.

Jeanne was in Hobart at the time and we had been in radio contact during my entire passage from Kerguelen.

The expression "living in the present", is well known, it is opposite may be termed multitasking.

Living in the present turns out to be exceedingly difficult to achieve for periods of time lengthier than a few seconds.

Sailing the worlds oceans has provided ample opportunity to lengthen these intermittent, elusive, and truncated periods of living in the present.

Various instances of sailing and anchoring during challenging conditions requires bursts of complete and focused concentration -living in the present- in conjunction with the necessary physical effort to ensure their successful achievement.

The first snatches of living in the present I experienced in the late 1970's when I would leave for a Georgia Strait weekend from Vancouver's Coal harbour for an adventure on my first sailing vessel, a twenty-four-foot fibreglass sloop “Alcidae”.

I found that I experienced a sense of fulfillment, accomplishment, and what I would later term living in the present when reefing the mainsail, replacing sails on the fore deck, developing, and utilizing single-handed anchoring techniques, or successfully performing immediately required and unforeseen structural, mechanical, or electrical repairs.

Scheduled boat yard repairs and maintenance also proved to be almost as enjoyable, possibly because their successful completion appeared to turn the page to the next chapter of nautical learning and advancement.

It is troubling when one’s vessel is near or just over the point of control, but relative comfort and satisfaction return when the necessary adjustments have been made and the vessel is again underway and back within an acceptable zone of control.

A mariner must learn through experience how to recognize the arrival of the point of control, this also requires a progressively rigorous training program.

Such progressive learning appears to assist in the creation of an inner voice, to which one develops a sense of confidence and ultimately obedience.

Due to the perceived necessity to create a financial base as well as an old age retirement package, I spent seventeen years accumulating the necessary nautical training and experience, although a similar amount of nautical skill could probably be achieved in a third of this time assuming one is following a concentrated training regime.

The progressive training program must commence with coastal onshore skills, many of which must be considered obligatory before their augmentation with offshore skills.

The initial years witnessed an almost physical sense of contentment, peace, freedom, anticipation, and fulfillment experienced essentially every time I left the dock and similarly later in my sailing career when I left an anchorage and directed the pointy end of the vessel towards the open sea and a lengthy ocean passage.

On many occasions during my last circumnavigation the conditions for arriving and leaving open coasts were far from ideal.

It is intuitive that the ideal time for leaving an anchorage and heading for the open sea would be in the hands of the mariner, there is some truth to this generality however in practice I found myself making for the sea to begin a passage, -often which was to be more than a thousand miles duration-, leaving the anchorage in conditions such as darkness, wind, rain, snow, or fog.

The actual departure time was controlled principally by the prospect of achieving a safe offing, which ideally include initial fair winds, a favourable tidal current and possibly some reduction in open ocean onshore seas.

These criteria often make it necessary to put to sea during adverse lighting and weather conditions, however there is no mistaking the sense of pride and accomplishment consistently experienced upon having safely achieved a successfully offing.

Perversely, my own degree of satisfaction may be related to the difficulty experienced while gaining a successful offing.

I have often found myself leaving just after the passage of a cold front, which almost guarantees a known direction of wind for a substantial period, although during high latitudes open coastal sailing local knowledge is often not available, thus one may hope to have initial fair winds, but the reality may be somewhat different.

Under such a situation the mariner will find themselves contending with an immediate beat into the wind on an open lee shore, although with prior planning, it may be possible to retreat and try another day.

If the departure wind direction is towards the safety of the open sea, the attraction to leave I have found irresistible, regardless of conditions often present immediately following cold front passage such as violent gusty wind, heavy snow, hail, or rain.

Such departures do not always include daylight; thus, the mariner must be comfortable with such conditions in darkness and have gained a suitable level of confidence and competence with navigation aids such as radar and GPS.

Throughout my sailing I did not have an electronic pilot onboard, such units have inputs such as radar and GPS, however in hindsight, such a pilot display would indeed be useful although the basic navigation skills discussed later are still required.

These initial potentially agitated ocean conditions are made more challenging because the vast majority of mariners subsequent to a lengthy period at anchorage, substantially lose their sea-legs, along with the required high level of balance and stamina, thus the sense of fear, nausea, dry mouth, and even loose bowels that the temporary seasickness syndrome can induce, must be foreseen and dealt with, thus a high probability of receiving an initial offshore wind is critical and should not to be squandered.

On the 3rd of March 1886 Joshua Slocum was leaving the Straits of Magellan in darkness with a favourable northeast wind.

Such a wind would likely have provided Slocum with a beam reach on a starboard tack, as well as relatively calm seas, the wind would have been off the land.

The entrance of the Straits of Magellan could probably rarely be considered as calm, however the wind generated waves should have been slight during Slocum's departure.

I am presuming he also had in his favour the tide and that the seas at this world-famous entrance were temporarily manageable, although he could not have called the Chilean Naval station -now at the entrance- and requested a sea condition report.

The point is, that he was leaving in darkness utilizing as many favourable factors as he could manage.

He had no radio, professional weather forecasting, GPS, detailed chart, nor motor.

Slocum writes that shortly after exiting into the Pacific Ocean his experience -possibly inner voice- told him that this might not have been an opportune time for leaving on a passage because he probably soon encountered a heavy swell and thickening cloud to the northwest, which was probably visible even in darkness.

He states, "there was no turning back even had I wished to do so, for the land was now shut out by the darkness of night."

This metaphor that a door and route of escape has been closed, is not a comfortable thought.

I am confident that if he had a weather forecast, he would have postponed his trip, and if he had radar he would have turned around and safely re-entered the Straits of Magellan, but thus began a most extraordinary five days at sea.

Slocum's experiences during the next five days prior to finding shelter several hundred miles to leeward indicate that in addition to stamina, endurance, ability, courage, and well-maintained equipment, a tiny modicum of luck may also be a useful passenger.

Slocum also added that he drove the ship to windward if possible, to gain sea room, aware that he was demanding maximum endurance from the vessel, it is the inner voice that notifies the mariner when the maximum capability of the vessel has been reached, during such windward beats.

As noted elsewhere, such unexpected as well as vessel straining windward beats may be required because one doe not often possess local knowledge of the actual wind direction which will be encountered due to local effects such as inlets, capes, tidal currents, and local mountains.

This is a price that must occasionally be paid by an isolated high latitude open coast mariner; however, the mariner must have extensive prior experience which will dictate just how much extra sail and extra list is necessary to provide the required forward drive, containing sufficient force to power the vessel through what are likely to be rough and irregular seas.

Slocum also made the humble admission "Confidentially, I was seasick!" during these first few hours in the darkness immediately after leaving the relatively protected waters of Magellan Straits into the open Pacific Ocean.

Fear and apprehension, I have found also contribute to seasickness, especially within such proximity as Slocum's to an unseen and dangerous lee shore.

It is a further tribute to Slocum that he was sufficiently ingenuous to admit such a temporary malady such as seasickness.

My purpose for adding this reference is because Slocum, who's calibre of mariner under sail is no longer encountered, also appeared to use a similar criterion of achieving the open ocean such as I have advocated, which is the possibility of leaving during inclement weather and darkness with the plan to achieve an offing under fair winds.

I have found making high latitude landfalls whether on an open continental coast or isolated islands, does not always provide the option of choosing the most favourable conditions, ideal conditions in high latitudes seldom persist for long periods of time.

Timing the most favourable conditions is not a difficult issue in trade wind belts when one can often closely predict vessel arrival times, often to include a favourable tidal current into a lagoon.

Cold front passage, low pressure system passage, and passing or stable high pressure wind patterns are highly predictable in the open ocean, however when one approaches and enters the region of coastal influence local effects such as actual entrance area wind direction, wind strength, visibility, shelving bottoms ability to create hazardous breaking seas, ocean wave generated surge, tidal current, coastal ocean swell reflection patterns, and wind in opposition to tidal current effects are not always accurately predictable and thus need be anticipated.

It is always an option to wait for optimal conditions before attempting the landfall, however practically other considerations seem often required.

I habitually applied an offshore X on the ocean chart and termed this X my arrival point, upon arrival in the vicinity of X, I could then decide to postpone the landfall or if a relatively small island I could elect to pass by. After passing this arbitrary X one becomes committed to the landfall, or possibly, if in a following sea and moderate wind one has the option to beating back to seaward.

Turning back to windward when making a lee shore landfall is not always an option due to wind strength and sea conditions thus commitment after the X position is an important decision.

The arrival destination X will be placed at different distances from the open coast landfall location depending on several factors.

Kerguelen was one of my most challenging landfalls, however the Chilean Patagonian coast and Aleutian Islands also present similar challenges.

At Kerguelen, I placed my arrival X three degrees of longitude to the west, which at this latitude equates to one hundred and eighteen nautical miles and was adjacent to the midpoint of the exposed west coast of Kerguelen. Specifically, my Kerguelen decision location was to be one hundred and eighteen nautical miles directly adjacent to the west end of that ecological gem named Ile d'Ouest.

Due to vessel drift towards a lee shore while hove-to

during high wind conditions, few long-term options for the singlehanded sailor to protect the ship during prolonged arrival point waiting periods, exist.

Waiting for more moderate or favourable conditions to arrive, heaving-to utilizing appropriate sails is my first choice however potential for a knockdown, luffing sail damage and leeway must all be constantly monitored because the leeward distance to the lee shore will be constantly diminishing and the point will be reached whereby it may be difficult to point at either extreme point of the island, in my Kerguelen example the northwest or southwest capes.

It must be remembered that near the end of what may have been a lengthy and difficult passage, one's decision-making ability may be less than optimum; thus, it is sound planning to prepare the arrival point and the bypass point well prior to arrival.

In the case of Kerguelen, even though I was still one hundred and eighteen nautical miles offshore, I thought I could feel Captain Cooke's presence, who had anchored for a few weeks at the northwest cape approximately two hundred and fifty years previously.

It was one of my many ships rules that I would not allow the vessel to enter a position whereby the apparent wind direction would be forward of a port or starboard beam reach.

If the apparent wind were permitted to become forward of the beam it could be difficult to ask the ship to stand up to such wind and seas, as well under such conditions I would not rely on the motor.

I will later introduce the concept of the mariner's arrival mental state of mind but will now introduce the mariner's physical state.

I have found that if I do not receive as regularly as possible, uninterrupted six-to-eight-hour periods of sleep, regular diet, regular exercise, regular radio contact and entertainment, it is likely after a lengthy ocean passage that I will arrive offshore in a mental and physical condition in which I am not likely to make the most useful or timely critical decisions.

The uninterrupted sleep is not possible every night but must be made possible most nights.

This does not mean that one cannot often be woken for a few minutes, to aurally monitor conditions from within the confines of one's bunk, however confidence must be achieved in the effectiveness of electronic aids such as the watchman mode on radar and a cockpit mounted low powered strobe light.

Presently mariners also have the powerful anti ship collision aid of AIS -Global Ship Tracking-, however numerous commercial vessels travel with disabled AIS equipment.

These systems are not fool proof but do greatly reduce the odds of a collision with another ship.

No aids to navigation including additional crew members, completely removes the possibility of a collision with partially or entirely submerged debris, although a steel hull greatly reduces the odds of serious hull damage.

One also often has the option to slow the vessel during hours of darkness or hours of sleep, however I have not found this option overly attractive.

Regular diet in my context includes routine eating times as well as a regular menu.

My regular menu may not be sustainable for people with a more varied, sensitive, and sophisticated pallet;

however, the human body does not seem to mind a repetitive diet, which if preferable need only be applied at sea.

I have also incorporated into me at sea routine, regular exercise of the same frequency and duration as on land. Such exercises entail running on the spot for twenty minutes followed by three complete cycles through a routine designed to maintain strength, flexibility and endurance, the entire process is completed in forty-five minutes.

One learns to stabilize oneself during exercise workouts by wedging the body into various locations on the sole, so that ship's motion becomes somewhat immaterial.

These routines could and were interrupted or even cancelled due to temporary weather conditions or immanent landfall, however most of the time they were completed as scheduled.

I did find after my return to Canada after my nine-year duration third voyage which included several long passages and lengthy intervals spent in very isolated locations, that I was in a somewhat less than acceptable physical and possibly mental state.

These physical and psychological issues were rectified after six months in Canada, thus the specifics of my exercise and diet plan may well require improvement although the physical issues possibly would have been ameliorated by a more frequent use of multi vitamins.

Regular human contact via radio, email, and musical selections were maintained throughout all three offshore voyages.

Sailmail and Winlink served in an effective manner for essentially daily emails from my Patricia, regardless of my position in the world's oceans.

The SSB radio along with the required amateur radio licence certification, could be obligatory prerequisites for offshore sailing.
The appropriate radio certification is obligatory for maritime mobile net participation, where as certification is not required concerning reception of weather surface analysis maps, grib files, and voice contact with other mariners, coast guards, navies, and related authorities.
The world's ham radio operators are a gift to offshore sailors, such operators are generous with their time, equipment, and assistance, however the offshore sailor is morally and legally obligated to comply with the basic licensing requirements.

The most frequent criticism I have encountered concerning singlehanded sailing is my physical inability to maintain a 'live body' twenty-four-hour watch.
A universal requirement of offshore sailing courses which are successfully completed by the majority of Yachties, requires the mariner to always maintain a twenty-four-hour visual watch.
This does not work for a singlehanded sailor; however, it also does not appear to work so well for two or even three person crews, such small size crews also typically arrive after nothing more challenging than trade wind passages and the entire crew is in a condition of physical exhaustion due to inadequate and interrupted periods of sleep.
Arriving in less than optimum mental and physical condition is almost a guarantee for making poor decisions, just when the landfall -which is possibly the most dangerous part of the passage- must be completed.
The optimum physical and mental level of alertness is

also critical throughout the passage, critical decisions are constantly required concerning sail deployment, reefing, and storm management as well as the constant awareness necessary to prevent slips and falls with their related high potential for physical injury.

The optimum state of mind approaches an attitude of ambivalence whether landfall is made tomorrow or next week.

There should not be a fixation to reach land, the landfall will be just as pleasant a bit further into the future.

It is often heard that "I must make landfall before the arrival of an approaching storm", the implication is the perceived need to proceed faster and this results in the increased probability of making a less than considered and controlled landfall.

Therefore, the nurturing of the recommended state of mind of becoming comfortable at sea even in storm conditions, is recommended.

The goal is to arrive off an open coast landfall whether as part of a crew or single-handed in the most perceptive mental condition and well rested physical state possible.

I often refer to my inner voice and this source of advice has become a more dominant component in my decision making in direct proportion to my age and experience.

When I was young, I essentially disregarded this inner voice, middle age found me at least considering this seemingly ephemeral source of direction and somewhere between fifty and fifty-five years of age found me essentially completely compliant.

I am now confident that without my lengthy nautical practical training program there would either be no inner voice, or possibly there might have been an inner voice, but it would have provided only trivial suggestions.

In my earlier years I took several hundred photos, however I came to the realization in my thirties that I had merely stored boxes of printed photos and thirty-five-millimetre slides but rarely if ever, viewed these images. Thus, I essentially gave up photography and during my three voyages have never owned a digital camera but rather continued to use my old Pentax analog camera, exposing a single roll of twenty-four exposures per year.

I had determined that I would hence forth attempt to more fully experience the sighting experience immediately, to store the visual, aural, and other sensual recollections into my memory.

The theory proposed, this action would also encourage me live in the present as opposed to fiddling with a camera, several years later this remains my philosophy.

SEAMANSHIP

I was raised in a family situation with no access to sailboats and I was 28 years old before setting foot on a bay racing sailboat as a member of the crew.

I was permitted to join the racing crew not because of any nautical experience or ability that I possessed, rather I was relatively strong and robust and able to haul on jib and mainsail sheets, as well as operate sheet winches.

I quickly found that it was much quicker to manually haul on a sheet with two or three wraps on a winch until at least eighty percent of the desired result was achieved, as opposed to slowly grinding away with a winch handle, thus robustness was an asset.

I performed these duties for two winter racing seasons and found it distasteful.

Rather than paying attention to the race I would often find myself gazing out to the open water on Georgia Strait.

I found most distasteful the almost total disregard for the well being of the gear and boat, versus finishing closer to first place.

I had previously observed sailboats in Vancouver's harbour since I was quite young, the possibilities of this type of activity had then first crossed my mind.

The second time it entered my mind -this time to stay-,

was a seminal moment on a solo hitch-hiking trip in 1972 between London and Tanzania's Lake Victoria by way of France, Spain, all North Africa, and the River Nile.

I was about to board a ferry from southern Spain to Ceuta in Morocco, early in the morning after sleeping in a park in this coastal Spanish city, I saw what I then perceived as an older lady in a bikini hanging up her laundry on the foredeck of a sailboat.

It appeared, she had most of what seemed important to her onboard, thus from mid June 1972 until I sold my third sailboat Alcidae III in March of 2016, navigating the worlds oceans singlehanded became my principal motivation in life.

I bought my first sailboat which was a lightly built twenty-four-foot fibreglass sloop in early September 1978, just six months after I began a position in the field of occupational health and safety which I was to hold for just over twenty-five years.

Also, at that time, I had just started romancing a lady who was to become my lifelong partner and who unfortunately is in the group of what I estimate to be less than ten percent of the human population who when at sea in a small boat become seasick when sea conditions approach what I term force six seas and remain so until conditions become almost completely calm.

Patricia never gave up on me and always supported my pathway towards my declared purpose in life, during the coastal and early offshore training periods she was to suffer numerous episodes of seasickness until we finally came up with an improved arrangement just after the start of the first ocean training voyage which was to be a twelve-month duration trip to French Polynesian in 1995.

The improved arrangement turned out to be Patricia would fly and I would sail, thus at the end of my third voyage I had completed what I perceived to be my main purpose in life and still maintained my lifelong partner.

Early during the first French Polynesian adventure, Patricia became very seasick off Cape Mendocino in northern California and demanded to be put ashore, thus in three days I landed her in Monterey.

The three day at sea delay was a result of my first offshore experience of placing a vessel into a defensive posture, I intuitively knew at the time there would be many more.

We had been among what I would even now consider impressively rough and dangerous seas in the region of Cape Mendocino, which were caused by that 1030 to 1040 millibar high which often can be found approximately five hundred nautical miles offshore.

At that time during the first offshore voyage, I did not yet know that I should have cuddled up more closely to the high's centre, until such time that I encountered manageable seas and reduced northwest winds, thus we suffered a bit.

I did not consider this experience as suffering, rather as a preview for what the anticipated future was likely to provide, I was not mistaken.

I was somewhat concerned by these large and dangerous seas however was keen to learn the appropriate defensive action which would greet them in a safe and harmonious manner.

Patricia advised me that she was returning to Victoria by plane from Monterey and inquired as to my intentions, to which I responded that my next stop would be

Nuku-Hiva in the Marquesas.

Thirty days after leaving Monterey I arrived at Nuku-Hiva in the northern Marquesas, and the single-handed ocean sailor that I had hoped was always present, had been born.

It was a very gratifying moment during that first ocean passage when I realized I adored the lifestyle I had dreamed of.

My first tropical landing was to be in the nine-foot rigid fibreglass rowing skiff which was to be put to excellent use during all three offshore voyages.

This first tropical landing was on the swelly, frothy warm soft sand, coconut, Casurina, Tamanu, Frangiopani, and Barringtonia lined beach in Taiohae Bay.

My enduring memories of this landing are composed of the welcoming warm tropical air that carried the pervasive fragrance of Frangiopani.

Frangiopani is in the botanical family Apocynaceae which only contains three species of small herbaceous plants in British Columbia, however this same family in the tropical pacific islands contains several exceptionally beautiful trees who almost universally contain very toxic and phytoactive compounds.

In Taiohae Bay at daybreak, one was greeted by the humid warmth, sound of gentle surge ascending the beach, ubiquitous wood fire smoke generated by early morning cooking fires and the ongoing crowing of roosters, all probably little different from what Herman Melville would have experienced on a whaling ship just over a century before when the whaling vessel from which he deserted, was also anchored in the same bay.

Upon landing for the first time at the end of this first offshore passage I experienced the unfamiliar necessity to immediately sit down due to temporary nausea and loss of balance, which is caused by the body having become one with the motion of the sea.

I then made my way along the beach to the rustic motel where Patricia had found lodging, she had arrived via air a week earlier, I was ordered to have a shower before I was permitted to fulfill my seemingly urgent amorous intentions.

Ten months later, after we had voyaged as far west as Bora Bora via the northern Tuamotus, Tahiti, Moorea, Huahine, Raiatea, and Tahaa and then returned to Nuku Hiva via Moorea, Tahiti, the central Tuamotus, Fatu Hiva, Tahuata, and Hiva Oa, I was to drop Patricia off in the same location where ten months earlier we had been reunited.

Afterwards, and thirty-four days out of Anaho Bay, located on the north side of Nuku Hiva, I was to find myself tying up in Victoria after having left Hawaii six hundred nautical miles to port.

I made a second training voyage in the spring of 2000, again into the Pacific Ocean and again crossing south of the equator, of fifteen months duration, and concluding with my first trip to the Aleutians Island chain after having left Japan one thousand nautical miles to port.

Shortly after buying the first sailboat in 1978, I started single handing the twenty-four-foot fibreglass sloop, first in Vancouver's Burrard Inlet, and then Georgia Strait.

I made many errors and damaged sails and gear but continually improved and continually increased the wind velocity within which I felt confident.

It was even then my goal to become habituated, confident, and feel secure in weather and sea conditions that were as violent as possible, thus as time passed my maximum wind threshold moved continually higher.

In those early days I considered Georgia Strait as a formidable stretch of water, however later it was to become somewhat trivial.

I would learn challenging entrances to several anchorages and found that I experienced the new gratification of entering under sail and during adverse conditions.

This source of gratification was to persist for my entire forty-year sojourn into sailing.

In this manner I increased the wind velocity into which I would purposely venture until in 1989 when we lived in the British Columbia north coast town of Prince Rupert and sailed an adored Spencer 31, when I was to reach the maximum wind velocity into which I would purposely enter.

This memorable occasion saw us at the south end of Chatham Sound leaving the Lawyer Island light station to starboard, Tim a long term and dear friend was onboard for what was to be the only time and continues to remember the details.

Lawyer Island during that period was a manned light station and had just reported the wind velocity as sixty-three knots and gusting.

I found the resulting sea and wind conditions permitted me only to go to leeward under a storm jib, the spray made it difficult to see further than a quarter of a mile and if necessary, it would not be possible to make a course to windward, thus one must find one's way into shelter to leeward.

I thus established what was to become a lifelong ships rule, sailing in winds more than fifty-five knots I must never permit myself to be too close to a lee shore unless downwind shelter was available which could be entered under sail.

During the ensuing years I was to successfully enter and anchor on several occasions within such wind velocities in conjunction with poor visibility, however I always assessed these actions on calculated decisions which considered visibility, tidal current, and the possession of the obligatory local knowledge.

There would be two serious near miss occasions in Chilean Patagonia where I did not have local knowledge and would violate this ship's rule.

It was a common practice during the training portion of my program whereby in calm weather I would anchor at the outer entrance of a shallow, rocky, kelp strewn, and convoluted anchorage entrance, then use the skiff for access to generate a hand drawn chart complete with natural shoreline marks such as notable trees, peculiar geological formations and if required, self generated range marks composed of similar natural objects.

Once such a chart was created, implemented, and mastered, safe entry could and would be achieved under particularly challenging circumstances including strong winds, fog, and darkness with the assistance of a powerful handheld flashlight.

The six-year period that I sailed out of Prince Rupert resulted in several such hand drawn charts concerning challenging entrances on both sides of Hecate Strait, Dixon Entrance, Chatham Sound and several other remote channels and islands.

Throughout my early and middle sailing training years I added many what my inner voice was to regard as ships rules.

In sequence with acquired nautical experience, unsolicited inner voice recommendations would be presented, such advice appeared to attempt to provide timely advice concerning approaching lee shores, safely leaving anchorages, acquiring a safe offing, appropriate circumstances to add and reduce sail, when to heave-to, when to deploy the series drogue, when to deploy an additional anchor or shoreline as well as when to increase anchor rode scope.

Early in my nautical training I did not always heed such inner voice advice, however during my later mariner years I discovered I had become essentially completely obedient to this inner voice.

The training portion of one's mariner endeavours must include skills of increasing complexity, always exploring the location of, and trying to increase one's upper limits.

To improve one must explore the boundaries of one's abilities and once found and established these boundaries may be expanded until a suitable level of confidence and ability is achieved.

I found I could not establish the actual maximum boundary limits unless these limits were physically approached and exceeded.

Does this philosophy render one vulnerable to the criticism of going looking for storms or potentially dangerous situations?

Yes, it does, because this is purposely the course of action being pursued and it is being pursued with a definite goal in mind.

It was during the winter seasons of the six years that I sailed out of Prince Rupert in my Spencer 31 that I truly learned many of the obligatory lessons of coastal sailing which routinely included conditions such as high winds, agitated seas, poor visibility, strong tidal currents, occasional poorly charted waters and numerous hazardous shoals and rocks.

Recall that two separate sets of skills are required for successful high latitudes voyaging, coastal and offshore.

During the first twelve years of my nautical training, I used only an appropriate nautical chart, clock, compass, sounding line and estimated vessel speed to determine my position.

In 1990 I bought my first LORAN and depth sounder and I still remember the sense of empowerment provided by the LORAN's provision of an X on the chart, which represented my position and it kindly did so regardless of visibility, sea condition, or wind strength.

The LORAN's capabilities were first fully appreciated during my second crossing of Hecate Strait to just offshore in the mist of the still hidden Haida Guaii.

These electronic aids were not added as replacements for the basic compass, chart, clock, estimated speed, and sounding line but rather as powerful additional tools.

Later the LORAN would be replaced by the GPS along with the extremely powerful navigation tool of radar.

During the Prince Rupert years, multiple day, and night crossings of Hecate Strait under a variety of weather conditions provided significant experience, this body of water must be considered as protected but is not trivial due to frequent strong winds, poor visibility, relatively shallow water, and strong tidal currents.

Such are the conditions which must be mastered to achieve a suitable competence level regarding coastal sailing skills

Post glacial sea level rise has provided both sides of Hecate strait with a significant number of all weather anchorages which are both secure and difficult to enter due to shallow water, extensive patches of kelp, strong tidal currents, and submerged rocks.

I improved and built on navigating and mariner basics through practical experience, however early in my sailing career I took what turns out to be one of the most useful courses of my life, which was the Basic Boating course offered at that time by the Canadian Power Squadrons where I first learned imperative theoretical skills such as aids to navigation, tides, and charting.

It became evident that my self-directed training program had succeeded when I first went offshore on the French Polynesian trip in the spring of 1995, it would be confirmed that I was already comfortable and sufficiently skilled in all aspects of vessel handling during high winds and rough conditions and had only to acquire the experience of long continuous periods at sea, along with open ocean seas and storm management strategies.

Unfortunately, many Canadian west coast sailors leave the Strait of Juan de Fuca bound for San Francisco or other west coast ports who do not have adequate nautical skills nor experience.

Some significant percentage become overtaken by seasickness, strong winds, and high seas only to make a radio emergency call to the US Coast Guard and plead to be rescued.

The US Coast Guard does indeed provide a significant number of such annual rescues, however occasionally such rescue attempts result in injuries and even fatalities to Coast Guard members.

The offending sailors usually have insufficient valid nautical experience but often have expensive gear, boats, and have onboard copious amounts of completed sailing course documentation.
A mariner's actual competence and ability at sea are greatly determined by their sense of confidence, harmony, comfort, and sense of belonging within such surroundings.

It appears that the facility to use hank-on head sails and main sail slab reefing routinely and effectively are being lost.
If these types of sails are not used on a routine basis in all types of wind, wave, light, and weather conditions, the mariner will not have the necessary skills, facility, nor confidence.
Thus, I promote that mariners of my sort should dispense almost completely with use of furling mainsails and furling head sails.
I included the word 'almost' in the last sentence because upon reaching my mid sixties I did decide that if my high latitude sailing were to continue, I should install an additional forestay upon which I would fit a furling one hundred and fifty percent light wind head sail.
This furling sail would have been used only during the appropriate light wind conditions and otherwise would have remained completely furled, all other head sails would be of the hank-on type and would have been bent as required onto the second forestay.
I conceived this unfulfilled strategy because I had found in my late fifties that the one hundred fifty percent head sail was starting to provide me with physical challenges.
My first sailboat in 1978 was of the hank-on variety, -

I do not think furling had yet been invented-, however the second and third sailboats were bought already fitted with furling head sails which were peremptorily removed.

I suspect that these rather abrupt furling system removals may also have possibly been due to a desire to avoid the temptation of becoming a cockpit sailor.

Prior to leaving on my third offshore voyage in 2004 I did purchase my first brand new complete set of hanks on sails, however I also maintained onboard a large selection of used hank-on head sails.

I carried such a large inventory of used hank-on head sails, possibly since most harbour sailors, coastal sailors, and offshore Yachties were converting to furling sails and thus used hank-on sails of high quality became very inexpensive.

Hank-on sails by their very nature approach the ideal sail size and material strength to provide the optimum match to the actual wind and sea conditions.

Furthermore, individual head sails cut and constructed for a defined purpose such as a working jib, storm jib and high aspect ratio jib with it is high cut clew are also constructed with a view to the likely sea conditions encountered during their use, whereas the furling sails must rely on a broad range of compromises which are required to match as well as possible a large range in wind and sea conditions.

Furling sails render the entire sail exposed to possible damage, regardless if only a small proportion of the sail may be use, if any part of the exposed clew, leach, or foot is damaged the entire sail becomes unusable.

If such a furling sail becomes unusable and the mariner carries a spare, removal, and replacement of such a sail at sea by a single-handed sailor, may well prove both infeasible and possibly dangerous.

Once the wind exceeds gale force, the elevated and furled portion of the furling sail becomes a significant source of drag and vessel heel and causes an excessive, continuous, and unnecessary lateral flexing of the forestay.

Partially and fully furled sails also place similar additional loads on heavy weather gear such as the Jordan Drogue, heavy weather management tools such as deployed heaving-to sails and anchor gear when anchored in powerful winds.

The fully or partially furled sails increase listing angle during yawing whether while hove-to or anchored and thus place an additional and unnecessary strain on gear and crew.

The almost constant lateral cycling on the forestay results in the furling sailor's not uncommon complaint of a broken forestay while at sea; the seldom inspected top furling swivel gear becomes cracked and finally parts.

Sail damage at sea whether due to sail overloading, chafe, tearing, poor construction, or poor maintenance is almost unavoidable, hank-on sails have simply to be lowered and repaired, or replaced with a spare, whereas furling sails are difficult to remove shorthanded and replace at sea in agitated and windy conditions.

Spare hank-on sails do require more of that limited and precious commodity termed storage space, however finding oneself located what could be thousands of nautical miles from a leeward port with a non usable furling sail, will quickly transform such limited storage into a minor inconvenience.

One may argue that furling is safer because one does

not normally need to leave the cockpit, however as noted elsewhere, this absence of the constant necessity to leave the cockpit and tend to head sails renders furling sailors without the confidence, balance, and skills to perform such foredeck duties safely and consistently.

Such foredeck skills must be kept current so that regardless of conditions such as wind, sea state, darkness, snow, rain, fog, and extreme cold finger numbness, the mariner may confidently proceed to the foredeck.

Terrified, may not be too strong of an adjective to employ to describe a furling sailor who is required to go onto the foredeck due to an unforeseen furling system malfunction, especially if the requirement occurs during strong winds, darkness, or high seas.

High end sponsored ocean racers essentially all have new and the most expensive equipment and do not typically use the same furling gear for longer than one race, thus their successful use of such gear may not be reasonably compared to a cruiser who may wish to maintain the same gear for many years.

Thus, for the ocean cruiser it is just a matter of time before the furling gear malfunctions and when it occurs the necessary skills, sails, and confidence to navigate without such gear are not likely to be found onboard.

When such a malfunction occurs synchronous with a common event such as a violent cold front passage, the entire sail may be quickly destroyed, the forestay or the mast may break, and the ensuing situation will be filled with terror, danger, and an almost total loss of vessel control.

An appropriately selected hank-on sail from the onboard inventory may at anytime and under any conditions be immediately made essentially powerless, thus immediately reducing strain on the mast, and rigging by simply releasing the jib sheet.

If the luffing head sail is not lowered in a timely manner sail luffing damage may occur, however this can be relatively easily repaired onboard and is much preferred to the sail damage and potential of personal injury for the furling sailor.

As well, an appropriately selected hank-on head sail can be lowered very quickly which essentially precludes damage and in the unlikely event of sail damage, a spare may be quickly and relatively easily pressed into service.

Therefore, possibly the most basic sailing gear decision is self furling versus hank-on, and in the absence of the correct decision, a mariner might not be born.

Mariners who become accustomed to performing all routine sail modifications from the confines of the cockpit, either lose what confidence to work on the foredeck while underway they had, or more likely, never develop such confidence and skills.

A sufficiently skilled mariner is habituated, content, and at ease for the entire amount of time required to perform all work on the fore deck and this habituation is to be found during even the most adverse weather and sea conditions.

These attributes are critical because the mariner must be at ease so that one is not encouraged to rush or hurry foredeck tasks, such haste leads quickly to mistakes, equipment damage, and personal injury.

I have never used other than the combination of a triple slab reefing mainsail and a selection of hank-on head sails.

Upon purchase, my second and third sailboats were already fitted with furling head sails, however these I immediately removed thus I have never stood in the cockpit and simply operated furling lines but always had what I termed the 'opportunity' to go to the foredeck to remove, stow, and change head sails.

The steel foredeck of the cutter with which I was to accomplish my third voyage was modified to accommodate five separately securely lashed head sails, which neither wind nor sweeping seas ever dislodged or damaged.

Literally hundreds of tons of seawater have poured over such foredeck individually stored head sails without any damage.

They were secured in such a manner that any one of the five could be removed or added without the need to disturb the remainder.

The validity and success of this method is best illustrated in the fact that the sails that I used throughout the entire nine-year duration penultimate third voyage were never off board for repairs at any time during the voyage, rather were subjected to the necessary and timely inspections as well as hand stitching repairs during the voyage.

Upon reaching an anchorage after a passage I would carefully inspect all sails, make the necessary repairs, and then carefully fold, bag, and store the sails ready for the next passage.

Often, I would remain in the same anchorage for up to several months and the sails would remain protected and secured on the foredeck under a water and ultraviolet light protective tarpaulin.

Heaving-to is the most often utilized defensive strategy but is only one of at least three imperative heavy weather strategies which should be onboard.

Except for one single bow deployment of the parachute type sea anchor, I utilized exclusively heaving-to until I encountered my first and only knock down off Cape Agullas, at the southern tip of the African continent.

Prior to this event I had already accomplished several thousand open ocean miles which had included very abrupt sailing conditions; however, the vast majority was in the North Pacific Ocean where one rarely if ever encounters the seas such as those that are regularly generated in the higher latitudes of the southern oceans.

In the North Pacific, the low-pressure centres can be very intense and large in diameter, however they tend to move relatively quickly, and another low does not routinely immediately follow in essentially the same tract as the previous.

Whereas, south of forty degrees south latitude in the southern oceans lows routinely track from west to east following a relatively narrow band of latitudes and thus generate the seas and resulting potential roll over hazard for which the southern oceans are well known.

Immediately after the knock down I had still to endure three days of successive passing cold fronts and the steep seas that such weather and the Agullas current creates.

Preferring not to experience my second knock down, immediately I fashioned an improvised drogue which consisted of a bow anchor, fifty meters of anchor chain, followed by two large coils of twenty-millimetre diameter double braid nylon anchor line, all attached to one end of a heavy-duty anchoring swivel and finally fifty meters of double braid anchor line made fast -including appropriate anti chafe protection- to the port aft mooring bit.

The vessel rode for approximately forty-eight hours on this makeshift drogue and did not suffer another knock down, as well the drogues coiled lines were never observed to break the surface nor did any seas again board the vessel.

The seas approached on the port aft quarter and the rudder was adjusted and lashed as necessary so that this would remain the case.

It was a major chore to retrieve this drogue and the line finally was led forward to the anchor winch and the whole affair including the final fifty-meter chain section was winched in an unceremonious manner over the stainless-steel rod capped bulwarks on the forward port side of the vessel.

Stainless steel is such a fine material, no less so when subjected to the extreme abrasive forces that were generated on this welded bulwark cap during this winching operation.

Shortly, I was to arrive in East London where I would assemble my first Jordan series drogue, thus I was never forced a second time to utilize such a difficult to retrieve impromptu drogue, although it remained in my mind and another such makeshift drogue could be pressed into service if I were to lose or seriously damage my Jordan series drogue, options for a single-handed sailor are an exceptionally good thing!

Subsequently, I was to credit the Jordan series drogue for permitting myself, Ede, and the vessel to survive the passage from Kerguelen to Tasmania.

Individual sailing vessels may present specific issues concerning heaving-to; however, it was to become evident that to successfully heave-to on all three of my sailing vessels, one could employ either a reefed mainsail/ trysail or the combination of the foregoing and a backed head sail hanked to the forestay.

The head sail if not backed, could also be sheeted as flat as possible with the clew in the vicinity of amidships or even over the centre line to windward using the assistance of a separate jib sheet positioning block and line.

My third sailing vessel which was cutter rigged also required that the backed or hard sheeted head sail option must be bent onto the forestay and not the inner forestay, because the inner forestay appears not sufficiently forward of the vessel's centre of effort to allow the vessel to remain in the desired orientation with respect to the wind and seas.

Under a similar hove-to situation, furling sailors will usually find the clew of the almost completely furled headsail located well above deck level which will generate excessive vessel heel, whereas a typical high cut clew storm jib or high aspect head sail maintains a much lower centre of effort as well as the desired minimum exposure to boarding seas.

The heaving-to option requires that the area of the mainsail and head sails be progressively reduced as the wind velocity increases until there is too much wind for both sails.

Hank-on head sails require one to physically change to a smaller area sail as the wind velocity increases however this places the relatively more delicate larger head sail which has just been lowered and lashed to a place of safety from possible damage, leaving the smaller and more heavily built head sail to face the more abrupt conditions, thus contrary to the situation for furling head sails, damage or wear to a smaller storm jib in no manner inflicts damage to other safely stowed larger sails.

When the conditions are reached whereby there is too much wind for even the smallest head sail, the final option is a triple reefed mainsail or trysail alone, to be followed by all sails lowered and lashed with the deployment of the series drogue, -which can be deployed just prior to lowering the triple reefed mainsail or trysail-.

In severe weather, the trysail set on its own track is probably the best option because it precludes any possible damage to the triple reefed mainsail, which will now be found safely flaked and lashed onto the boom, which itself is securely sheeted amidships and securely lashed to a substantial boom gallows.

There is a feeling of security, relative comfort, and a job well done when the point is reached whereby all sails are stowed and secured in a manner whereby it is no longer possible for the wind nor seas to cause damage.

If the reader will excuse the anthropomorphism, the sails will wait patiently until the weather moderates and the arrival of the appropriate conditions to again get underway.

The maximum continuous period that I have kept all my active sails lowered and stowed on deck during severe weather was five days, although over the duration of a long high latitude's ocean passage the sail stowed duration may well extend to several multiple day storage periods.

Throughout this down time there should be no damage or wear inflicted on any vessel equipment other than anti chafe gear.

Significant personal satisfaction and even exhilaration are experienced when one is again successfully underway, with the heaved-to condition removed or the Jordan drogue retrieved, and the appropriate undamaged sails are transferred from deck storage, hoisted, and again pressed into service.

An inherent flaw regarding heaving-to is that the vessel continually yaws, at the end of every up wind cycle the holding sail will briefly luff before the vessel again falls off the wind.

The more overpowered the vessel's mainsail the longer and therefore more damaging is such luffing, if excessively over canvased with respect to the wind speed the hove-to vessel may have enough momentum to come completely through the wind to where the mainsail is now backed, and the vessel will be found to be in irons and heavily listing.

My third vessel was fitted with intermediate shrouds which I altered to create running intermediate backstays which were alternately maintained under suitable tension using the windward jib sheet winch.

Once deployed such an intermediate running backstay was at an excellent angle to counteract pumping of the mast which is caused when sailing hard on the wind in rough seas with a sail bent onto the inner forestay.

To provide a stable and stiff mast I also employed the windward running backstay when I was hove-to, thus if the vessel came unexpectedly across the wind the now backed mainsail must be suitably prevented from contacting this windward running intermediate backstay, otherwise serious structural mast damage is likely to occur.

A preventative precaution requires attaching the boom vang to a secure anchorage on the leeward bulwarks, then when the vessel is unexpectedly put in irons with the mainsail aback, the mainsail and boom is held clear of the windward running backstay, the situation may then in a calm manner sorted out.

While hove-to, if the wind becomes greater than forty knots the brief yawing cycle and resulting mainsail luffing can rapidly damage the luff of the mainsail as well as damaging the tied down line of reefing crinkles.

If the triple reefed mainsail employed to heave-to is damaged on the luff edge or line of intermediate crinkles the entire sail is not usable, which indicates the advantage of a trysail on its own track during powerful winds.

In view of preventing damage to the mainsail while hove-to I prefer to not tie tightly the reefed sails crinkles securely against the boom but rather secure them in such a manner which only prevents the bagged lower portion of the sail from luffing and therefore chafing, as well as preventing the bagged portion from collecting significant amounts of seawater from spray and boarding seas.

Sails deployed while hove-to are also vulnerable to almost instantaneous debilitating damage caused by the often brief but potentially violent and extreme wind speeds attained during the actual cold front passage.

Such brief violent wind conditions are difficult to predict therefore it is most prudent to lower and lash all sails prior to all actual frontal passages, lash the tiller to leeward and temporarily lie a hull -unless a sea is running which can cause vessel rollover-.

This temporary halting of the vessel will add to the length of time spent at sea during a passage however will greatly raise the odds of arriving without rig or sail damage.

In the tropics I tend to apply this same lower and lash

precaution to approaching thunder clouds because even though they often present gentle winds, occasionally they present very violent and instantly sail damaging wind velocities.

I do not routinely recommend lying a hull, however vessel rollover or knock down during such relatively short periods appears not to be an issue during the final approaches and passage of a tropical thunderstorm or an open ocean cold front passage because seas in the tropics do not often generate a roll over hazard with respect to thunderstorms and seas in the higher latitudes seem to become reduced in size and actually attain a partially confused and more flattened state temporarily during the relatively quickly changing wind and sea direction which is related to a transiting cold front.

The temporarily confused and slightly pacified sea condition however does not last for an exceedingly long period of time and when the violent frontal passage winds subside it is prudent get underway or heave-to.

An appropriately adjusted radar operating on the watchman mode during daylight or darkness will normally alarm when the heavy rain of an approaching thunderstorm or heavy rain squalls usually contained in an approaching cold front5 enters the predetermined radar guard zone.

Such an alarm would probably not be given by a darkness hours crew member sitting in the cockpit.

I have conceived a method of heaving-to which eliminates the yawing cycle and the resulting potential for sail luffing damage.

To enter this mainsail luffing free state while hove-to, one sheets in the main sheet so that the boom is as close to the vessel's midline as possible, I have also often used a separate line to haul the mainsail boom across amidships onto the windward side.

The vessel hove-to with the mainsail in this configuration in combination with a backed head sail and the tiller lashed to leeward, will no longer perform the yawing cycle but rather lie constant with respect to the wind.

Along with the vessel continually cycling upwind when hove-to in the conventional manner, also goes the mainsail luffing and therefore potential damage to the mainsail.

This alternate hove-to configuration of the mainsail and head sail also appears to forcibly flatten the sails and thus reduces their power which slightly extends the upper wind velocity within which this sail arrangement is useful.

There is however an upper limit of wind velocity where this method of heaving-to is not useful, the limiting factor involves vessel listing.

Under this modified hove-to sail arrangement the vessel holds its position and releases energy not through mainsail luffing but rather via vessel listing.

I have found therefore that this method of heaving-to must be abandoned when the constant vessel listing approaches forty-five degrees, at which time there remain two viable options.

First, to revert to heaving-to using the triple reefed mainsail or trysail and suffering the resulting luffing induced potential for sail damage, or second, to deploy a Jordan series drogue.

As will be explained further, with practice an admirable attribute of the Jordan series drogue is that it can be safely, efficiently, and effectively be deployed as well as retrieved in reasonably severe conditions, thus conditions may be permitted to deteriorate through all the stages of hove-to sail area reductions, always maintaining the final option of drogue deployment.

As well, sailing downwind in heavy conditions the Jordan drogue final option permits one to continue underway until only a poled-out storm jib remains, before finally stopping and deploying the drogue.

This Jordan drogue attribute of successful deployment in rough sea conditions is especially useful south of forty degrees south latitude where one must attempt to continue moving east when conditions permit, because there often appears a continuous series of following deep depressions and associated cold fronts and the distances to be crossed are exceptionally large.

Heaving-to versus deploying a series drogue is very tempting because heaving-to is quite easy to initiate and exit, thus one can again get underway quickly and with relatively little deck work, often without being required to leave the cockpit whereas onerous labour is required to deploy and retrieve the drogue.

Thus, the philosophy of not trying to make sailing too easy or entirely free of possibly arduous physical work, will not encourage the mariner to seek easy and work free methods of navigating the world's oceans.

Once the Jordan series drogue is deployed, the vessel's leeward drift is in the order of one and a half knots, whereas while hove-to at least double such drift will be experienced, thus both options are no longer viable if the vessel is too close to a lee shore.

If one finds the vessel too close to a lee shore the final option is not the stern deployed Jordan series drogue but rather the bow deployment of a parachute type sea anchor.

Considering the excellence of weather forecasting one should not find oneself too close to a lee shore, however late in a long passage mistakes and miscalculations can be made and the human brain appears hard wired to naturally be encouraged to attempt to make a landfall and attain a secure anchorage thus potentially leading to the miscalculation and the resulting insufficient sea room.

I am recommending that it is highly desirable while at sea to maintain a routine schedule of sufficient continuous periods of rest, regular diet, and mealtimes as well as regular exercise during a passage so that the probability of making a landfall in a sufficiently functional state of mental and physical acuity remains high.

If one finds oneself in hazardous proximity to a lee shore the purpose of carrying a suitable parachute type sea anchor, the necessary ancillary gear and the knowledge of its deployment and retrieval become apparent, although deploying a parachute sea anchor in heavy weather conditions will be incredibly challenging, any mistakes probably will result in serious equipment damage, loss of the sea anchor, and potential serious personal injury.

Due to the extreme and almost immediate tension on the bow deployed parachute anchor rode during deployment, any fouling of the parachute system will result in the necessity of cutting the parachute adrift and finding oneself drifting out of control towards a potentially perilous lee shore.

The deployment and retrieval of the parachute type sea anchor does not share the characteristics of the Jordan series drogue because the parachute becomes much more difficult and dangerous to deploy and retrieve as the sea and wind conditions increase.

The ability to safely retrieve a Jordan series drogue in very rough conditions of both wind and seas does not apply to the bow deployed parachute anchor, therefore if the parachute anchor is used at sea far away from a lee shore, the mariner will be forced to squander the possible advantage of a fair wind due his inability to safely retrieve the deployed parachute until wind and sea conditions have substantially moderated.

In the southern oceans this forced delay in again getting underway until conditions have drastically moderated sufficiently to retrieve a bow deployed sea anchor may well entail a period of several days delay and then another system will usually be following close on the heels of the last.

Safety and health at sea are large, varied, and related subjects of concern, however probably the most important and controversial is the possibility of becoming a single-handed mariner overboard, thus I would be somewhat incomplete if I did not broach my practices concerning prevention of unintentionally going overboard.

I must also state that the following views are my own and I present them in terms of completeness rather than as an absolute recommendation to others.

Single-handed sailors have been lost overboard and have no one to pull them onboard or more importantly to stop the vessel if they have the misfortune to go overboard, although many persons have also been lost overboard from multi crewed vessels.

It is somewhat understated, going overboard must be avoided!

If the vessel is drifting to leeward while hove-to the mariner armed with a plan, is likely to find his way back onboard.

To illustrate, I have often deliberately gone overboard in the open ocean while hove-to, -usually just before leaving warm tropical waters-, to clear goose neck barnacles, upon completion ascending the transom mounted ladder, the whole time using as added safety insurance a line dragging on either side and a third off the stern.

These three lines may also be used as resting stations for us older mariners who no longer seem to be able to clear the entire underwater hull area without a few rest periods.

It is an enduring and slightly haunting visual image when the scrapped off barnacles spiral down through the warm and almost transparent tropical water, passing between numerous vertical shafts of darkness.

It is also occasionally necessary to make such an open ocean cold water high latitudes entry using a wet suit to clear debris that has fouled the propeller shaft or ships rudder.

I performed all my offshore sailing protected by a steel hull however those with fibreglass hulls might be prudent to foresee the possibility of the necessity of going overboard within the open ocean to plug a hole caused from collision with a large piece of floating debris.

The standard man overboard preventative options are suitable guardrails, harnesses and lifelines, or a combination of the two although furling sailors may argue that furling sails assist in overboard prevention since in most situations, they are not required to leave the relative safety of the cockpit.

I have made the acquaintance of possibly many more furling type sailors than necessary; however, the vast majority are habituated to entering the cockpit where they immediately attach their harness to a cockpit anchored lanyard and then proceed to perform all necessary sail handling, the entire time remaining within the confines of the cockpit.

There is however a significant proportion of the above who must leave the cockpit going as far as the mast, thus, to reef the mainsail, although a large percentage rigorously avoid leaving the cockpit when conditions are anything more robust than light to moderate wind conditions, such furlers often therefore extol the benefits of sailing without the use of the mainsail.

Sail reefing is only one example of several routine issues for which leaving the cockpit may be necessary, other reasons would include daily rigging, sail, and running line inspections, on deck repair of sails or equipment, immediate rectification of line or sail chafing issues, or simply going to sit on the bow pulpit seat to observe albatross or bow wave surfing dolphins.

It is certain that all mariners including furling sailors will be required to leave the confines of the cockpit when sea, wind, and light conditions are less than ideal, therefore ongoing routine practice in all weather and sea conditions and a methodical sequence of their safe and confident performance is critical.

The ideal overboard prevention method would ensure that all necessary deck work could always be safely and efficiently performed while tethered to a harness and lanyard, which itself is attached to a suitable on deck anchoring system.

I have not been able to discover such a functional overboard prevention system which results in the mariner remaining tied to the vessel in a continuous manner, remaining able to perform all necessary deck work from the point of leaving the cockpit forward to the bow and return.

It is possible to attach a lanyard once the specific deck worksite has been reached, however this I have found also excessively restricts the necessary range of unimpeded motion.

I attempted the use of various lifeline systems and configurations on my first offshore voyage to French Polynesia in 1995, as well, previously during my several years of self-administered coastal sailing training however I continued to find that I fouled the harness lanyard on myself and other gear and thus the smooth, efficient, and therefore safe performance of the required deck work became an insurmountable issue because I found I was continually creating tripping and snagging issues.

I often discovered that to clear the fouled lines, it often requires both hands and thus I found myself braced or balancing, thus exposing me to the hazard of being thrown into other on deck structures or equipment.

Restricted mobility caused by an attached lanyard also presents an increased risk of being hit by luffing sails, clews, jib sheets, or worst of all the main boom or spinnaker pole.

There are unforeseen situations which develop on deck which require timely and rapid rectification, thus speed and efficiency in clearing fouled equipment may become important considerations.

Thus, I have developed and implemented specific 'ships suggestions' designed to mitigate the possibility of continually snagging the lanyard, falling into unforgiving gear such as bow mooring cleats or the anchor winch and thus possibly sustaining personal injury, or actually going overboard.

The learning and implementation of this mindset and skill set cannot be achieved via a few expensive offshore sailing courses, nor the installation of a complicated fall arrest system but must be achieved over a significant amount of time spent gaining experience and confidence in constantly more severe sailing conditions.

The goal is to become equally comfortable and confident during all previously noted conditions whether one is within the cockpit or anywhere else on deck.

Once this incremental course of training has been achieved one is able to perform safely and confidently all necessary on deck duties without experiencing the mishap of falling or going overboard.

Throughout my entire sailing experience, I have never unintentionally gone overboard, furthermore during all three of my offshore voyages in Alcidae III, I did not experience a single near miss with potential of being thrown overboard.

It was always clear in my mind that if I went overboard, there was no one to stop the vessel nor assist me back onboard.

I must stress that the method chosen for person overboard prevention may well be the most critical decision and learned survival skill.

Thus between 1978 and 2004 I continually augmented and modified my on deck skills and slowly became confident, efficient, and even relaxed and comfortable in the performance of tasks such as changing and stowing sails on the foredeck, reefing the mainsail at the mast, inspecting all on deck gear for chafe and damage, attending to issues with the standing rigging, attending to the ongoing securing of on deck gear and equipment and responding to unforeseen events such as deck leaks and broken or adrift critical gear.

During the period that this necessary skill is under development, other on deck practices will also be implemented to augment the level of security.

Such additional practices include reducing all sails based on the latest weather forecast to a size whereby it should not be necessary to perform deck work during darkness.

As well, it is always prudent to stop the vessel prior to leaving the cockpit to perform deck work by temporarily lying a hull, heaving-to using both sails, mainsail alone, and head sail alone.

I have broken this rule more than any other in the spirit of permitting the vessel to continue its course, however on occasion the mariner will find the vessel too close to a lee shore when it will become necessary to reduce sail area without completely stopping the vessel, therefore the skill and confidence must be gained to change head sails and reef the main sail while the vessel is still underway and on course.

This of course presents the hazard that if the single-handed mariner goes overboard there will be no one onboard to stop the vessel, there is no denying that this presents a risk, thus confidence and ability are the major safeguards.

As well I have developed a trailing line system which will force the vessel into the wind by hauling on a line trailed astern, this line is attached to the self steering servo oar, however I must admit I have never had occasion to use or rigorously test this method.

Thus, the recommended method, if circumstances permit, is to place the vessel in a hove-to configuration before going forward to change or reef sails.

In such a hove-to state, if one were to go overboard without a lifeline, one should have only to hold on to the gunnel and float oneself back onboard under the guardrail as the vessel lists to leeward.

If one finds oneself falling off the high side while hove-to, the vessel will be stopped in the water and one can make their way to the vessel's stern whereby they can ascend via a stern ladder or the transom attached steering gear, however, recall that the vessel will be stopped and only drifting to leeward.

If the vessel is not stopped prior to going forward the risk of going overboard is greatly reduced if one chooses the windward and therefore higher side of the vessel on which to go forward, if one then looses one's balance he will fall -due to gravity- towards the vessels midline where there will be found a myriad of gear and equipment from which an emergency handhold will be found.

If the vessel is off the wind a heavy roll to port and starboard is probable, in which case the mariner going forward will stop and hold fast during the more hazardous portion of the roll cycle when temporarily he finds himself on the low side.

While going forward it is usually possible to be holding or maintaining a sliding hand contact with predetermined hand holds such as cabin top rails, guardrails, and shrouds, which must become sufficiently familiar to be used in complete darkness.

One hand for the ship and one for yourself is not always

workable, thus it must become instinctive through practice to wedge the body into braced positions against equipment and structures such as gunnels, mooring bits, bow pulpit, anchor winch, forestay, or shrouds so that both hands are available to perform the required task.

Mast pulpits which are designed for wedging the body between the pulpit and the mast are also indispensable because one requires both hands to raise a sail, however if one were to go overboard during this sail raising task it is likely the person holding onto the halyard would continue to go overboard and the sail would continue to go up.

During the multitude of tasks performed more efficiently using both hands, if it is found that whole body bracing is not possible it is prudent to have one arm looped around a guardrail, pulpit, forestay, or shroud.

In summation, concerning personal lifelines I prefer mobility to mobility restrictions and have successfully accepted the increased risk of going overboard which have been reduced by the adoption of practices and procedures which have been noted, however such a decision by others must be carefully considered.

Finally, it would be preferable to develop a system which has eluded me whereby one can be tied off from the point of leaving the cockpit, perform all necessary work without the snagging and restricted movement issues created by lifeline systems.

An enduring task which must be experienced to be suitably shared is performed in total darkness and involves leaving a condition of deep sleep and coming from the warm and secure bunk to the interior cabin dressing station followed by deck work.

When fully and appropriately clothed -in total darkness to preserve night vision- for all necessary deck work, the mariner enters the cockpit, latches closed the companionway door from without and often finds the vessel charging along at an excessive speed and quite probably near or even beyond the upper limit of steering gear control to see and hear the foamy white wake being forced outward from both sides of the vessel as well as the surrounding breaking seas.

If sailing downwind the vessel will also be regularly rolling deeply to port and starboard and if to windward the vessel may list to leeward with luffing sails and the lee deck partly awash.

If one is fortunate, you will also be greeted by the sparkling illumination emanating from the bowled aside phosphorescent plankton which are mixed with the white outward tumbling and spreading wakes.

This phosphorescent phenomenon is potentially present in the tropics as well as at certain times of year in the higher latitudes.

Such excessive vessel speed renders the servo pendulum steering gear near it is upper limit of control, resulting in servo control lines and their turning blocks emitting the unmistakable sounds of strain, which along with the exaggerated vessel motion may have been the indications which instigated leaving the bunk.

Arriving in darkness in the cockpit one will find that the sense of sight is somewhat reduced, however other senses such as hearing, skin sensitivity to wind and spray direction and the whole-body balance which is sensitive to the ship's physical motion will all be available and ready for duty.

It should be noted that at such potentially critical times

these just noted senses will optimally serve the decision-making process only if the mariner has been well rested, fed, and entertained, preferably over the period of the entire voyage.

If one finds oneself suffering from conditions such as sleep deprivation, dehydration, malnutrition, or haste, sensory and decision-making abilities will be reduced.

If the vessel is bowling along off the wind it will also have started yawing in increasingly wider arcs as the servo steering gear incrementally over corrects due to the increased force of the wind on the sails with the imminent potential of coming across the wind and backing either the mainsail or poled out headsail.

Both possibilities entailing the potentially catastrophic result of a broach, thus vessel speed must be reduced as quickly as prudence will allow but also in a controlled manner.

Once the darkness hours deck work has been successfully completed and the vessel is again bowling along under reduced sail, the mariner along with maintained night vision may sit on either transom box and gaze pensively over the stern at the swirling plankton phosphorescence created by the ship's motion, ship's rudder, and servo pendulum oar motion until the arrival of the well-earned urge to return to the bunk.

While sitting in such periods of darkness one not uncommonly will see the silhouettes of storm petrels as well as larger petrels who are also interested -for nutritional reasons- in the vessels swirling plankton containing wake.

When sailing at sea with a wind direction aft of the beam, I prefer employing only a larger than normally necessary head sail.

Regardless of the head sail area it is set poled out on the forestay and the mainsail will be found lowered and securely lashed to the boom which itself is secured onto the boom gallows.

The inner forestay was not used to set any sail under such downwind conditions due to the vessel's apparent preference to self steer with the vessel's centre of effort the maximum distance forward.

Sailing with only a poled-out head sail, when conditions deteriorate to where the vessel was overpowered, I had simply to release the jib sheet and the sail would luff harmlessly to leeward, the pole remaining fixed by its three support and positional lines.

Just prior to releasing the jib sheet, -which will immediately reduce the vessel speed through the water-, I untie the figure eight knot which normally prevents the sheet from passing through the jib sheet lead block, thus the jib sheet as well will be found luffing harmlessly to leeward along with the headsail.

The vessel will quickly slow down however the steering gear will continue to steer the boat on course due to wind pressure on the vessel.

Therefore, with a reduced vessel speed through the water one will find himself working on the dark foredeck with wash streaming at a reduced speed by on both sides of the vessel.

A safer option if the seas permit is to disconnect the steering gear prior to going forward and lying a hull, the luffing head sail and free flying jib sheet will not be damaged.

Under such circumstances I prefer to let the jib sheet with the removed figure eight knot fly free because on occasion it can foul on the vessel or attached equipment and cause the jib to open and close in a very violent manner.

Under such circumstances if one chooses not to stop the vessel, occasionally the vessel will come beam to the wind while the mariner is working on the foredeck.

This is not an onerous situation and can be sorted out once the smaller replacement head sail is bent and raised.

If one chooses to sail downwind using the mainsail along with a head sail it can be a delicate task to slow the vessel sufficiently, especially if one has waited too long to reduce sail area.

This is because even after the jib sheet has been released the vessel may still be overpowered.

Reducing speed on a vessel which is sailing directly downwind under only a mainsail requires executing judicious hauling on the main sheet while manually keeping the vessel directly downwind.

Once the boom has been hauled into alignment with ships fore and aft axis the mainsail will see less wind.

This procedure will slow the vessel to the point where one can come beam to the wind and seas without the fear of broaching, while simultaneously releasing the main sheet.

This potentially tricky and dangerous manoeuvre can be avoided if one is sailing without the mainsail, however I have successfully performed such a manoeuvre many times without significant issues.

Caution must be exercised with this method because there is the potential to come too far across the wind with a resulting damaging and dangerous mainsail gybe.

I also prefer not to use the mainsail off the wind due to

its propensity to chafe on the aft lower shrouds.

Thus, even though greater speed can be achieved through the water during downwind sailing using both mainsail and head sail I prefer to use only the poled-out head sail, especially during hours of darkness.

VESSEL MAINTENANCE

Hull sheet replacement due to inside corrosion, repaired in San Fernando just up rive from Buenos Aires.

Sailboats do not usually turn out to be sound financial investments, defined as capable of being sold for substantially more or usually anywhere near the original cost of the initial acquisition and subsequent equipment additions, maintenance, and repairs.

Thus, it would be my recommendation that the minimum be spent on the initial acquisition because one is very unlikely to see even a moderate percentage of that investment upon the inevitable resale or uninsured physical loss of the vessel.

A secondary reason for not spending a large amount of money on a high-end sailing vessel is because aboard an immaculate vessel, the owner is more prone to become overly fastidious and timid regarding using the vessel in a rough and ready manner and in areas of the world's oceans where extreme weather is likely to be encountered both at sea and at anchor.

Secondary anchors, chains and kedging weights all require to be transported along the deck, often during much less-than-ideal conditions which can result in damage to furniture quality teak decks, pristine gel coats, and cabin mouldings.

As well, maintenance within the vessel often entails providing access to various hard to reach areas and this damages interior pristine cabinetry.

Thus, as well as a simple exterior of the vessel I would also recommend a plain interior which is functional, durable, easily removed and then replaced if access is required.

Again, I would point to certain French interior layouts for both functionality and ease of maintenance.

A final environmental motivation, sailing the world's oceans within a second hand, easily repairable, and rather plain vessel avoids purchasing a major new object and thus provides the opportunity of repairing and breathing new life into an existing object, which is an important component of an environmentally conscious lifestyle.

Replacement insurance would certainly be a route to potentially recoup total loss or major damage costs, however the cost of high latitudes offshore insurance for a single-handed sailor I found prohibitive.

The annual premiums that I saved over a period of eleven years which includes all three of my offshore voyages, would have paid for substantial repairs, although such expensive repairs were not required.

The interior of my vessel was far from yachty magazine photo material; however, it was functional and did not seem to mind a bit of rough treatment.

As noted elsewhere I bought my first sailboat in September 1978 and from that time until just before my first offshore training voyage in April 1995, I had always maintained valid vessel insurance, however during that entire period I had never submitted a claim and thus after 1995 until I sold my third sailing vessel in 2015, I did not have vessel insurance.

Offshore insurance companies also have issues with single-handed sailors, especially those who venture south of forty degrees south followed by two voyages into the Bering sea.

I will allude in other parts of this book to the importance of developing and maintaining the state of mind of contentment and well being during ocean passages.

This attitude questions the quite common conception that the vessel must be fast.

I will define fast as the ability to average one hundred and fifty to two hundred nautical miles per day rather than my humble one hundred nautical mile average, some passages achieving substantially less.

The choice of hull material is probably equally as controversial as vessel insurance, man overboard prevention, and furling versus hank-on sails.

My first two vessels were fibreglass, however due to my goal of surviving extreme weather likely to be encountered in high latitudes, I concluded that fibreglass was just too fragile.

Steel became and remains my choice although if fibreglass is indeed another mariner's choice the necessary repair skills will be equally essential and achievable.

Very admirable, seaworthy, and cost-effective repairs can be made to a fibreglass hull while the vessel is purposely beached for this purpose, as well emergency repairs are possible while the vessel is in the water.

The world is replete with suitably protected bays which would well serve the purpose of beaching a vessel to make repairs.

Routine beaching is practised in all parts of the third world as well as in first world countries such as Chile.

The mariner who intends to venture into isolated high latitude regions will be prudent to learn as much as possible concerning the necessary maintenance and repair skills for all types of equipment found onboard.

These skills I consider to be almost of equal importance to the nautical abilities noted in the seamanship and other sections of this book.

Lacking nautical, repair, and maintenance abilities an aspiring mariner cannot realistically and consistently remove themselves for lengthy periods of time to some of the world's most isolated, unaltered by humans, and therefore pristine locations.

I have learned little from British Columbia commercial fishermen under the heading of seamanship; however,

I have been heavily influenced by their philosophy and actual practices concerning maintenance and repair.

Their philosophy is essentially to attempt to become familiar with as much ship's equipment as possible and when any piece of equipment or portion of the vessel's structure requires repair or replacement, access is achieved regardless of what interior equipment, cabinetry, panelling, deck head, or flooring must be removed. Thus, one cannot be timid about cutting a hole in the deck or removing interior cabinets, however aforethought during vessel construction regarding the potential for future access, is recommended.

A high percentage of yachts contain magnificent interior design and cabinetry, and the owners are very reluctant to permit a necessary interior partial tear out which would be necessary to repair a damaged hull.

A steel hull encourages the mariner to learn steel fabrication and welding skills as they apply to a steel hull, including repair and installation skills regarding welded stainless-steel attachments.

I made a mistake buying my thirty-nine-foot steel cutter in that it was not sandblasted and painted on the inside during initial construction.

I did not pay an exorbitant initial price; however, I did replace twenty square meters of below waterline hull before leaving in 2004 as well as another twenty square meters in Buenos Aires, followed by the final twenty square meters in East London, South Africa.

After a pitiful experience concerning my hired welder in Buenos Aires, I was determined to conquer the overhead welding portion of the required skill set, subsequently I successfully performed all the welding and fitting hull repairs that were performed in South Africa.

I use the term conquer overhead welding with caution because I would fail to find a job as a professional welder, however none of my welds have leaked or broken.

The motivation of my caution concerning acquiring a properly constructed steel vessel is an attempt to prevent others from a similar mistake, because an appropriately finished interior hull surface would have precluded the necessity of all the steel hull sections that I was obliged to replace.

Such a well constructed steel vessel would initially cost more, however these would be funds well spent and may preclude the necessity of learning structural steel repair skills.

I mentioned previously the enviable ability of fibreglass hulls to be repaired in isolated locations throughout the world, all that is required are relatively few and inexpensive repair materials that can readily be carried onboard.

One would need only to carry a small amount of fibreglass mat and roving, polyester resin, catalyst, simple manual application tools and the correct solvent.

In contrast, a steel hull would be difficult to repair in such an isolated anchorage location without the onboard addition of large, bulky, and expensive equipment as well as primed steel plate, however due to the penetration resistance of steel versus fibreglass it is also much less likely that such hull repair would be required.

Specific maintenance and repair skills must be combined with a sufficient inventory of spare parts, necessary onboard tools, as well as the competence and knowledge in their usage.

At sea repairs are often performed during rather turbulent conditions, thus facility concerning the usage of hand tools is essential.

This will apply to structural, mechanical, and electrical systems, and a thorough understanding of the motor and its maintenance and repair is of prime importance.

Offshore sailing vessels turn out to contain complicated mechanical, electrical, and electronic systems, thus in addition to mechanical skills electrical and electronic skills should also be available onboard.

Anti fouling strategy is a subject where substantial money may be saved if one does the work themselves.

I routinely applied forty litres of ablative anti fouling paint during each haul out, this volume of paint would result in approximately six thick coats.

Such haul outs occurred once every three years, I applied extra coatings in the vicinity of the water line and the entire rudder.

At anchorages in the tropics, it is not an issue to clean the bottom prior to a passage using only a mask, fins, and snorkel, whereas in higher latitudes one must carry a wet suit and weight belt.

One soon develops the sensitivity to scrub applying only the necessary pressure; thus, the anti fouling paint's useful lifespan is prolonged.

On lengthy tropical sea passages goose neck barnacles are an issue which usually require removal at sea because they will drastically reduce vessel speed through the water.

This is best performed in conditions of minimum seas and less than ten knots of wind, however in some regions such sea conditions do not often exist, thus the mariner must exercise prudence when clearing the overhanging stern sections which have a propensity to move up and down with the seas generating the hazard of the vessel striking one's head.

One stiff arm should be continually employed propped against the hull to prevent such a hull head collision.

The skill of using one hand as a brace against the hull and the other for scraping, while the legs and fins maintain contact with the hull is soon acquired.

Watching the scrapped off barnacles slowly spiral down into the seemingly infinitely clear ocean water among hundreds of vertical dark shafts of darkness creates a sensation of vulnerability and apprehension.

I would often be reluctant to look downwards because I would find myself becoming preoccupied with imagining passing shadows, although during such open ocean cleaning projects I did not see a passing or approaching shark.

Beaching the vessel is also possible and is a useful method of cleaning the underwater portion of the hull in a suitably protected bay, with an acceptably sloping sand beach, suitable tidal range, and cooperating hours of daylight.

It was ship's policy that all the standing rigging be inspected prior to any ocean passage, this always entailed going up the mast.

I used a four-part block and tackle system to haul myself to the two steps permanently installed near the mast head.

The two steps are necessary because one must be able to stand at the masthead in relative comfort, to service at waist level equipment such as the anchor light, vhf antenna, and wind direction indicator.

It is a bit of a chore to pull oneself from the bosom's chair sitting position up and onto the masthead steps,

however at sixty-five years of age, I remained capable.
It is recommended that one become relatively comfortable standing on the two mast head steps because such tasks are best not rushed.
A suitable safety belt and lanyard is recommended so that the masthead worker can lean back into the safety belt and easily use both hands for the task at hand.
At sea, I attempted once to go aloft as far as the lower spreaders because a lower shroud was stranding where the wire exited the compression fitting.
This assent was accomplished but with much difficulty due to vessel rolling, sea conditions were less than moderate thus reinforcing the prudence of a thorough inspection prior to leaving the anchorage.
I replaced all my standing rigging just prior to my nine-year duration third voyage, and had kept all the removed rigging as spares, however during the nine years I only replaced one running backstay and repaired one stranding forward lower shroud.
Possibly, steps fitted the entire length of the mast would be a more suitable solution, however I always assumed such steps would continually create a fouling obstruction for lines such as the external portion of halyards, telescoping headsail pole vertical control lines, and possibly flogging jib sheets.
A majority of what could be considered obligatory maintenance skills, require several years of practice to acquire, and should be learned throughout the same period the aspiring mariner is learning the necessary seamanship skills.
Such skills are also financially advantageous as noted by my savings account, which was higher after my third voyage than upon embarking nine years earlier.

This favourable balance was also due to my simple lifestyle, frugality, adoration of isolated locations where money is of no use, and my philosophy of negligible vessel and equipment damage.

Electrical repair performed anchored in Rio Chorcha in Panama, note mosquito net on bunk.
Mosquito net effective against mosquitos however nocturnal tiny biting flies pass easly through.
Such flies found both in Panama and Brazil.

COASTAL SAILING

"An adventure is a sign of incompetence"
Vilhjalmur Steffansson,

If one is to successfully navigate the worlds high latitude oceans, two sets of skills and knowledge are required, coastal and offshore.

Coastal navigation requires piloting skills although the new electronic chart pilots with inputs such as GPS and radar seem to render this skill largely redundant, until of course the pilot, radar, or GPS malfunctions.

Other areas of coastal compulsory cruising knowledge will include competence predicting local tidal currents and wind direction based on topography, anchoring skills, and the immediate course of action to be implemented if the motor or other critical equipment fails when the vessel is immediately adjacent to land.

Efficiency and thus speed of deck work may be an important issue during coastal cruising because one is frequently remarkably close to shore or offshore rocks and drying banks, thus where it is acceptable to be blown out to sea, it is not acceptable to be blown or carried onto an exposed portion of earth's crust.

There are many areas in the world where detailed and accurate charts do not exist, as well there are many areas which are entirely uncharted, -this also applies to a few isolated areas on the Canadian, British Columbia coast-.

Electronic pilots are based on nautical charts; thus, such pilots are only accurate if the local charts are sufficiently detailed and accurate, therefore caution may be in order with electronic pilots in many areas of the world.

Therefore, the basic coastal piloting skills are still required if one is inclined to safely navigate in several isolated locations in the world.

An apparent contradiction between the usage of traditional piloting skills versus electronic pilots is that proficiency regarding the prior is unlikely be achieved while relying on the latter, thus I would suggest an initial period is required whereby electronic pilots are not permitted onboard.

Immediate assistance, or more likely the complete dearth assistance of any kind will be found available once one ventures into remote and isolated locations, thus one is again encouraged to foster an attitude and skill set promoting self sufficiency, simplicity, and self reliance.

Specifically, piloting skills include those that place one accurately on a paper chart, employing the use of nothing more than the nautical chart, ship's clock, estimated ship's speed over the bottom, ship's compass, and the mariner's ability to correctly combine and interpret such data.

An extremely uncomfortable state of mind, possibly bordering on panic is experienced if one is close to land within shallow water in combination with tidal current and numerous submerged rocks when the mariner is not absolutely assured of the vessel's position.

As well, serious damage to the vessel such as holed hull, broken keel bolts, bent or broken rudder, and destroyed propeller shaft and propeller can occur if the boat runs aground, such a collision may instantly disable the vessel.

Worst case scenarios which are not uncommon, entail a vessel running aground during a falling tide whereby not only the vessel is damaged, but it is also left high and dry and in the precarious position of possibly falling over on its side.

A hand bearing compass is a significant addition to the onboard navigation tool kit, unfortunately I have found the hand bearing compass to be an almost useless instrument on a steel hulled vessel, however on non-ferrous hulls I have found a hand bearing compass to be particularly useful.

On any coastal or offshore sailing vessel a properly adjusted ship's compass complete with deviation chart is obligatory.

One must be able with equal facility to fix one's position from the chart to land converting true to magnetic bearings, including the deviation correction and from the land to the chart using magnetic to true bearing conversion, again including deviation corrections.

Known points on charts such as lighthouses, beacons, capes, points, and mountains may all be utilized to chart a bearing line from land to the vessel, it is for such bearings that a hand-bearing compass is almost indispensable.

The skill of fixing the vessels position on a nautical chart must be perfected so that it can with confidence be correctly and consistently accomplished in a timely manner, when the visibility is less than ideal, in turbulent sea conditions, in rain driven by gale force winds, and in the company of emotional and physical conditions such as fear and seasickness.

It is important to create the ongoing habit while coastal cruising of identifying natural range bearing lines between successive points of land, lighthouses, charted mountains, and offshore islands, in an unofficial uncharted manner as one proceeds along a coastline, the purpose is to keep a 'feeling' for the vessel's location.

Such approximate positions are only bearing lines, thus will only indicate that the vessel is somewhere on this bearing line, however they must correspond and make ongoing sense with respect to your most recent plotted chart position.

The coastal mariner must always be aware that vessel drift due to wind and tidal current are always a possibility.

Mariners who use only electronic chart plotters seldom develop such an 'unofficial' sense of the vessels position.

Speed, distance, and time are interrelated and knowing two of the three, one can always calculate the third.

With practice one becomes very adept at estimating the speed of the vessel through the water, however one must be acutely aware that the vessels speed through the water is not always equal to the vessels speed over the bottom and it is speed over the bottom that is one of the critical metrics.

In the early nineteenth century Joshua Slocum who must be considered one of the gold standards in locating oneself on a chart upon arriving on an unfamiliar shore, succeeded in correctly identifying the entrance into Cockburn Channel in southern Chilean Patagonia after having being blown to leeward for over three days with very limited visibility, very poor chart, no electronic aids to navigation, flirting with sea sickness because he had lost his sea legs after having spent a period of months within protected waters, and the fear of certain destruction without the possibility of rescue if blown ashore.

The two most powerful sources of fear I have experienced have been created by the possibility of being swept ashore on an open coast and of being run over by a freighter.

Piloting skills must be practised and then practised some more, first practised where accurate charts exist and in conditions that progress from ideal to poor and violent, and then practised in areas where accurate charts do not exist, only then is one prepared to venture into isolated high latitude locations.

There is nothing that focuses one's attention on the present such as when one is off a lee shore and is fixing the vessel's position preparing to enter a narrow entrance of an anchorage for the first time.

Lee shore off the wind entrances can and should be sailed into, however if under power raised sails which are appropriate to the wind conditions must be kept raised so that the mariner retains the ability to immediately turn and sail back to windward and safety.

This is prudent because if one decides for whatever reason to abort the entrance, it may still be possible to sail immediately back to windward.

The motor can and should be idling with the transmission not engaged, as well, our ever-present final safety device which is the anchor must be ready for immediate deployment.

Be aware however that on an open coastal approach in

gale or above wind conditions, a sailing vessels anchor is unlikely to hold the vessel from being driven ashore. Gale force or stronger onshore wind and sea conditions always present the point of approach concept, after which no retreat is possible, and onward is the only option.

After relinquishing the sea, I am still somewhat covetous of situations which force one to live fully focused on the present and a final well-planned approach and successful entry into an open coast anchorage during gale force conditions is one such situation.

I have successfully entered numerous potentially very hazardous open ocean narrow anchorage entrances, often becoming humbled by the successful entry, the vessel having purposefully passed less than a boat length of disaster.

Prior to the actual entry, one must preferably memorize the entry route to be followed and then completely focus on its completion, always suspecting that changes may occur such as expected wind direction and strength, tidal current speed and direction, and the possible unexpected appearance of rocks, patches of kelp, or other obstructions.

It is not a sin to dry out wet and crumpled charts after such an entry because some entrances are complicated requiring the use of several tight turns which must be performed adjacent to previously selected specific shoreline markers.

Expensive commercial nautical charts are much more forgiving of such treatment than photocopied paper copies, however a suitable number of commercial original charts are also prohibitively expensive.

Such skills, insights, and actions must become as close

to routine as possible, on occasion they must be immediately implemented.

Prior to embarking on a passage when I was not in possession of an adequate printed chart for the proposed area of landfall at an isolated and exposed location, I would boot up my pirated CMAP program and hand draw an 'arrival' chart with sufficient shoreline information and bearings so that I could safely enter and anchor within a sheltered location, although it must be remembered that such electronic charts may contain less than sufficient information.

Published coastal pilots can be useful in this respect, however such pilots are typically written for use by deep sea freighters and other large ocean-going vessels, not under powered sailing vessels.

Local tidal current strength and direction is another important variable which can be provided by digital world tide and current tables, although successful implementation of such information still relies on the ability to use the previously noted three basic pieces of coastal piloting equipment.

I have invested the modest personal brain power which I have available concerning the determination of local tides with respect to published sun and moon positions, but without consistent success.

The skill to effectively interpret natures freely provided aural and visual indications of seawater covered rocks, tidal currents, gusty winds, and surging water must be learned, practice is necessary.

In another section of this book, I deal with the subject of selecting an arbitrary arrival point located a suitable distance offshore, where one must decide either to proceed, heave-to, or alter course.

The coastal piloting skills of the mariner along with the functional onboard equipment, useful charts, and of course the weather prognosis and conditions must then guide the decision to proceed.

I am not recommending that the latest electronic aids to navigation are not utilized, rather that they are used in conjunction with functional and well-maintained traditional piloting skills.

I suspect that most ocean mariners under sail do not have onboard such functional and basic chart and compass coastal piloting skills, but rather rely on electronic pilots, GPS, radar, and a powerful motor.

I would add to this insufficiency the fact that most ocean sailors who are also furling sailors, do not possess the necessary functional and ready for immediate implementation foredeck experience, confidence, nor equipment to change sails or deal with unforeseen events such as torn sails, fouled sails, or fouled rigging. Such problems occurring during the final stages of open ocean anchorage approaches can quickly escalate and end in near or actual disaster.

Alcidae III was not fitted with an electronic chart plotter, however after graduating from Alcidae II I did add GPS and radar to my navigational equipment inventory. I left Victoria in 2004 on my third offshore voyage with approximately nine hundred and fifty paper charts, as well as a recently professionally adjusted ship's compass and deviation chart.

I also had installed a variable vertical magnet located beneath the binnacle compass, so that I could adjust for the change in the dip of the earth's magnetic field after I had entered the magnetic southern hemisphere.

The digital CMAP copy which appeared to be standard

on most cruising boats, is a wonderful bit of software which I would not recommend being without.

The ability to place the cursor at the ship's position with the aid of the GPS and confirmed by radar is at the same time seducing, powerful, and useful.

Seducing, in the sense that a prudent mariner should also rely on the agreement of as many indications of position as possible, which would include plotted position, compass bearings, water depth, regional topography, and inner voice.

I do not advocate the avoidance of using the latest piloting electronic advances, I do advocate learning, developing, and maintaining the basic coastal piloting skills which do not utilize such electronic aids.

There are also other problems concerning total reliance on the electronics, for example in Chilean Patagonia a chart datum is used which is dissimilar to other areas of the world, and the vessels GPS position is approximately 1.5 nautical miles from your actual position which presents a potential problem at night or in poor visibility when transiting the narrow Patagonian channels.

The years that I sailed on the British Columbia south and north coasts, I accumulated and made notes of significant amounts of local knowledge.

The most important bits are items such as anchorages with good and known anchor holding characteristics, the actual direction of gale and storm force winds within anchorages before, during, and after cold frontal passage.

Local knowledge also includes documented information concerning entering bays and channels where the direction and strength of currents is affected by wind direction.

Local knowledge contains information regarding the quality of the holding bottom which is best assessed by collecting a sample.

I found a useful tool for sampling the bottom conditions of an anchorage was to use a 0.3-meter piece of 50 mm diameter stainless steel propeller shaft, to which a line has been attached with the opposite end drilled with a 10 mm diameter hole to a depth of at least 10 mm.

This device may then be bumped across the bottom as the vessel is drifting to leeward along the surface, one develops the hand sensitivity to distinguish between rock, gravel, sand, muddy sand, firm mud, and sloppy mud.

Often in mud conditions, an actual sample of the bottom material will appear in the drilled hole.

The actual bottom material characteristics are important regarding choosing the correct anchor design and minimum scope of anchor rode to be deployed.

Ship pilots which are issued typically by governments as well as those written by cruisers may both contain particularly useful anchorage information.

Anchoring in storm force winds with possibly of the presence of williwaws, is also an obligatory coastal skill.

I have always sailed single-handed and have always utilized a pitifully under powered motor, therefore I have been obliged to develop anchoring strategies and techniques which are suitable for such a limited crew and motor.

Solo mariners, especially those with low powered motors have limited ability to safely haul anchor and move to a more sheltered position or reset anchors once gale to storm force winds or williwaws have entered the anchorage.

I instituted another ship's rule which indicated that if gale or storm force winds entered or were likely to enter the anchorage, moving the vessel would not be an option, thus I always prepared plans to defend the vessel without the necessity to move.

This illustrates one of many reasons why I always prefer an anchorage where I am the only vessel because most of my problems in anchorages have not been due to my own inadequate practices, rather to other vessels with dragging anchors.

Therefore the strategy of staying in place throughout the storms duration is my preferred course of action, one must consider ahead of time what will be done if the main anchor starts to drag, where might additional anchors be placed before the arrival of strong winds, which direction will winds take subsequent to frontal or low centre passage as well as having a standby anchor prepared for immediate deployment in the event of main anchor dragging, or an unexpected wind direction change to an unprotected quadrant.

These scenarios often lead to the placement of multiple anchors along with related gear, which results in substantial manual hauling of such gear at the termination of strong wind, however this is much more desirable than dragging one's vessel off the shoreline.

My prepared standby anchor in the event of the main anchor dragging or wind blowing from an unexpected quadrant, is always a different type of anchor than that deployed because dragging has often resulted because of an inappropriate anchor design about holding potential of the various bottom categories.

A significant component of my storm force anchorage strategy is the presence and immediate availability of my precious rigid rowing skiff.

The skiff on Alcidae III had been substantially modified and was never to be a welcome site approaching alongside other cruisers topsides, however commercial fishermen the world over have not been concerned.

The fibreglass constructed skiff was 2.8 meters in length and weighs about 100 kg, was fitted with heavy stainless steel oar locks and oar lock holders, as well as a separate stainless-steel stern and bow mounted skiff hoisting attachment.

The stern fitting was also designed to accept without abrasive damage the deployment and retrieval of ample lengths of anchor chain during manual anchor deployment and retrieval.

Essentially unbreakable oar locks, oar lock holders, and oars are obligatory because if any of these components break at an unexpected moment of exertion, very perilous circumstances may be experienced.

A young robust single-handed sailor during moments of fear or other powerful motivations can exert large forces onto such skiff rowing fittings.

The oars were in the order of 70 mm in diameter and greater than 2 meters in length, of which I carried three pairs made in Chile as well as one pair made in Brazil, all were fitted with their own set of heavy-duty stainless-steel oar locks.

I was to demonstrate on numerous occasions that a motivated mariner can row to windward in anchorages experiencing strong winds, wind generated waves, strong tidal currents, darkness, snow, and rain while transporting and deploying a substantial load of an-

chor, chain, and attached nylon rode.
If necessary, such ground tackle can be skiff deployed in the most advantageous location to prevent that experience that I want to complete my life without experiencing, being blown ashore.
The crane in the Buffalo River in South Africa that finally succeeded in lifting the vessel from the water only did so because I was forced to unload almost three tons of gear, a significant portion of which consisted of anchors and the necessary chain.

Once heavy loads are put on the anchor rode or shorelines, effective anti-chafe gear is critical.
On several occasions after a long period of violent wind gusts, I have repeatedly been amazed at the strain that a properly set anchor system will withstand, the entire time maintaining the anchored vessels position.
In 2008 I arrived in Chilean Patagonia after numerous years of anchoring experience, at that time I considered the use of shorelines as being beneath my dignity, however that has all changed, since Patagonia I have used shorelines in combination with anchors whenever I have the opportunity, mainly because of the additional security provided by using a combination of both anchors and shorelines.
Attaching three anchor rodes, each set in the order of one hundred and twenty degrees with respect to each other and all attached to one end of a heavy-duty underwater swivel is a powerful combination which allows the vessel to maintain bow to what may be frequently and violently changing wind directions.
This three-anchor swivel arrangement -because it permits the bow to always face the wind- also provides a hedge regarding anchorages for which reliable local

knowledge concerning expected wind direction is not known.

Such swivel usage is also eminently successful when anchoring in rivers or tidal estuaries where the wind is not always from the same direction as the potentially strong tidal or river current.

Conditions such as this can be uncomfortable and even dangerous because the vessel will lie to the current direction even when strong wind and steep and breaking wind generated waves may strike the vessel on it is beam.

Such wind and wind generated waves can cause the vessel to maintain a list to port or starboard and the resulting waves will break over the vessel.

The most dramatic such situation I experienced when I was anchored well up the tidal estuary in Puerto Deseado in southern Argentinian Patagonia, the boat due to tidal current would lie broadside to extraordinarily strong wind and the wind generated waves which would break and throw spray athwart-ship to leeward passing over the entire vessel.

The vessel end of the three-anchor swivel arrangement is attached to the vessel using two separate large diameter lines, each moored to a separate bow mooring bit.

The three anchors rode swivel method also requires that the three lines be held underwater, therefore the use of weights hanging from each anchor rode are employed to prevent fouling by the anchor rodes on the vessels keel, rudder, zinc anodes, or propeller during vessel swinging.

I used a combination of beach combed fishing net which were fashioned into bags, into which suitable rocks were placed.

These separate bags were suspended from individual anchor rodes at one to two ship's lengths from the swivel.

These hanging weights also fulfill the gratuitous role of kedges on the anchor rode, which increase its effective scope, thus extra rocks in the net bags were always welcome.

On occasion, I would reserve the right to use one or more shorelines attached to the swivel and if this were the case, similar rock bags would be tied to the shorelines as well, although be aware that shorelines are usually floating polypropylene, thus the hanging weights may need to be heavier to overcome the buoyancy of the shoreline when it is not under strain.

I carried three one-meter-long stainless-steel angle iron pitons (50mm x 50mm x 7mm thick) which I would use if needed to drive into rock crevices to serve as shoreline anchors, if a suitably located natural shoreline anchor was not present.

Shorelines were always polypropylene due to it is floating ability and lengths of chain are required to overcome chafe issues between the shoreline anchor point and sufficiently deep water.

All this gear must be transported and retrieved using the skiff, also shoreline topography in the desired location of the shoreline anchors is not always ideal, which is one more justification for a robust skiff.

I also had protected the bottom of the skiff with three lengthwise stainless-steel strips to provide increased hull protection while driving the skiff up rocky shores.

Polypropylene's ability to float also explains why thousands of meters of such line can be economically beach combed in open ocean locations such as the Aleutian Islands, thus there appears not to be financial reasons not to carry several hundred meters onboard, as well as providing a valid reason to visit the Aleutian Islands.

One should exercise caution during beach combing as there seems to be a communicable infection which compels one to scour beaches for useful and not so useful jetsam, this communicable infection often seems to require several decades to be cured and can result in several hundred kilograms of onboard ultimately useless material.

Having provided this disclaimer, beach combing is a very agreeable method of passing the time and finding innumerable treasures.

When one finds oneself in an anchorage concurrently with storm force or stronger winds, the well being, and accessibility of the skiff are critical.

Storm force and stronger winds can generate in the order of one-meter waves even within a fetch of less than one hundred meters, therefore mooring a rigid skiff along side is not a viable option when anchored or utilizing a combination of anchors and shorelines.

The only viable option I have found is to allow the skiff to trail up to ten meters to leeward off the stern, all oars and floating equipment are removed.

In such a position the skiff will often partially or even completely fill with spray and rainwater, which turns out to be a useful weight which prevents the skiff overturning due to high wind velocities.

I do not recommend the skiff be stored on deck because it must be available for immediate use.

As noted, a properly built and equipped skiff with sufficiently strong oars and oarlocks can be used to row out an additional anchors or shorelines if required.

The standby anchor, chain, and rode to be potentially deployed from the skiff are placed along the appropriate deck for immediate transfer into the skiff.

I tend to be understandably criticized for being somewhat excessively "what if" in life, however I interpret the disorder as preparing for all eventualities and I credit my success in avoiding most "adventures" in my later sailing career, to just such a personality disorder.

I am attracted to the quote that "Luck is when preparation meets opportunity".

FOOD

Eight different species of fruits on the Marquesian island of Ua Huka.

Food turns out to be a critical component of voyaging under sail and I was fortunate to have many options which were unavailable to Captain Cook, as well as nineteenth century whalers and sealers.

Captain Cook as well as the whalers and sealers had a

crew which included a cook, thus regular hot meals were provided, this is not always the case with present day single-handed mariners however regular meals of nutritious food are equally important.

Regular nutritious meals are a critical factor if one is to expect to arrive on an unfamiliar open coast in a suitable physical and mental condition so that correct decisions are taken, and so that the physical body will be capable of the necessary exertions.

Nutritious food also appears to be an important factor concerning the physical bodies capability to withstand cold temperatures.

The onboard refrigeration system may at anytime fail and thus a diet which does not require refrigeration must be considered.

As well, an alternative method of heating and cooking food should be established in the very unlikely event of an unsolvable problem concerning the main galley stove, even though an extensive list of stove spare parts will be onboard.

I tended to spend from a few weeks to several months without any opportunity for resupply, thus provisioning the ship is a critical issue.

I am possibly fortunate in that if a bell curve distribution exists with those who live to eat on one end and those who eat to live on the other, I find myself close to the latter extreme.

This is not to say that I am not routinely in awe, satiated, and inspired by the French, who contribute not only competent single-handed mariners but also an abundance of mariners who seem able to make extremely palatable gastronomic creations quickly and efficiently, often from remarkably simple ingredients.

Since my early twenties I have eaten my own variation of Red River Cereal, a brand which will be recognized by many Canadians.

At sea and throughout my voyages I used a German made manual whole grain cracker with which, following twenty minutes circular manual labour provided a two-week supply of breakfast material.

Red River cereal is a mixture of flax seeds, cracked wheat grains, and cracked rye grains to which I add a quarter cup of raisins.

Upon leaving Canada, -where all ingredients are readily available- my vessel contained four ten litre snap sealed plastic pails, each containing wheat and rye whole grains, as well as another identical ten litre pail containing flax seeds.

These five pails, without the need of resupply, provide almost three years of breakfast material.

Resupply of rye turned out to be a problem outside of Canada however whole wheat grains as well as flax and raisins were available, thus during the last two thirds of my nine-year duration third voyage, rye was to be missing from my onboard version of Red River Cereal.

As mentioned, to this breakfast material I add only water and a small handful of raisins, the raisins are also stored in their own ten litre plastic pails and can be easily sourced in many countries.

My vessel was not noted for its stylish interior; however, it was purposefully altered to stow in the order of twenty ten litre sealed plastic containers which contained my health sustaining staples.

The principle of a relatively monotonous breakfast menu was also to be applied to my lunch and dinner menus.

Lunch would often entail my own canned sauerkraut, wholewheat bread – made from using whole wheat flour to be found in four ten litre plastic pails-, cheese, dried or canned soup, and canned or my own dried and pickled tuna.

When transiting tropical waters, I often landed tuna, wahoo, mahi mahi, and barracuda.

These fish would provide fresh meat, relatively long-lasting refrigerated ceviche, and almost indefinitely lasting dried strips.

The steel deck in the tropics turned out to be superb for drying fish strips which were arranged to facilitate drying upon stainless steel cooking sheets.

Both arrivals in the Aleutian Islands as well as the arrival at Kerguelen witnessed two or more recycled rice sacks filled with dried strips of fish, such dried fish filled rice sacks would continually beat out the motion of the sea while suspended from the ceiling salon hand holds, as well as possibly providing a fishy odour.

Landing Mahi Mahi was not without hesitation, it is not uncommon to see a second unhooked Mahi Mahi attend the hooked individual and apparently attempt to get it off the hook.

Mahi Mahi, Yellow Fin tuna, and Waho are probably the most delicious fish that I have ever tasted.

Dinners would usually entail dipping into one of the two ever present four litre plastic containers at the bottom of my cold box/refrigerator.

The contents of these two containers would probably not taste noticeably different had one a typical palette, both contained a mixture of cooked white beans, soybeans, peas, lentils, mung beans, and kidney beans, -all of which are easily sourced throughout the world-, stored in yet more of my precious ten litre snap lid plastic pails.

In addition to the above pulses, I also carried mung beans, alfalfa seeds and mustard seeds for the purpose of sprouting.

To the cooked pulses I would add my own onboard canned tomatoes, canned smoked and non smoked pork, beef, and hamburger along with tomato sauce and various spices.

I carried onboard approximately two hundred reusable glass one litre canning jars as well as a large aluminum pressure canner, which could hold seven one litre jars and carried onboard what I termed a lifetime supply of single use jar sealing lids.

In locations such as Puerto Montt in Chile, Buenos Aires in Argentina, and East London in South Africa I was to find markets where I would buy large quantities of fresh foods such as meat and tomatoes, which I would then process on board into my sealed and carefully stowed glass one litre containers.

In such locations it was not an uncommon site to see me carrying my two large El Salvador reusable plastic shopping bags from market to bus, bus to skiff, skiff to vessel, and then proceed to process onboard.

Once aboard, the priority was to process and stow this precious cargo before spoilage could degrade the market fresh quality.

Throughout all three of my offshore voyages, I did not break a single sealed one litre glass container, rather only a few empty jars were broken entirely due to my carelessness.

I had fabricated specialized western red cedar wooden trays which could contain exactly two dozen glass jars

and stored the majority of these in my below floor bilge area.
The metal screw tops are only necessary for the actual canning process and not desirable for storage due to their propensity to corrode, which will result in rusting between the screw top and the metal vacuum sealing lid.
Properly processed and stored produce filled jars remain viable, sealed, and useful for well over three years, thus storage to prevent metal to metal corrosion is important.
The metal screw tops which are removed immediately after processing are stored in a large pot submerged within paraffin wax which has been momentarily melted.
In this manner enough metal screw top lids are kept corrosion free and available for immediate usage, after reheating of the paraffin.
I also maintained a separate supply of paraffin coated metal screw top lids stored in sealed plastic bags.
In higher latitudes cabbage, garlic, and onions linger for extended periods of time without refrigeration, however in tropical and subtropical latitudes refrigeration can extend the useful life of these vegetables in a significant manner.
Thus a few cups of my refrigerated bean concoctions would be added to a pan of freshly sauteed cabbage, garlic, and onions with the whole lot being placed on a layer of freshly steamed rice.
It is not an understatement to say such repetitive meals were the main source of evening nutrition throughout my several years navigating the world's oceans.
In locations such as the Chilean and Argentine Patago-

nian coasts, Aleutian Islands, and Kerguelen, I would add various plants found onshore, most of whom belonged to the Brassicaceae family which was a practice not dissimilar to that implemented by Captain Cook two hundred and thirty years earlier.

A mariner such as I spend almost equal time in the subtropics and more temperate higher latitudes, thus two pieces of equipment become indispensable.

The wood burning stove in the higher latitudes and refrigeration in all regions, but especially the tropics.

A new refrigeration system was installed before my second offshore voyage in 2000 and was to remain trouble free throughout offshore voyages numbers two and three.

I installed a standard 12-volt DC hermetic compressor which supplied hot refrigerant gas to a standard fan cooled aluminum condenser followed by a stainless-steel glycol containing holding plate type evaporator, which was mounted at the bottom of my cold box.

The cold box was fitted with a suitably sized top mounted removable lid, 250 mm of rigid polyurethane insulation, waterproof fibre-glassed interior surface, and an interior volume of 0.15 cubic meters.

The upper half held a removable shelf, half of which was composed of wooden slats and half of stainless-steel grate.

As noted elsewhere, ship's policy dictated essentially total abstention concerning the motor from the departure anchorage until destination arrival, even though this often required between one and two months at sea, therefore a functional non fossil fuel electrical supply system for the battery driven hermetic compressor was imperative.

The battery charging system, which was exclusive of the ship's engine, consisted of two seventy-five-watt solar panels and a KISS wind generator, both mounted on the transom arch.

The combination of solar and wind is imperative, it is also imperative to harvest all available power when the opportunity presents itself, which often means running the refrigeration compressor at night whenever battery charging wind has been provided.

Such pragmatic energy harvesting requires the compressor's thermostat to be bypassed, thus the compressor is run continuously when there is sufficient power available, providing the opportunity for the holding plate and insulation to maintain the cold inner temperature between periods of energy availability.

Such refrigeration operation greatly reduces the electrical load and therefore extends the useful life of the expensive ship's lead acid batteries.

One must be cautious not to run the compressor excessively which will result in freezing items in the cold box, although my beans did not seem to mind.

The other critical bit of gear noted above is the wood burning stove.

I intellectually conceived the design for the perfect wood stove which would be made to fit the location that was available, however the vast majority of my theoretically efficient non creosote creating wood combustion system did not actually work.

It is clearly understood that on an ocean sailing vessel there are no unused locations available for a wood stove and chimney, however one must be found or created for this purpose.

The result was a mixture of 5 mm mild steel plate, 5 mm

stainless steel smoke baffles, and 25 mm fire bricks, all of which, minus the fire bricks required two strong men to move.

The stove was through bolted to the vessel's sole and fitted with a 250 mm diameter by 4 mm wall stainless steel pipe, which was welded both to the stove and fitted into a specially made stainless steel deck insert.

Fitted also, was a suitable heat shield in conjunction with an integral interior wood drying rack.

As noted, this equipment undergoes no usage within the tropics and subtropics however I elevate its presence to critical within all higher latitudes.

Mussels collected in Chilian and Argentinian Patagonia were stored in a sack suspended from the transom.

The flat stove top which is fitted with welded stainless-steel fiddles can be used for heating food and large energy consuming applications such as steaming clams, mussels, crabs, and heating full buckets of wash water for the odd occasions when I wanted a full body wash. A bucket of hot water would be emptied into the solar shower which would be affixed to the boom in the cockpit and a great deal of steam would conceal the bather in the often-frigid cockpit.

I must admit that this shower capability was not overly exploited when Patricia was not onboard.

French mariners do not appear to concern themselves with nudity while showering or washing on deck and I have often had a hard time recognizing a fully clothed 'neighbour' when encountered onshore.

The stainless-steel bucket used for water heating applications was to enjoy a constant presence on the wood stove.

The warm and dry heat generated by a wood stove fitted with an adequate diameter chimney creates a comfortable and welcoming interior, even though the vessel's exterior may be covered with snow or pelted by driving rain and wind.

Such a system operates only within a secure anchorage due to the two-meter-long removable exterior section of smokestack which is attached on deck along with three supporting guy lines which are attached to both sets of upper shrouds and the port side back stay.

The immense joy achieved immediately upon arriving in a secure anchorage after a long, rough, and cold heatless passage, is to erect the smokestack, start the fire from the weeks supply of dried firewood found aboard, leave the stove access door ajar until one sees the base of the stainless-steel smokestack become cherry red, and then begin to sense the dry and welcoming warmth.

This is always followed by consumption of my arrival hot rum followed by a few more libations in the company of my habitual arrival opera.

The same arrival ritual minus the wood stove and hot rum would also be rigidly observed for all tropical and subtropical arrivals.

Other than at Kerguelen, I have always found an abundance of firewood freely available within the upper range of the inter-tidal zone.

Australia and New Zealand are two locations in the world where my philosophy towards provisioning the ship were certain to present problems.

Prior to my entrance into the Southern Indian Ocean, I had intended to travel from South Africa directly to New Caledonia, leaving Australia to port and New Zealand to starboard because I was fully aware of the customs policies in these two countries.

Visiting Captain Cook's anchorages in Tasmania and New Zealand as well as the indigenous botany in both countries attracted me immensely however the entry regulations concerning my onboard food supply of whole grains, legumes, self processed canned foods -as well as certain professionally processed canned foods-, made this untenable, as well my cat and several pairs of handmade wooden oars also would present insurmountable issues.

It was in view of these restrictions I had originally planned to voyage from Kerguelen directly to New Caledonia without stopping in either Australia nor New Zealand, however damage sustained within the first two days after leaving Kerguelen, as well as six subsequent gale and storm encounters during this forty-nine-day passage, necessitated a repair stop in Tasmania.

I therefore established an email contact with the Australian authorities via Winlink -Sailmail is not functional in this region of the Indian Ocean-.

The email contact concerned my damage issues, my numerous onboard issues concerning prohibited items, and the fact that nautical prudence necessitated a stop for repairs.

I was given permission to stop for repairs in Hobart and the authorities were fully aware of my numerous contraventions of their entry requirements including what turned out to be more than twenty litres of gin and excessive quantities of South African wine and beer.

Tongue firmly in cheek and careful to avoid sarcasm, I thanked the customs officers for providing such a thorough inspection because after eight years of my third voyage even I had lost track of the exact onboard locations of my spirit supplies.

Prior to my arrival in Hobart, I had been in radio contact for several months with Jeanne Socrates on SV Nerieda who was in Hobart when I arrived, and who also nudged the authorities on my behalf as well as finding me a boatyard to perform my steel repairs.

I arrived at the appropriate dock in Hobart and was immediately visited by customs, agriculture, and immigration.

The agriculture inspectors were noteworthy in seeing, but then again apparently not seeing all my prohibited forms of wood, cat, and food.

Customs and immigration inspectors wanted me to prove I had accomplished the passage that I claimed and requested to view my digital plotter position record.

I did not have such a device onboard thus they finally accepted my daily noon positions indicated by a daily 'x' noted on the very small-scale ocean chart.

They then inquired if I had a locker they could seal, in which they would place all my illicit alcohol, whereby I provided the chain locker which was soon filled followed by the necessity of an additional galley locker.

Thus, the inspectors generously permitted me to retain my entire supply of alcoholic beverages with the proviso it remained sealed in the two lockers.

The inspectors made it clear that they would temporarily waive all my contraventions with the understanding that I would only be permitted to moor to a buoy and only as necessary temporarily moor alongside to make structural steel repairs.

The cat was to remain on board and was required to be kept in a cage during periods when I was moored alongside for repairs.

It was also made clear that when my repairs were complete, I must immediately leave the country.

I remain grateful for the many accommodations made by the Australian authorities as well as to Jeanne for finding me a buoy on which to tie, which turned out to be owned by a local boatyard which very generously provided me access to their repair dock, welding electricity, scrap stainless steel, and usage of their repair shop.

I had the additional good fortune to meet two 'Tassies', Margarite and Peter, who greatly improved my well-being via transportation, logistics, and friendship.

I had first met them prior to checking in on my second night anchored at the south end of Tasmania.

My meeting with Margarite and Peter at the south end of Tasmania was also the first people I had seen -other than a single-handed French sailor who is not overly dissimilar to myself-, in just over five months since leaving South Africa.

Shortly after my arrival back in Canada in the fall of 2013 after the nine-year duration third voyage, I was to find that long periods without fresh fruit and vegetables as well as long periods of confinement while at sea, did have a temporary negative impact on my physical health which was reasonably quickly rectified upon the restoration of access to the necessary foods and exercise.

Throughout my travels I have made it a priority to gastronomically experience all possible local fruits and vegetables and I will conclude my subject of food by presenting my favourite fruit, which is the grapefruit (Citrus maxima) found in many tropical Pacific Ocean environments, especially French Polynesia.

This precious fresh fruit has travelled many thousands of miles swinging in one of my salon hammock style storage nets and would easily remain edible without refrigeration for periods more than two months.

Another member of the same genus with similar storage characteristics are limes (Citrus aurantiifolia), which I would place second only to the grapefruit.

OFFSHORE & HEAVY WEATHER

As previously noted, two broad sets of nautical skills are required, this section is concerned with offshore skills however many specific skills presented equally apply to coastal sailing and the mariner will already have achieved an admirable degree of competence regarding these skills before heading offshore.

Open ocean passages north of forty degrees north latitude and south of forty degrees south latitude present a significantly higher risk of abrupt weather conditions than passages completed between those two parallels of latitude, however all open ocean passages within all latitudes must be undertaken with respect for the forces of nature and all such passages will provide the opportunity to view sea mammals and pelagic seabirds which cannot otherwise be experienced.

One of the most precious aspects of voyaging some of the world's oceans in a sailing vessel, is viewing pelagic mammals and seabirds in their natural offshore habitat.

This habitat is essentially totally hostile to humans, in that humans would survive for a truly short period of time without several technical precautions, whereas the ocean mammals and seabirds are in their element and are perfectly adapted to thrive.

I have several precious mental images concerning whales, dolphins, penguins, and pelagic fur seals.

Fur seals can be a regular and always welcome visitor to offshore sailing vessels, I have observed the highest numbers in April off the Washington, Oregon, and Northern Californian coasts.

These agile, curious, and seemingly nonaggressive to mankind -while in their aquatic natural element-, are delighted to behold.

I was to find that on isolated Southern Ocean islands such as Kerguelen, one must be overly cautious in the vicinity of fur seals when they may be encountered on land.

I have made three passages down the west coast of North America, Victoria to Monterey, California, Victoria to the equator south of Hawaii, and Victoria to Ensenada, Mexico.

Upon leaving Ensenada bound for El Salvador, I have a mental image which does not appear likely to diminish with time, which entails two breaching side by side adult Blue Whales which appeared at approximately forty meters from the vessel.

They appeared to be travelling and breaching at the same speed and were not dissimilar in synchronization to two choreographed perfectly synchronized swimmers.

This enduring mental image includes both images of the two whales in perfect side by side unison, and their colour which is what I termed Mediterranean blue.

The combination of size, power, coordination, and colour of these two mammals are the principal components of this memory.

I spent most of the fourteen months duration of my second offshore training voyage traversing the equator between the Line Islands and the Marshall Islands, during which time I had several opportunities to view sea turtles mostly at sea, but also on atoll tropical beaches.

These reptiles are wonderfully adapted to the open tropical ocean and when encountered at sea, like large whales also provide the sense that one is in the company of gentle ocean creatures.

They are occasionally encountered sleeping on the surface and can then -under sail- be approached quite closely, although otherwise they are usually quite wary and cannot be approached closer than fifty to one hundred meters.

My final entry at this time concerning sea mammals must be left to the many species of dolphins to be found throughout all the world's oceans that I have visited.

I will not provide a favourite species because whenever a single animal or group of dolphins would cross the oceans surface to 'greet' me, I would always drop what I was doing, regardless of the weather and go and sit on the bow pulpit seat and observe, softly whistle, wave, speak, smile, nod, and enjoy these magnificent animals.

While engaged in such bow pulpit activity, there seems little doubt that these sea mammals were also aware of my presence and behaviour.

They would often hold station with the bow of the vessel, not more than two meters from the observer and often distinctly appear to be looking you in the eye.

The joy and sense of contentment experienced when one is in relatively close contact with dolphins is enduring, in that the final group of dolphins I observed during my entire period of sailing resulted in a similar level of joy and sense of well being as the first I had observed several decades previous.

I stated that I would not provide a favourite species, however I do rate very highly the Pacific White Sided Dolphin.

One of the most critical concerns when navigating the world's open oceans is heavy weather, if inappropriately managed can result in serious vessel, equipment, and personal damage.

Once the mariner is in possession of the necessary repertoire of coastal skills, it is time to develop the necessary offshore skills although both skill sets are closely interwoven.

The major difference between coastal and offshore heavy weather skills must be that offshore, one cannot hide but rather must implement suitable defensive action.

The prudent mariner must recognize when it is time to reduce sail or to take other more extreme defensive measures, most of these skills will already have been developed to a suitable level during the coastal sailing training period.

One must become tuned to the vessel so that it is immediately apparent when the self steering, and other ship's gear starts to become strained.

To be able to accomplish this the mariner must be familiar with the normal sounds generated by all ship's gear.

Regarding the self steering gear, in addition to the sounds of strain such as control lines and turning blocks there will usually commence an increase in vessel yawing which will result in increasing off course increments steered, along with the corresponding increasing steering over corrections as well as excessive vessel speed and listing.

The mariner only acquires the suite of obligatory vessel awareness through progressive practice and experience, it is not developed to the necessary degree from solely reading or attending sailing courses.

The first course of action is usually reducing sail area in a manner which maintains sail balance and reduces or normalizes the strain on the steering gear and rigging.

Recall that the priority is to arrive without damage to the vessel, gear, or oneself, thus reducing speed and lengthening the time spent at sea must not be considered as items to be avoided.

This discussion of heaving-to may well have been placed in the coastal sailing section of this book because it is during this initial phase of training that the essential heaving-to skills in conjunction with its limitations must be acquired, however it is closely related to heavy weather management in the open ocean thus is presented in this section.

When it is necessary to reduce sail area by reefing, sail change, or their combination, the pressure must first be removed from the sails and rig and way taken off the vessel.

The safest method of reducing the pressure on a sail is to stop the vessel in the water and heave-to, perform the necessary deck work and then continue course.

I will discuss later in this section specifics of action to be taken if vessel speed has been allowed to increase excessively thus creating the potential for a broach if sailing off the wind, however at this point in the discussion we will assume a timely decision has been made to reduce sail and the vessel speed is not excessive.

Achieving a hove-to configuration, the vessel becomes much more stable and wallows in the water drifting to leeward at a rate which depends on the velocity of the wind but is usually at least one knot and can increase to approximately five knots.

Heaving-to is also considered desirable because if one was to fall overboard, one could likely climb back on as the vessel rolls back to whichever side one may find oneself, although to increase the degree of safety during hove-to deck work I endeavour to access the bow on the leeward side of the vessel, so that if I were to fall overboard the vessel will be drifting towards me and I will find myself on the low side where the gunnel may well be rhythmically dipping into the water.

Alternatively, the overboard mariner could hand over hand oneself along the gunnel to the stern and climb up the steering gear or a fixed stern ladder.

The foregoing is simply a theorized rescue proposal which was never utilized because I have never fallen overboard, however I am very attracted to advance mental preparation.

Lying a hull without any sails raised and with the tiller lashed to leeward is a viable option if the seas are such that one is not likely to roll the vessel, otherwise lying a hull is not a viable option, in which case the vessel will be held in the hove-to position using either a headsail, mainsail, or both.

Pole work on the foredeck is exacting, physically demanding, and time-consuming work and is best completed with the vessel held in check hove-to using only the mainsail, thus when pole work is completed if the mainsail is no longer required for propulsion, it must be lowered and furled while the raised, luffing, and unsheeted headsail, is waiting to power the vessel.

From the cockpit the luffing head sail sheet can be hardened, and the vessel is brought underway and on course, the vessel having been in control and not lying a hull during the entire process.

All facets of heaving-to must be mastered throughout the entire spectrum of wind velocity increases in conjunction with the series of decreasing sail area changes. The speed of sail changes while hove-to is are not critical in the open ocean, rather organization, vessel control, and safety are considered the priorities.

The two main additions concerning offshore compared to coastal sailing heaving-to skills concerns the offshore increase in vessel motion and the related increased difficulty regarding the telescoping pole.

Coastal sailing often occurs mostly in relatively protected water where there is a direct relationship between wind increase and an increase in vessel motion due to wind driven waves, however in the open ocean the mariner also must deal with swell and wave trains from often multiple directions.

Heaving-to is the most useful and frequently selected option however like all other aspects in life, heaving-to is not without unwanted side effects.

The main heaving-to issue is mainsail luffing during each upwind hove-to cycle and the resulting potential for sail damage.

Such luffing is very destructive and can quickly damage the sail in winds more than forty knots, in addition to the violent shaking visited on the entire standing rig.

Therefore, speed and efficiency when performing deck work while hove-to within wind greater than forty knots is encouraged, however long-term heaving-to as a defensive measure with winds more than fifty knots is not recommended.

Speed and efficiency of hove-to sail changes can be important during coastal cruising due to drift towards a possibly nearby lee shore.

Sail changes and reductions attempted where insufficient distance to leeward is present, leads to panic, stress, and the increased potential for physical injury or equipment damage, therefore sail changes must be considered prior to approaching a lee shore or before the wind increases.

When hove-to, one is often making sail area changes during rapidly changing weather conditions and once the sail changes have been made and the vessel is back underway, it is not uncommonly determined that the vessel remains overpowered and thus further changes must be immediately made, thus one is encouraged to think of the next stage of sail reduction defence continually proactively.

I have found, concerning all three of my sailing vessels that in strong winds using only a mainsail that is appropriately reefed is the most effective means of heaving-to.

The optimum amount of sheeting of the main sheet will be determined with practice and is somewhat vessel specific.

The mainsail is precious and usually a spare is not onboard, therefore if damaged from a short period of violent luffing experienced during the brief passing of a cold front, serious issues are created.

I have already discussed tactics in the Seamanship chapter concerning lying a hull during brief potentially violent winds which may be encountered during thunderstorm or cold front passage.

If one is voyaging south of 40 degrees south latitude the vessel is likely to be subjected to the incomparable and magnificent southwest seas, which, when subjected to the appropriate conditions can morph into seas which are both impressive and imminently dangerous to sailing vessels such as Alcidae III, writers such as Joseph Konrad may have best described these Southern Ocean seas and the winds responsible for their generation.

The opportunity to view such Southern Ocean seas usually presents itself to mariners such as myself after a cold front has passed and the strong and sustained southwest wind which usually follows immediately on the heels of such a cold front, continues to blow for several days.

It is exactly the remnants of such winds and the resulting seas that the mariner can utilize to make good one's course downwind, once the wind and seas have suitably moderated and the Jordan Series Drogue has been retrieved.

When the time arrives to again get underway, the seas will remain quite simply immense but the dangerous breaking upper third will have ceased, however the following wind will likely remain strong for several hours to a few days thus the decision to again get underway requires prudence, experience, confidence, and practice.

The 19th century sailing vessels were designed, equipped, and crewed so that they were rarely required to enter a defensive posture in the southern oceans, rather they could continue to utilize the favourable seas and winds until they arrived off Bass Straits.

More than fifty knots wind speed my most viable option

for continued vessel, sail, and crew damage free existence is deployment of the Jordan Series drogue.

I have included my experience of being obliged to deploy and retrieve the Jordan Series Drogue seven times during the forty-nine-day passage between the west coast of Kerguelen and the east coast of Tasmania.

In the South Indian Ocean, this precious piece of equipment and my learned ability in it is use saved the vessel, myself, and Ede from multiple vessels roll overs.

The following procedures were developed during the seven deployments and retrievals in 2012 during the latter part of my nine-year circumnavigation (2004-2013) which saw the vessel both south of the Antarctic Convergence and within the Bering Sea.

The Jordan series drogue deployment and retrieval ideas are offered as a basis to build upon, the procedures presented have been demonstrated to be effective however I am confident other mariners will provide several improvements.

I constructed the drogue from purchased cones along with three different diameter double braid nylon lengths of rope that I had onboard, however very limited instructions in the actual use of the drogue came with the cones, as well, sparse information was available on the internet thus my purpose here is to share what I have learned in the hope of improving the actual heavy weather usage of this precious piece of survival gear which in effect permits mariners such as myself to safely transit potentially very rambunctious stretches of ocean.

The drogue cones that I received in South Africa appeared to be made of light spinnaker rip stop nylon type material, these cones would reveal obvious wear after each deployment and after seven deployments approximately ten percent of the cones appeared too frayed and worn to function.

Once I arrived in Hobart Tasmania, I ordered additional replacement cones, these had been made from a heavier and more rigid material.

The light material cones would more easily pass the sheet winch during retrievals however I preferred the heavier material.

In the interest of assisting other mariners, in 2014 I sent a copy like what will follow to the Seven Seas Cruising Association who replied that they could not publish this information in their newsletter because I was not a member, as well the Blue Water Cruisers Association and 48 North both indicated they may put the information into their data bases and thus make it available to members.

As noted, while in South Africa I ordered two hundred cones and proceeded to assemble my first drogue.

Upon completion this mixture of cones and rode resulted in a pyramid shaped pile in the order of one-meter high by almost one meter at the base, thus a storage issue.

I have subsequently observed a ready-made series drogue provided by an American supplier which all fits neatly into a small satchel.

This supplied drogue is much easier to store, deploy, and retrieve compared to my drogue, although my drogue was built as per the original Jordan instructions which I had found on the internet.

Mr. Jordan had stressed the importance of the ability of the rode to reduce shock loading by the stretching characteristics inherent in double braid nylon rope.

The manufactured drogue which I observed which was ready for deployment was contained within a laptop computer sized bag and included a single diameter non stretchable rode approximately 10 mm in diameter.

The single-handed sailor who owned this drogue reported to me that she had deployed two such manufactured drogues and both times the rode had broken.

My series drogue rode was constructed of 12 mm diameter double braid nylon for approximately the first into the water 30 meters, followed by 15 mm diameter double braid nylon for the next approximately 30 meters, followed by 25 mm diameter double braid nylon for the remainder of the drogue which in total contained one hundred and fifty cones.

I initially used the number of cones recommended on the website but found when the wind got above seventy knots, this number of cones would not hold the stern to the weather but rather the beam would start to come around to the seas, therefore in Tasmania I increased the number of drogues by approximately twelve percent.

I was not to use the drogue again because I did not again encounter suitable weather during my return trip to Canada via the Tasman Sea, South and North Pacific oceans, Aleutian Islands, and Gulf of Alaska.

All sections of the three different diameter double braid nylon rodes are connected with a carrick bend.

I had used a double sheet bend initially, however not even tools would loosen the tightened knot and during the sixth storm I lost the terminal third of the drogue because the line broke at the double sheet bend.

I had previously successfully used the double sheet bend knot to attach sections of conventional anchor rode as well as sections of shorelines, these knots had often been under considerable strain however the severe load imposed by the series drogue is in another category and I would now only use the carrick bend, what a magnificent knot!

I would not use shackles for fear they may cause injury to myself or damage to the vessel during drogue deployment and retrieval.

Careful thought and planning prior to drogue deployment are an absolute necessity due the extreme potential hazards of serious injury to the mariner, structural damage to the vessel and equipment, and potential loss of the drogue.

The potential for damage and injury must not be underestimated because the strain that is very quickly applied to the drogue system is quite simply immense.

Alcidae III's fully loaded displacement of approximately eighteen tons in addition to its forward momentum would be physically arrested by the fully deployed series drogue.

The system would create a counter force into the rode which appeared to physically haul the vessel backward through the sea against the combined forces of wind, waves, and vessel forward momentum.

Such a counter intuitive sensation of being pulled to windward backwards by a bungy cord, simply must be experienced!

During the entire forty-nine-day passage from Kerguelen to Tasmania -except when it was deployed- the drogue found itself piled in the cockpit in a manner such that it would not roll around, become tangled, or be swept overboard by boarding seas.

On the sole of the cockpit the drogue system was stored

ready for use, such that the end attached to the anchor chain section was kept secured on the port side cabin top and the last to be deployed end at the bottom of the cockpit pile was led and attached to the port side stern mooring bit in such a manner that it would not foul the vessels guard rails during deployment.

A retrieval line is attached prior to deployment to the main drogue rode and feeds out with the drogue while the inboard end of the retrieval line is so adjusted so that it contains excessive slack and is attached to the port amidship mooring bit.

Retrieval line slack will be removed once the drogue has been deployed.

I found the retrieval line most useful if attached to the main drogue rode at one to two boat lengths from the drogues main aft port mooring bit anchor point.

The first and main function of this line is the initial drogue retrieval, this line is attached to the main drogue rode using a six-wrap rolling hitch with the dead end whipped to the main drogue rode to prevent unwanted knot unravelling which is likely to occur due to the constant motion of the drogue after deployment.

The second retrieval line function is to permit positioning of the vessel once the drogue has been deployed, positioned such that the stern cannot yaw to the extent where it will directly face the oncoming seas, rather the advancing seas will be forced to remain on the aft port stern quarter.

Thus, the retrieval line maintains the vessels position during yawing at the most advantageous angle so that seas can be deflected along the port side and thus discouraged from boarding the aft and exposed vessel cockpit, however a sufficiently robust companionway

door remains a prudent safeguard.
The inboard end of this retrieval line is anchored and adjusted for the correct vessel angle at the amidship port side mooring cleat, which must be of similar strength to the stern drogue mooring bit because it will occasionally experience high tension due to the momentum of the yawing stern.

I have used two different methods of drogue deployment and have found that both are useful.
The first is deploying the drogue while the vessel is underway with just enough boat speed to permit the self steering gear to steer the vessel once the drogue is deployed the head sail -if used- is immediately permitted to luff and lowered.
The second method is to stop the vessel and heave-to, preferably using only a triple reefed mainsail.
The second method requires that the sea conditions be carefully assessed, in the southern ocean's heavy seas with the potential for boarding as well as causing a possible athwart ships rollover may be encountered.
The roll over potential hazard exists during the portion of the hove-to cycle when the vessel is essentially beam to the wind and seas.
Both methods have advantages and disadvantages however I have used mostly the second method because I wanted control of the vessel to remove the stern mounted steering gear prior to deploying the drogue and lowering the mainsail.
Once drogue deployment has commenced, one must be extremely careful that a cone, cone attachment strap, or rode section connecting knot does not foul any equipment or structure on the vessel nor any part of your body.

Each cone contains three nylon webs at each end therefore there is ample available to snag, as well in the vicinity of a sailing vessels cockpit there is not a shortage of items capable of creating additional snag points.

If one is fouled by the outgoing drogue, I suspect the mariner would have one brief chance to free yourself before the deployed portion of the drogue tensions, although a greater opportunity for freeing oneself exists if deployment option two is selected.

A system to allow the rode to self deploy would contain a much greater degree of safety, however I was not able during my seven deployments to conceive of such a procedure.

To repeat, if the drogue fouls on any of a myriad of potential sites during deployment you will likely loose the drogue, damage vessel gear, sustain personal injury, or all three.

The potential for fouling during deployment is made more extreme due to the contrary motions of vessel and the deploying drogue, as well the sea and wind conditions are certain to be quite rough, as well, in the hove-to state seas may occasionally sweep the vessel.

To reduce the possibility of fouling during deployment I initiated a procedure to physically guide the rode and cones clear of the guard rails and other potential snagging sites by using an extended and braced wooden two-meter-long oar, I would stand on the port side of the vessel adjacent to the cockpit.

The deploying mariner must then be suitably braced and during the entire deployment remain out of the deploying drogues bight while guiding the rode using the outstretched wooden oar, which also assists in keeping the outgoing rode aft and above the deployer's aft facing body.

Prudence must also be employed during deployment so that the drogue does not get fouled on the rudder, propeller, nor underwater attachments such as anodes.

This latter proviso applies only during the hove-to deployment method because the vessel will cycle on and off the wind resulting in less control of deployed drogue location with respect to the vessel.

This proviso does not apply when the drogue is deployed while the vessel is underway, however if the drogue snags while using the underway method it will tension immediately whereas during the hove-to deployment method the drogue will require some seconds before it tensions.

I have successfully used the underway deployment method with the vessel powered solely by a poled-out storm jib, further reducing vessel velocity by allowing the storm jib to luff almost completely to leeward, to where just sufficient vessel velocity remains so that the servo steering gear will function.

The forward motion of the vessel is thus reduced, however is still significant and will result in absolutely no possibility of freeing a potentially deployment fouled drogue.

The hove-to method of drogue deployment method results in the deploying rode alternating between loaded and unloaded conditions which provides an increased level of drogue rode control and thus an increased degree of safety during deployment.

If the hove-to method of deployment is selected provision must be taken to prevent the mainsail boom from gybing when the drogue is fully or partially deployed and stops the hove-to motion of the vessel when the stern is brought to windward.

As noted previously, speed and efficiency are desirable during such a hove-to deployment because it is probable that the wind will be more than fifty knots and thus up cycle hove-to luffing of the triple reefed mainsail will rapidly result in sail damage.

After heaving-to and prior to deployment of the drogue I would physically remove and stow the stern mounted steering gear due to fear of fouling the drogue rode on the outboard transom mounted steering gear.

A distinct advantage of the series drogue compared to the parachute sea anchor is that one can delay the series drogue deployment and keep the vessel moving if possible, thus making excellent on course mileage while the conditions remain manageable, however when it is finally deployed the sea and wind conditions are almost certain to be abrupt and probably rapidly deteriorating.

If using the hove-to deployment method, once the drogue is deployed the mainsail is lowered, the boom is sheeted and lashed amidships to the boom gallows, and then the sail is lashed to the boom.

If using the poled-out headsail method, the jib sheet will immediately be released upon full drogue deployment followed by the storm jib being lowered and stowed.

At this point the slack retrieval line attached to the port amidships mooring cleat must be adjusted so that during a portion of the vessel yawing cycle it tensions and physically prevents the vessel from yawing to a position whereby seas may directly strike the stern.

This may result in temporary extreme loading of the retrieval line thus as noted the amidships mooring cleat must be very well anchored.

Finally, the rudder is adjusted so that the vessel greets the arriving following seas as close to the port stern mooring bit as possible.

Once this final rudder adjustment is completed the rudder must be secured in position for the duration of the drogue deployment or until an additional rudder re-adjustment is required.

At this moment, one becomes acutely aware of the contrast from just before drogue deployment when the vessel was at or just beyond it is upper limit of control, to the present situation where the vessel, it is movement, and even the ocean seems momentarily relatively restrained.

This sense of calm will be somewhat transient because conditions will likely rapidly deteriorate as the cold front or low-pressure centre approaches and passes, followed by several more hours to days before the centre passes a sufficient distance which results in a sufficient reduction of wind velocity and sea conditions which will in turn permit the series drogue to be retrieved.

It is not an entirely pleasant series of experiences watching the barometer needle rapidly decline until low centre passage, although the much anticipated and confirmed change in barometer needle direction is always greeted as an encouraging thumbs up moment.

At this point, the thumbs up moment is always tempered by my inner voice which states the "third shoe is about to fall", meaning that with cold front passage in the southern oceans the southwest winds are about to commence, and thus the creation of those majestic southwesterly Southern Ocean seas.

The rate of barometer needle movement may well be substantial just prior to cold front passage as well as just

after a depression centre passage, on the contrary barometer needle movement can become painfully slow if the low-pressure system reduces its velocity or if the four millibar pressure isobar lines are well spaced.
The rate of barometer needle rise may also be dramatic immediately after an intense Southern Ocean low which has passed directly overhead, when the vessel will experience that section of very compressed isobar lines which often follow just aft of the low-pressure centre.

My first drogue deployment entailed the use of a stern anchoring bridal as per instructions available on the internet, however during the first such deployment from my aft cockpit sailing vessel, a sea soon boarded and caused damage to the rigid companionway dodger, binnacle, and transom arch.
Immediately after this sea boarded, I detached the stern starboard leg of the bridal, the vessel then rode receiving seas on the aft port quarter, during the remainder of this drogue deployment and the following six deployments a second following sea did not board the vessel.
The vessel is fitted with a stainless-steel companionway door, if fitted with the standard wooden companionway door several hundred litres of seawater would have probably entered the boat during this single aft boarding sea event.
My brain appears to be wired in such a manner that I am more content deploying the drogue from the port side rather than the starboard side of the vessel, thus my drogue anchor point entailed a meter-long section of galvanized 18 mm chain attached directly to the port side aft mooring bit which then passed through a chafe proof 16 mm diameter stainless steel rod chock which

was welded to the deck.

Thus, all possibility of chafe at this critical and high wear anchor point was eliminated, although the chains zinc galvanizing was quickly damaged.

Yaw is not insignificant while riding a deployed series drogue, thus as noted previously I physically removed the stern mounted servo pendulum steering gear prior to each drogue deployment, if such steering gear is fouled during drogue deployment or while the drogue is deployed it is probable that the stern mounted steering gear will be destroyed, and the drogue will be lost.

As noted, the preferred procedure prior to deployment was to have the entire drogue piled in the cockpit in a manner whereby it would not become tangled during whatever number of days there were between deployments, thus the drogue was to be found in the cockpit almost the entire south Indian Ocean passage.

It cannot be over stressed that all possible precautions must be taken to prevent fouling the drogue, it is resulting loss in the southern oceans will likely lead to multiple vessels roll overs.

Drogue retrieval is initiated with the retrieval line which will be removed from the amidships mooring bit and then wrapped twice around the largest port side cockpit sheet winch.

This sheet winch will intermittently experience the full drogue load thus it must be anchored in not a dissimilar manner as is the aft drogue mooring bit.

After several retrievals I now prefer to commence retrieval under a triple reefed mainsail in the hove-to configuration, which will maintain the vessel within a port tack heaved-to position and will result in the drogue rode cycling between loaded and a partially unloaded condition, possibly even allowing the drogue rode to be hauled manually at rode lengths up to a meter at a time between loading cycles.

It was my experience that this manual retrieval could only be accomplished with two wraps on the sheet winch.

Three wraps on the winch provide much greater control concerning the tail end however the additional wrap resulted in both fouled cones and the rode forming unwanted half hitches on the barrel of the winch.

Using the hove-to retrieval method, utilization of the winch handle and manual winching may be required for the first third of the drogue retrieval, however single-handed sailors will require one hand to tail at the winch and the other to operate the winch handle.

This is the case because the cones will not pass through the sheet winch self tailing device, therefore the mariner must be well braced and able to anticipate the vessel movement.

As noted, once approximately a third of the drogue rode has been retrieved utilizing two wraps during the hand winching phase, the drogue line may then be manually hauled during unloaded portions of the cycle which will preclude the necessity of manual winching with the winch handle.

It was during such winching operations that I was finally able to visualize a single possible reason for the presence of a foot operated electric sheet winch or a crew member.

Caution must be exercised during such manual winching during the loaded portion of each cycle so that the mariner always maintains the two sheet winch wraps, tension on the tailed portion of the rode, and maintains the body suitably braced into position.

The mariner must stand in such a manner that if necessary, the rode can be released and allowed to run free without fouling the mariner in the outgoing rode.

Remember, throughout this retrieval procedure the vessel end of the drogue rode remains attached to the port aft mooring bit, thus if control of the portion of the rode which is undergoing retrieval is lost, the entire drogue will not be lost rather one simply starts the retrieval a second time.

Once the rolling hitch of the retrieval line reaches the winch, a short temporary load bearing line must be attached to the main drogue rode, -again using a rolling hitch- and take the full strain of the drogue while the retrieval line's rolling hitch is removed.

At this time, the unloaded drogue retrieval line is removed from the winch and the main drogue rode is wrapped in its place followed by the release and removal of the short temporary load bearing line.

The cones will then come around the double wrapped sheet winch without damage however as noted will not pass through the winch self tailing device.

The entire drogue may then be hauled into the cockpit using a combination of initially manual hand winching using the winch handle to be followed by manual hauling without use of the winch handle.

During the entire retrieval procedure, the vessel continues to be hove-to and patiently awaits again getting underway, however if the mariner has attempted retrieval before conditions have adequately moderated, seas may still be too dangerous with respect to a possible boarding sea or a possible vessel rollover, in which case the drogue retrieval must be postponed.

Even though the vessel is hove-to -which substantially reduces the load on the drogue-, manual hauling of the drogue requires extreme caution because of the alternation between the fully loaded and partially loaded states of the drogue.

If the rode becomes fouled on the winch it is again necessary to remove the load on the winch using the same short line which was used to take the load while the retrieval line rolling hitch was removed.

The initial sixty meters of 25 mm diameter double braid nylon drogue rode to be hauled does not contain attached cones, therefore cones will remain submerged and thus the drogue will remain at full load tension, thus during this initial phase of retrieval maximum loads can be expected to place on the sheet winch.

Such cycling of full drogue load on the cockpit sheet winch requires extreme care be taken to keep body parts clear of winch nip points, this is not a trivial matter because the vessel movement will be lively and will become livelier as the drogue is retrieved.

As noted, during the first third of drogue retrieval the loaded portion of the cycle creates a tension on the rode which requires a minimum of two wraps around the sheet winch as well as substantial tailing tension supplied by the right arm.

This is but one more of the multitude of single-handed tasks onboard whereby there is not an extra hand to brace mariner, thus body positioning, whole body bracing, practice, balance, and aforethought are required.

I preferred to get underway when wind and sea conditions had moderated sufficiently to where they would just permit a poled-out storm jib, thus the wind conditions remain strong however if my proposed course were downwind, I usually permitted the wind to diminish only to the upper forty knot range.

Prior to retrieval, of greater concern than wind velocity is the assessment of a suitable reduction in hazardous breaking seas which could potentially engulf or result in vessel rollover.

Throughout the duration of a Southern Ocean storm, seas will have been very hazardous whereby the upper third of the possibly greater than fifteen-meter-high seas will have been breaking.

Therefore, the most critical decision concerning getting underway is the status of the breaking seas, however in the southern oceans where the probability is high that an equally intense depression will be following the present low-pressure system, motivation is thus provided to get underway and make full use of the existing decreasing fair wind.

In the southern oceans as opposed to the north Pacific Ocean I have found that it is not uncommon for the wind to decrease enough to be able to get underway, however the seas often remain too unsafe to attempt getting underway.

It is also important to get underway because there may remain several thousand passage miles to complete and a fair but still strong wind is an opportunity not to be squandered.

Recall that a major advantage offered by the Jordan series drogue is that it may be deployed and retrieved during harsh conditions of wind and seas.

The mariner will be confident that little wind has been squandered when hull speed is immediately achieved after hauling the drogue and getting underway under solely a poled-out storm jib.

The hove-to drogue retrieval option thus involves drogue retrieval with the assistance and vessel control provided by the triple reefed mainsail, just prior to the final portion of drogue retrieval, a poled-out storm jib hanked onto the forestay is set with the jib permitted to luff, the drogue retrieval is completed, the triple reefed mainsail lowered, the head sail is sheeted in and away we go.

It will be found that this process of successfully getting underway after a prolonged period of successfully protecting the vessel and its gear, creates an enduring sense of satisfaction and accomplishment.

The longest period of continuous riding under drogue during the seven-drogue deployment forty-nine-day passage from Kerguelen to Tasmania, was five days, the sensation and memory of again getting successfully underway under poled out storm jib, remains acute and precious.

A sense of accomplishment is also experienced emanating from the fact that all sails during the defensive interlude under drogue, had been carefully stowed on deck in a way they do not sustain any wear or damage, regardless of the tons of seawater that may have passed over the deck, thus once again gets underway with the knowledge that neither the vessel nor any of its equipment has been damaged and that all is in the same seaworthy condition as before the gale's arrival.

Immediately after getting underway, the lowered but still unsecured mainsail and boom must be securely sheeted and lashed to boom gallows followed by effective lashing of the triple reefed mainsail to the boom.

This sequence is recommended because the vessels rolling motion at this time will likely attain such violence that during the mainsail lashing operation the mariner can be thrown overboard.

The entire retrieved drogue at this time will be found in a heap on the bottom of the cockpit waiting to be prepared for its next deployment.

In harmony with ship's philosophy, multiple drogue deployments and retrievals must be accomplished without damage to the ship's gear, drogue, or crew.

I am convinced that Don Jordan through his invention has given single-handed sailors such as myself the ability to protect themselves and the ship during almost any severe weather conditions, and it is in this spirit that I wish to share my practical experience concerning the drogue.

Please understand that "almost any severe weather conditions" does not include hurricanes, freezing spray, nor where sufficient sea room is not available.

An additional piece of heavy weather defensive gear which should also be carried onboard is an appropriately sized Para-Tech type sea anchor along with the necessary rigging and connecting devices.

I carried a six-meter diameter Para-Tech Sea anchor which I have used only once, when I believe it did prevent the vessel from rolling over.

This experience was early during my third voyage before I had acquired the series drogue, although the series drogue would also have saved the vessel regarding the specifics of this incident, however the sea anchor must still be considered obligatory gear because one may miscalculate and find oneself off a lee shore with insufficient sea room to accommodate use of the series drogue.

Such miscalculations are made at sea in inverse proportion to the mariner's experience, abilities, as well as mental and physical state, however the possibility of such a miscalculation may not be ignored.

An example of such a miscalculation would be to have approached too closely to an open coastal lee shore during winds that are too strong to permit the vessel to sail to windward, thus creating the potential of being blown ashore even if the series drogue is deployed.

One may take the position that such a mistake will not be committed, however a possible mitigation strategy would be preferable to such a position, the sea anchor is one such mitigation strategy.

The sea anchor is also useful to hold a vessel off a lee shore with respect to other unforeseen events, such as an untimely loss of the mast or a motor failure.

The major difficulties concerning a sea anchor with respect to the single-handed sailor are sea anchor deployment and retrieval, as well I have experienced erratic and violent vessel yawing while riding at sea anchor, as well as heavy loads placed on the rudder.

Rode loaded and unloaded cycling while riding at sea anchor compares with the series drogue, however the anchor winch can be used to advantage during bow deployed sea anchor retrievals, however all sea parachute type anchor retrievals must wait until wind and seas have greatly diminished thus relinquishing the potential opportunity to utilize favourable winds.

The mariner often can approach the landfall in relatively calm conditions, however open ocean landfalls usually entail very turbulent waters due to tidal currents, shoaling ocean waves, and other local effects.

Such agitated ocean surface conditions can cause clogged motor fuel supply or airlock issues for even the most well-maintained fuel supply systems, therefore sailing without engine assist into the lee of shelter has always been my first choice, although I also switch to a secondary gravity fed fuel supply which is supplied from a day tank guaranteed to contain no sediment.

If the wind direction permits, I prefer using the smallest head sail that provides steerage and thus sail into protected waters, the mainsail being suitably reefed and secured so that gybing is not an issue.

Prior to making any final approach towards shelter, another ships rule has been to retrieve from the at sea stowage location, the main ship's anchor and rode and prepare for immediate anchor deployment.

I also will ensure that all engine isolating through hull valves are open, change the fuel supply to the day tank, and ensure the motor is running with the transmission not engaged.

Approaching shelter in violent wind conditions one must be ready to engage the transmission because alternate gusts and calms along with potential unexpected head winds may be encountered.

Noted in another section, during the entire passage the motor is protected against internal engine flooding by a closed through hull valve on the exhaust system and a closed through hull valve on the cooling raw water system, in addition to closed engine fuel supply valves.

Such a motor protection condition at sea is critical because if adequate motor protection is not provided internal flooding of the shut down engine can easily occur during the violent waves and the subsequent extreme vessel listing conditions.

After several thousand offshore miles I have adopted a functional, if not fashionable high latitudes deck dress code which closely resembles British Columbia commercial fishermen.

This includes what may be several layers of T-shirts, long underwear, and sweaters, all covered by the heavy duty Helly Hansen jacket fitted with a permanent hood along with the bib style pants which reach the arm pits.

At sea during rough weather, the safest location below is in one's bunk within the protection of a substantial rigid leeboard, or otherwise in a predetermined and braced position.

While underway at sea one becomes tuned to the vessel, it is sounds, the wind, the sea, vessel motion, and the resulting constantly changing myriad of such sound and sensual inputs.

The desired result of these constant inputs is a useful output initiated possibly by your inner voice.

This inner voice will advise you as to what needs attending to, as well as specifically what is to be done, it will become apparent that one ignores or postpones such inner voice advice at one's peril.

Such advice will include when to change sails, reef sails, shake out reefs, adjust a jib or mainsail sheet, adjust steering gear, change tacks, gybe the mainsail or headsail pole, remove all sail, heave to, and when to deploy the series drogue.

Trades winds sailing often requires the mariner to become accustomed to only static wind and sea conditions, as well possibly of the necessity of removing all one's clothing during deck work so that boarding spray or waves may be towelled off upon task completion.

High latitudes sailing requires a decision on how much clothing is necessary underneath the rain gear so that perspiration is discouraged, as well as constantly changing sailing decisions based on the wide range of wind and sea conditions to be encountered.

It is very tempting while clothed in one is preferred below deck jogging pants and t-shirt type bunk dress, to simply don rubber boots and quickly open and then close the companionway door to perform brief tasks such as adjusting tension of a jib or main sheet, or slightly modify a steering gear control line tension or wind angle.

The mariner thinks he can time the interval between boarding seas and spray and often succeeds, however perhaps my recommendation may be gleaned by the pile of sea water-soaked bunk clothing usually present upon such a high latitude passage completion.

As noted, I did not have high tech underwear, clothing, nor rain gear, and like completing the entire nine-year circumnavigation with the same sail inventory which had never left the vessel for repairs, I also completed the entire voyage with the same pairs of Canadian Stanfield's wool grey long johns and grey sweater, suspender supported Red Strap denim pants, and Helly Hansen commercial fisherman's rain gear pants and jacket.

The rain gear jacket attached hood I found obligatory because it allows one to simply turn ones back to boarding seas, spray, and wind driven rain resulting in totally dry underclothes even after several hours of very wet exposure.

I often used the same rain gear when onshore, thus upon return to Canada the rain gear did contain several sewed-on patches not dissimilar in nature to the sails, however it was the same set of rain gear as nine years previous.

Challenges arise when one must exit the cabin during

darkness to perform deck work.

One is reluctant to turn on a light to suitably dress for the conditions, thus before retiring to the bunk I place all necessary deck clothing in a location and order from which it can be donned in complete darkness and while maintaining a braced position.

Such a plan is critical if one wishes to exit the cabin with night vision intact.

The South Indian Ocean necessitated the institution of an additional piece of gear which must be donned just before opening the companionway door.

This entailed a length of rope which contained an eye at one end and the use of a slip knot at the other, this I would cinch tightly around my waist outside of the rain gear jacket, the tail end then passing through my legs and securely tied at the waist.

Without such a cinch around the waist on the rain gear jacket, whenever one turned frontwards or backwards to the wind, the rain gear jacket would be blown open or blown up to the upper back area and be steaming to leeward, held only by the out turned sleeves.

Under such conditions the hood must also be tightly sealed around the face utilizing the two draw strings provided for this purpose.

The other lasting physical memory of the Indian Ocean concerns exiting the cabin during storm conditions.

The sensation is not dissimilar to leaving an airport waiting area through tight fitting doors to enter upon an outside boarding area where an operating nearby jet engine plane is nearby, one experiences a similar roar and pressure difference upon cracking open the companionway door.

Upon reaching the cockpit, which is in darkness, securing closed the companionway door, one experiences a sensation of being in complete oneness with nature and again the opportunity of living totally focused on the present.

The darkness can appear almost complete, one is in the company of only the sound and feel of the wind, spray, passing and breaking seas, as well as the luminescence which may emanate from foam generated by the breaking seas.

During such precious moments, one must compose oneself and quickly acclimatize to this external environment only moments after leaving the protected and warm bunk.

Under storm conditions due to extensive cloud cover, illumination from the moon and stars is often not present, thus except for the luminescence one is greeted by almost total darkness, the roar of the wind, and the swish and collapse of the passing seas.

Within this cumulative exhilaration of seemingly flying through the seas in total darkness with the vessel near or possibly just beyond the upper limit of steering control, thoughts and actions must be channelled to the immediate task of safely reducing vessel speed through the water.

I will present in a different section of this book that the first and best option is to immediately release the jib sheet.

I would usually attempt to complete all darkness deck work except for final sheet hardening without artificial light, however prior to final sheet or halyard hardening I would temporarily destroy my night vision and perform a spreader light, flashlight, or head lamp inspection.

Once all the necessary darkness hours deck work has been successfully completed, the vessel is back in control, and the mariner is safely seated either in the cockpit or more preferably on the leeward transom box - with an arm for safety reasons looped around a back stay-, a powerful sense of well being and accomplishment arrives.

COMMUNICATIONS, ENTERTAINMENT, & OTHER GEAR

Communications, Entertainment, and Other Gear

Generally, I tend to be somewhat predicable, me at sea tastes concerning entertainment turn out to be almost identical to my onshore routine and contain twice daily BBC World Service news broadcasts on the SSB, Friday afternoon finds me listening to one or more acts of one of Wagner's ten operas although the Ring Cycle, Tristan und Isolde, and Parsifal became my main repertoire, as well Act 2 of Beethoven's only opera Fidelio has also been inserted into this Friday rotation.

The Friday rotation may be considered a weekly warm up for the main opera event of the week, Saturday Afternoon at the Opera.

My Saturday Afternoon at the Opera entailed the curtain going up at the same time as it would have happened in Canada, which was usually at 2 PM, subject to change depending on the length of the opera.

I have used capital letters concerning Saturday Afternoon at the Opera because this was one of the seminal influences on what has turned into a life long musical interest and I could almost hear the Canadian Broadcasting Corporation's Howard Dick introducing the chosen opera and singers.

I had brought onboard a selection of eighty complete operas recorded on cassettes, along with a pile of photocopied libretti for most of these operas as well as a large selection of post opera encore CDs and cassettes.

Like a negligible formative year's exposure to sailing noted in another section, a similar lack of formative exposure was experienced with respect to opera and classical music, thus my technical musical sophistication is somewhat limited.

The CBC was seminal is my musical appreciation, however in later life my sense of reverence concerning the CBC would disappear, although I will always credit Clyde Gilmour the host of the CBC radio program Gilmour's Albums for my introduction to both opera and classical music.

Unfortunately, CBC is now but a shadow of its past brilliance which included personalities such as Clyde Gilmour, Barbara Frumm, and others.

To complete my onboard weekly entertainment routine I would, when the opportunity presented itself, download six months of the most recent podcasts of Eleanor Wachtel's Writers in Company and listen to each interview at the same local time on Sundays that they would be aired in Canada, the same would apply to Quirks and Quarks which I always listened to at noon on Saturdays.

The above has also been a major component of how I have entertained myself throughout my entire adult life, thus it turns out that my at sea lifestyle was to be just more of the same.

Onboard entertainment also contains the subject of literature and technical studies.

Every evening in the bunk would find me reading novels and several hundred daylight hours were spent in the study of botany, geology, as well as French, Spanish, and Portuguese grammar, and vocabulary.

I do not consider myself overly fluent in my ability to speak and write languages other than English, but I did make major efforts before my offshore sailing period to learn French, and then during the third voyage Spanish was my major focus.

I was to find that all I needed to acquire the basics before landing and beginning to interact with the local people was a book on verbs and their conjugation, a dictionary, and a book containing the rules of grammar.

A powerful and well used tool of learning was also my ever-present pocket notebook, which was mostly used for botany, geology, to do lists, but was also replete with lists of foreign words and phrases learned while onshore.

I also adopted and maintained my own form of phonetic abbreviations concerning pronunciation, to be used when new words were encountered while onshore, although it has many similarities to that system used by the Larousse French dictionary.

If one were to review my past several years of notebooks it is apparent that at a certain entry point, the list of foreign words learned onshore declined and then essentially ceased, at this point I had become what I would term functionally fluent.

This point was reached in both French and Spanish, however after six months spent in Brazil, I admit I was still far from considering myself fluent in Portuguese which I found to be a romantic language which is difficult to pronounce.

I found Spanish speaking people very considerate and helpful towards a foreigner trying to learn their language, as well possibly fifty percent of French people could be equally complimented, however a significant percentage of French males could be very unhelpful as they would often take the view that they could not understand my pronunciation or choice of words.

Granted French is a difficult language to master, however I had spent a significant number of years learning French in a formal setting and although I always made mistakes in pronunciation, verb conjugation, and word selection, I was always certain that they could indeed understand.

This significant percentage of French however would expect me, the English speaker, to always understand their broken English even where it was obvious that they had made little or no attempt to formally learn the language.

Nevertheless, when I encounter an ocean mariner whom I consider a peer, they are most likely to be French and I would not consider my sailing experiences to have been complete without the many French nautical acquaintances that I have been fortunate enough to acquire.

As noted, I went to sea equipped with more than eighty recorded operas and will now add a few hundred classic novels in both the physical book form as well as in digital format.

Throughout the course of my nine-year voyage, I worked my way through Charles Dickens, George Elliot, Thomas Hardy, EM Forrester, Virginia Woolf, both Bronte sisters Emily and Charlotte, Oscar Wilde, Robert Louis Stevenson, Rudyard Kipling, and several more English writers.

French literature included writers such as Emil Zola, Maupassant, Victor Hugo, Balzac, Flaubert, and George Sand.

The other major nationality read was Russian writers such as Leo Tolstoy, Turgenev, the father of the short story Anton Chekov, as well as Gogol, and Pushkin.

I have found that I my intellect does not seem to include re reading a book that I have already read with two short scene exceptions which have been re read several times, those sections are found in Dicken's, David Copperfield and Charlotte Bronte's, Jane Eyre.

American writers such as Steinbeck, Poe, Faulkner, and Mark Twain have also been read.

I would look forward daily to rejoining many their literary characters and personalities as well as the on going plots each evening during my allotted reading period and arrived at the conclusion that in addition to plot and character development, the greatest authors create characters who are as we are, -made up of characteristics and personalities which contain a mix of agreeable and not so agreeable attributes-.

Within the category of electronic equipment and the single-handed sailor, I have referred to radar and its necessity in conjunction with the watchman mode.

Radar is not only useful for collision avoidance but also as an accurate range finder, a warning device concerning objects such as approaching squalls containing rain, hail, or snow, as well as approaching ships, large floating debris, and land.

Upon reflection, I upgrade the installation and knowledge of radar's usage regarding single-handed sailing to obligatory.
My radar contained three interval settings within the watchman mode, which are five, ten-, and twenty-minutes intervals and emitted peak power of 1.5 kilowatts.
While operating at full power when transmitting it consumed 2.5 - 3 amps, and 1.5 amps on standby within the watchman mode.
I found I used the twenty-minute watchman standby interval only when sea conditions were less than one-meter seas, otherwise I would use the ten-minute interval until seas attained the three-to-four-meter height and afterwards the five-minute interval was selected.
One becomes acutely aware of having chosen an excessively lengthy watchman interval when upon arriving on deck after an alarm and experiencing the unpleasant realization that the freighter has already passed.
Without rigid obedience to such time intervals the radar cannot be relied upon to detect even freighter sized objects in seas larger than three to four meters height, which is due to the relative motions between the small sailing vessel and the large vessel, which results in the target reflection not being consistently detected.
Of course, the watchman mode may always be left on the shortest standby interval however this results in an unnecessary use of the batteries stored energy.
I did not have the addition of the AIS collision avoidance equipment; however, I would now not put to sea without such electronic gear.
I had close calls with freighters on several occasions regardless of their reported professionalism, watch keep-

ing ability, or their state-of-the-art onboard electronic equipment.

One must expect such encounters when crossing busy port inbound and outbound shipping lanes in such areas as off San Francisco or the Panama Canal, however outside of such busy and restricted shipping lanes such encounters are much less expected.

It was always my practice to plot major shipping lanes on my ocean charts and I would then endeavour to cross these plotted lanes at an angle as close to ninety degrees as possible, and during darkness utilize the five-minute radar watchman mode regardless of sea conditions.

In such areas I would also endeavour to forego the ship's rule concerning minimum necessary hours of uninterrupted sleep.

Approaching the end of my third and final offshore voyage in 2013, I had just left Saipan in the Northern Marianas bound for the central Aleutian Island chain and found that for the first time in my radar assisted sailing career, my precious Furuno was returning a weaker than expected echo, which quickly degenerated to a complete absence of returning echoes.

I tried all actions available which included checking all signal handling cables and connections, supply voltage check, replacement of the rotating antenna drive belt, followed by replacement of the magnetron, all to no avail.

The radar was repaired much later in Victoria and found to have a faulty circuit board which controls the display; thus, I was putting out the proper radio frequency signal and the echoes were bouncing back, however the receiver section of my radar display was unable to provide the necessary display.

A few weeks into this passage, -now without a functional radar- I was approximately six hundred miles east of Tokyo and was sitting having my second coffee at about 7 AM.

Ede in her customary vantage point was sitting on my chart table keeping an eye on me while I was sitting at the same chart table downloading the mornings weather fax on the laptop.

It has never failed to amaze me the way a cat can sit without being braced on a flat surface such as a chart table in a seaway and maintain both balance and position simply by leaning alternately to port and starboard, apparently taking no notice of the constant and sometimes abrupt motion of the vessel.

The cockpit companionway door immediately behind me was propped open less than one quarter of its full opening width.

I had hove-to the previous night for seven hours because I was being nudged by a passing low and associated cold front, thus the vessel had been closed and was somewhat stuffy, although I am not sure that Ede nor I really noticed the stuffiness.

After the fronts passage, the vessel was now in sloppy five-meter seas and temporarily light, unstable, and finicky winds that are quite normal immediately following a cold front passage.

Wind was in the order of 5-10 knots and I had raised a double reefed main and a staysail was set on the vessel's forestay.

This was admittedly insufficient sail, but it provided minimum steerage as well as minimum unwanted opening and closing of the sails.

I was thus plodding along at two knots or so when I

heard Ede growl, when I looked at her, she was looking out towards the partially open hatch with concern.

I had long before learned to take immediate note of what concerned any one of my cats, their sense of smell, sight, hearing, and vigilance were much more effective than mine.

I looked out the stern only to see the North Pacific Ocean post cold front mist and fog, visibility was less than one hundred meters.

I sat back down at the chart table and Ede was still concerned and intently looking out the open companionway, then I heard a swishing sound, not dissimilar to the sound of an approaching tropical downpour during windless conditions.

I informed myself there were not such windless tropical downpours to be heard in the vicinity of my present latitude and again looked out the open companionway, and there just coming into view out of the mist and fog heading directly onto my stern was the obvious white wing logo centred on the black bow of a rapidly approaching freighter, complete with it is highly visible, hissing, and surging bow wave.

It was now obvious that it was this bow wave which generated the swishing sound that Ede had first heard.

For a reason I still do not understand I took my half full cup of coffee from the chart table beside the weather fax downloading laptop and with it in hand went out into the cockpit without any sort of appropriate deck clothing and immediately disengaged the servo steering gear.

The sailing vessel had been plodding downwind while wallowing in the previously described seas and the freighter at full cruising speed was rapidly approaching directly onto my stern.

My first thoughts concerned which way to turn, the freighter still appeared bound directly onto my vessels fore and aft axis.

I chose to turn to starboard because the sails were set on a starboard tack and thus less likely to be backed or collapse in the light wind and sloppy seas.

Later it became apparent that my immediate actions had become automatic and it seemed that the time taken making decisions approached zero.

It had been my philosophy throughout my sailing lifetime to plan when determining possible actions, however in this present imminent likelihood of a collision, I found myself taking immediate unplanned action.

I turned the vessel ninety degrees to starboard and over my right shoulder watched the black bow with the white wing logo bear directly down on me, I maintained my new course with only slight control of steerage due to the low boat speed.

Within what could not have been more than two minutes the bow was upon me, but the sailboat had responded to it is helm and I was now pointed ninety degrees from the freighters course.

Just before the bow wave struck, I was just able to sight along the starboard side of the freighter, thus I was possibly four meters outside of the freighter's centre line.

The bow wave struck my stern and filled the cockpit as well as spilling through the mindlessly left open companionway door.

The power of this wave then took the sailboat out of my tenuous control and instantly the vessel was pointed parallel to the starboard side of the freighter with the bow directed towards the freighter's stern and it is now

visible and quickly approaching light coloured overhead flying bridge.
If this life persists, I will likely never forget the sound of the water hissing along the freighters side, or the image of the full length of the starboard side of that freighter's black hull passing along my starboard side at not greater a distance than half my vessels width.
I was convinced my vessel was going to physically bump along the freighter's hull, I possessed no steerage, however this did not occur.
I could see the relatively low flying bridge on this fully laden vessel approaching and was concerned it would be struck by my mast, however the mast head passed untouched directly underneath the unoccupied flying bridge.
As I reached the freighter's stern my vessel which was still completely out of rudder control turned another ninety degrees to starboard and now, I was looking over my right shoulder directly up at the freighter's stern.
I left the cockpit in this churning sea, turned on the vhf and called the freighter on channel 16, no response.
My coffee cup was broken, I had been soaked with cold seawater when the bow wave boarded, and the laptop was destroyed by the bucket or so of sea water that entered through the open companionway but otherwise I was spared.
This probably would not have occurred had my radar been operating or if I had AIS.
The freighter was either not watching their radar, did not have their radar set on a guard zone, or more likely the sloppy seas had resulted in the freighter's crew tuning out the waves and thus small targets such as myself.
Upon reflection, Ede and I were incredibly lucky to sur-

vive as there is little chance the freighter would have stopped and upon further reflection, it has become apparent that I may owe my life to the companionway door being propped partially open and my Ede.

I clearly remember the black hull with a white wing-logo painted amidships on the bow, the white superstructure, and the white flying bridge.

The ships name in big white block letters went right past my eyes, first on its starboard bow and secondly on it is stern, however I must have been somewhat terrified because I cannot definitively be certain of the name, the ship quickly disappeared into the mist and fog.

Later I wrote down what I thought I saw (RIUKU) but the date (28 April 2013), time (0730 local time), and position (41 52' N & 162 2' E) are accurate.

Self steering gear which obtains its power from vessels velocity through the water and its direction control from the wind, are for a single-handed sailor similar in importance to the mast.

I have always been acutely aware of the importance of such a powerful and nonelectrical energy consuming piece of equipment; however, an illustration of its importance was presented on my second ocean training voyage.

I was just about to enter the Inter Tropical Convergence Zone (ITCZ) south of Hawaii on a planned passage from Victoria to Samoa.

Within the ITCZ conditions include high temperature, high relative humidity, immense towering cloud structures from sea level to several hundred meters of altitude, lightening, thunder, immensely heavy rain showers, squally winds, and turbulent waves which are due to contrary wind which meets strong ocean currents.

The ITCZ is a singular zone which contains conditions that my intuition informs me may well be like the type of environment within which life on earth first originated.

This second ocean voyage was to witness Alcidae III on both sides of the ITCZ as well as the equator over a period of ten months, enroute visiting Palmyra Atoll, Christmas Island, Kanton Atoll, Butaritari, Majuro, and finally Likiep Atoll which itself is just outside of the northern edge of the ITCZ.

This turbulent area was also one of the areas where the whalers hunted sperm whales and although I constantly searched for this whale species, I was not to see my first and only two sperm whales until near the end of my third voyage.

Just before dark on 10 July 2000 just south of 10 degrees north, I was below deck and noticed the boat steering in an erratic manner, upon reaching the cockpit I immediately noticed the broken self steering servo oar dragging aft held only by its safety line.

The folding hinge apparatus of the oar on the 24 mm diameter stainless steel shaft had broken.

I was approximately five hundred and forty nautical miles south of the west coast of the island of Hawaii, and I had just passed out of the north east trade winds into the ITCZ.

The next two days saw me trying all means that I could conceive to convince the vessel to sail to windward by means of bungy cords and jib sheet cords, all to no avail.

I had great success with this method of self steering during my coastal sailing training period aboard Alcidae II, which was a tiller steered fibreglass Spencer 31 sloop.

I soon found in my present situation aboard a wheel operated hydraulic steering vessel, that I could only progress if I hand steered, which was soon found to be a non option.

It was required to hand steer as close to the wind as the vessel could manage, therefore continuous spray was generated and rain gear was required to prevent loss of body heat due to rapid skin evaporation, even though I was within the tropics.

The rain gear however resulted in excessive and continuous sweating which quickly resulted in dehydration and brown coloured urine.

It became apparent that if I did not conceive of an effective jury steering rig, I must make instead for the Marshall's or Christmas Atoll.

Upon arrival several months later at Christmas Atoll, I found a sparsely equipped steel fabrication shop where I could have made the necessary stainless steel welding repairs using welding rods and bits of stainless steel that I had carried onboard; thus, this should have been my new destination and not Hawaii.

I finally did conceive a jury rigged self steering temporary repair using a second-hand bench vice which I almost had not brought along, and subsequently did manage to sail the five hundred and forty nautical miles to windward, finally passing almost exactly one mile to windward of the west coast of the island of Hawaii and was very content to anchor within the inner bay at Hilo.

Well protected tropical anchorages such as the inner bay at Hilo are indeed intrinsically welcoming.

The original point, however, was the extreme importance of robust, effective, reliable, and nonelectrical powered self steering gear.

After the twelve thousand nautical mile first voyage in 1995 to French Polynesia I had made structural changes to the ship's rudder to render the pendulum servo steering system more effective, I then went on my second offshore training voyage of thirteen thousand nautical miles in 2000 and upon returning to Victoria made further structural changes to the ship's rudder, after which the self steering system was passable for my penultimate third voyage.

I utilize the adjective passable because I would now not recommend such a servo pendulum self steering system but rather the trim-tab system, often employed by French mariners.

The trim-tab system requires a transom mounted ship's rudder, a modification I was not willing to install however in hindsight a transom mounted auxiliary rudder with a trim tab mechanism attached should have been my choice.

In conclusion, even though a high quality and powerful electronic steering pilot system is required for conditions such as motoring and sailing with less than ten knots of following wind, an effective and powerful non-electrical steering system is critical for those single-handed sailors who wish to navigate without an on-board auxiliary diesel generator.

Artificial light provided for deck work during darkness hours is a subject on which there are several options.

Spreader mounted deck lights can be used, however if one is tempted or required to look upwards night vision is instantly destroyed.

Furthermore, external halyards and jib sheets require final checks before hardening, which may require one to look to the masthead which will not be visible above the spreader mounted deck lights.

I am partial to spreader mounted deck lights because they impart a feeling of comfort and security at night in the open ocean when the mariner finds themselves alone on deck but within this cocoon of comforting and almost protective light.

Deck lights are also highly effective in certain circumstances such as when approached too closely by other vessels during hours of darkness.

A small flashlight in the pocket which can be transferred to the mouth has been used with success along with a larger flashlight left under the cockpit dodger, used to observe that all is as it should be before final halyard and jib sheet hardening.

My final years at sea witnessed a vast improvement regarding head mounted lamps, I suspect these may now be the best option, however usually the moon and or stars will provide sufficient light to perform the required deck work without artificial light.

If possible, I prefer not to use any artificial light when performing darkness hours deck work, however one must be confident that halyards, sheets, and sails are not fouled prior to final application of line tension because serious damage will ensue.

I have previously discussed the necessity of a poled-out head sail when sailing with the wind aft of the beam, therefore a telescoping whisker pole of sufficient strength is another critical piece of gear.

My first two offshore voyages witnessed me using a fixed length spinnaker pole, the length of which was equal to the vessels J measurement.

I was never content with this pole because it never

seemed the ideal length for any of my head sails.

Prior to my third voyage I purchased a jewel of a telescoping American Forespar four-inch diameter pole which had an adjustable length from thirteen through twenty-one feet, this pole was magnificent!

Once the inboard end had been lowered in its track towards the deck and the attached headsail was permitted to slightly luff, the length of the pole could be adjusted in place provided the pole was sufficiently unloaded due to the luffing sail.

This is an important adjustment which saves completely disconnecting the head sail when one wishes to slightly change the point of sailing when the wind undergoes slight shifts in direction.

Although an easily achieved alternate pole adjustment procedure involves lowering the head sail without releasing the jib sheet, the temporarily dropped sail will harmlessly hang into the water and over the side until the pole length or angle is adjusted and the headsail is again raised.

This adjustable pole perfectly accommodates the decreasing foot length from the one hundred and fifty percent genoa all the way down to the storm jib, as well as providing an adjustable vertical angle which will accommodate the changing headsail clew height.

Vessel yawing at sea under self steering gear when there is a constant swell from at least one direction is a reality, without a properly set pole head sails will open and close, commonly in a violent manner, a properly set pole minimizes this destructive problem.

As well, a properly set pole will minimize the nuisance and even danger involved when the head sail is backed by reducing its occurrence.

The pole is heavy, and the deck is most often quite unstable, but a procedure must be adopted to safely set, gybe, and stow the pole.
This procedure must be practised and mastered so that it can be safely and efficiently performed in all weather, sea, and lighting level conditions.
In all cases it is necessary to lift only one end of the pole while the other remains securely attached to the vessel.

The SSB's usefulness is manifold, although many of its functions can now be quite well accomplished by a satellite communication system.
The SSB system requires little cost after purchase and installation, other than Sailmail's annual fee.
The SSB in conjunction with a laptop computer, appropriate software, functional antennas, functional ground plane, and a modem will provide free of charge weather maps, grib files, emails, BBC World Service broadcasts, and long-distance voice communication including ship to shore, ship to ship, and phone patches.
If one has an appropriate amateur radio licence one can tap into an especially useful land-based group of radio nets and amateur radio operators.

INDIGENOUS PEOPLE

The lifestyle and environmental impact of aboriginal peoples before the period of European contact forms a keen portion of my interest.

Prior to European contact aboriginal people lived in harmony with nature in terms of their ability to adapt, this ability to adapt to existing natural conditions was not qualitatively dissimilar to plants and animals.

A common attribute observed in most countries visited is that our species always seems to want to consider themselves superior to another visible or ethnic group, regardless of the actual judgment providers level of poverty.

Thus, even the most abjectly poor people also seem driven to consider themselves superior to someone or some group, the usual recipient of the final stage of subjugation appears to be the present descendants of the original aboriginal peoples.

The first nations people also do not appear immune to this mind set, they can often be unflattering of adjacent groups of first nations peoples, thus we all seem to suffer from a similar cerebral hard wiring, and all must work towards improvement.

In countries such as my own we have a history of first

nations miss treatment which is also common to other countries.

Equal opportunity will probably be a major factor in the final solution of this issue, but this is indeed a complicated and long-term concern.

Comments I am about to make do not apply to all members of the societies visited, however they were commonly encountered.

Panama contains an example of this unofficial aboriginal marginalization which manifests itself in day-to-day practical issues.

Patricia and I spent almost one year anchored in a river adjacent to a tiny village called Chorcha which is a one-hour bus ride south of David on the west coast of Panama.

In this region of Panama, one commonly sees a local northern Panamanian aboriginal group the Ngabe-Bugle-Comarca, travelling in small groups and essentially keeping separate from the local population.

This group has a distinctive manner of dress and seem to function in a manner almost as if the other Panamanians do not exist.

Upon passing members of this community in David or in rural locations, they will often not respond to greetings, although most I was informed speak Spanish.

We took a day bus trip to the Panamanian east coast whereby the bus passes over interior mountains to descend into a very humid and hot tropical forest on the Caribbean side.

In the David region I would see small mobile groups of this ethnic group engaged in travelling and shopping, on the tropical east side of the interior mountain range we were to see the actual tiny, isolated villages and house structures often containing no road but rather only footpath access.

Houses are made almost entirely of forest materials and were constructed in an elevated manner supported by posts, often greater than two meters above the ground.

This may be due to snake avoidance, however it is not a common form of Panamanian construction, for example Chorcha did not contain one such structure but rather masonry as well as split bamboo structures built on grade.

In Chorcha, snake entry into split bamboo house structures is a relatively common occurrence.

I was interested in the possibility of sighting snakes, however the locals who lived in daily and often intimate contact with these potentially dangerous reptiles understandably did not share a similar curiosity.

This learned attitude is very understandable because a poisonous snake bite would necessitate an immediate visit to central medical services at David and the majority of Chorcha residents were relatively poor and without any form of vehicular transportation, other than the two scheduled return bus trips per day.

Snakes are often nocturnally active creatures and split pole bamboo structures which provided residence to many lower income individuals and families cannot be considered snake entry resistant.

The practice of killing crocodiles, collecting body fat and thus the oil and then spreading this liquid around the outside of the bamboo house structures is still the major method of preventing snake domicile entry.

Like bamboo structures most residences constructed of masonry building blocks have an exterior toilet facility as well as an exterior shower facility to which snakes

can and do gain entry and it is not uncommon to find a poisonous snake coiled on the floor such a structure.
The Ngabe-Bugle-Comarca people of Panama appeared to prefer physical and cultural separation from Panamanians.
They appeared to employ many of the adaptations such as housing, dress, diet, and language that they would have found successful for possibly several thousand years before the Europeans appeared in Panama.
I came away with the distinct impression that this east coast and central Panamanian indigenous people might prefer this separation, however all people would welcome useful standards of necessities such as housing, transportation, education, and medical treatment.

While transiting Chilean Patagonia I anchored in front of Puerto Eden, my principal intentions were picking up a few cabbages but most of all a new feline shipmate.
The physical environment in this section of Chilean Patagonia can aptly be described as environmentally harsh.
Within the regions channels one commonly observes floating ice which originates from several local area inlet calving glaciers.
The ice appears in no great hurry to melt as the physical environment appears to be routinely cold and wet.
The approaching lows from the west bring initially powerful northwest winds followed by more powerful southwest winds.
The channels are completely protected against the entry of ocean seas however due to the strength of the winds an anchorage fetch of greater than one hundred meters must be considered excessive.
I was in this area during the southern summer and

the apparently continuous series of passing cold fronts which also brought strong wind, rain, and wet snow, indicated that the winter weather would be substantially more challenging.

While in Puerto Eden I was able to observe local people likely of Kawésqar ancestry, of very modest means, who would arrive in open homemade wooden skiffs of heavy construction with an overall length in the order of five to six meters.

These open boats would often be propelled solely by handmade Chilean oars, which are made from indigenous Chilean woods such as Alerce (Fitzroya cupressoides), Avellano/Walnut (Gevuina avellana), or Manio \Southern Yew (Podocarpus nubigena).

On occasion they would also be propelled by a motor of a type I have seen only in Chile, it consists of a one-cylinder diesel engine without a transmission and is fitted amidships in the open skiff, thus when the motor is started the prop shaft immediately turns and the vessel is immediately propelled forward, there is not a reverse.

I recall one family group composed of what appeared to be a mother, father, and three young daughters who appeared to all be below the age of twelve, arrive, purchase food, other supplies and depart.

I was told that there are several such people who live in skiff only access areas of the nearby coastal region and conduct all necessary business in Puerto Eden.

Puerto Eden itself is not serviced by any roads, rather a twice weekly passing supply ship from Puerto Montt and the village has a population of a few hundred.

At departure time the family experienced strong wind along with mixed rain and snow, as well as a strong contrary tidal current, all of which they appeared to take no notice.

The two adults and three children wore no rain gear, occupied a completely open engine-less skiff, the oldest daughter continually bailed during what was probably a several mile trip.

Chilean houses in this part of the country are almost entirely heated by inefficient wood burning stoves, thus the family would likely have returned both cold and wet to an unheated and a non insulated house.

This family emanated an attitude that I interpreted as one of complete acceptance regarding the nautical and environmental conditions.

I carried onboard quite a weighty cargo of reference books, one was a large volume of black and white photos, many taken during a French nineteenth century expedition (reference 1), this reference also contains actual photos of almost exactly what I described near Puerto Eden, although the Kawésqar people in the photo -which was taken at least one hundred years earlier- shows a similar family but clad in very scant clothing and clearly indicates their almost complete immunity to inclement weather.

This photographic reference also contains dozens of other photos of Kawésqar, Yamana, and Selk'nam peoples of both Chilean and Argentinian Patagonia which were taken in the late 19th and early 20th century, it is images such as these that Slocum would assuredly have observed and described in his book.

Aboriginal people's lifestyles before the contact with Europeans has formed a keen area of my interest, in that before European contact aboriginal people lived in tacit harmony with nature in a high level of adaptation along with a virtual absence of environmental degradation.

I have referenced the publication of late 19th century photos, which to my eyes clearly provides graphic images which assists the modern reader to achieve a sense of the loss and the misery suffered by the original indigenous peoples.

Individual images capture emotions such as despair, pride, dignity, courage, fearlessness, poverty, hunger, desperation, and graphic images of genocide.

The Yamana, Kawésqar, and Selk'nam of ancestral territories of Chilean and Argentinian Patagonia probably arrived shortly after the last glacial ice receded from the coastal areas, this would be in the order of possibly eight to ten thousand years before the present.

Conditions must have been difficult as it would require a significant period for the complete succession of plants that we see today to re-colonize after the ice retreat.

A similar chronological scenario of human aboriginal habitation immediately after glacial retreat in the interior of British Columbia, Canada is substantiated by dated ethnological remains along the Thompson River between Lytton and Ashcroft which respectively indicated 7400 and 8400 years before the present.

The original groups of humans which crossed the Bering land bridge to North America during the last glacial ice maximum in the order of 19,000 years before the present, managed to colonize not only the Thompson River area in British Columbia but also the Beagle Channel in southern Chile in the southern limit of South America.

Therefore, the entirety of North and South America must have been colonized without any form of modern transportation, within a span of a few thousand years.

Quite impressive for groups that communicated verbally but had no formal form of written communications.

I am reluctant to use the term spiritual, regarding the thought process which I experience when I am sitting quietly alongside a long ago abandoned pre-European contact indigenous people's habitation site.

I have visited many such sites throughout my travels which includes the coast of British Columbia, Aleutian Islands, Marquesas, Moorea, New Caledonia, and the Beagle Channel.

Such habitation sites may well have been occupied for several centuries to millennia before the arrival of the Europeans.

The feelings I experience when sitting at such sites includes a sense of the spectrum of human life experiences such as birth, death, procreation, violence, sickness, happiness, despair, contentment, future planning, past recollections, as well as the more mundane daily occurrences such as eating, drinking, food preparation, food storage, tool fabrication, and food processing.

Such sites on the coast of British Columbia may be found on the west coast of Vancouver Island, west coast of Graham Island in Haida Guaii, and both east and west coasts on Moresby island also on Haida Gwaii, as well as interior BC sites along both sides of the Fraser River from Yale to the mouth of the Chilko River.

The sites in coastal British Columbia include rectangular middens with centrally located depressions upon which would have stood man made Western Red Cedar structures.

One of Captain Cook's many precious gifts to posterity has been the drawings made by the ship's artist of such habitations, which the artist observed and recorded in locations such as the west coast of Vancouver Island, southeast Alaska, Aleutian Islands, and many locations in Polynesia.

These graphic images often include habitation structural details, nearby physical surroundings, clothing, indigenous peoples, and their tools and equipment.

I have had an opportunity to study such drawings from Cook's visit to Nootka Sound, Haida Gwaii, the English Bay area on Unalaska island in the Aleutian Islands, as well as in the Southern Marquesas, Moorea, and Tahiti.

It is also these details of such images that enter my mind when I am pondering beside one of the actual sites, I have been fortunate enough to visit.

The Aleutian Island sites are striking also due possibly to their sheer number, Amchitka has greater than seventy such sites some of which may contain in the order of twenty house depressions, some sites within the Aleutian chain still contain portions of the collapsed roof and upper wall structures.

Cruising the Aleutian Island chain in a sailboat, the eye is continually attracted by what Cook termed Lyme Grass (Elymus arenaria).

This grass essentially signals the site of a former Aleut habitation site because this indigenous member of the grass family seems to thrive on the calcium, phosphate, and protein rich organic refuse concentrated at such sites.

During both of my early May arrivals to the Aleutian Islands, Lyme grass was observed to be just starting to emerge from the brown shrivelled remainders of the previous year's growth, about to demonstrate its diagnostic lime green colour.

This species of grass which the Aleuts also used to line their boots and house structures can attain a height of two meters.

The Aleutian occupation site depressions are very visible in late April and early May, however by June they are much more difficult to discern due to Lyme grass but also the several species within the carrot family (Apiaceae).

The sites on the west coast of British Columbia are often marked by high numbers of closely spaced and stunted Sitka Spruce and Western Hemlock.

Such stunted trees, which often reach less a third of a meter in height appear to be many decades in age and grow on midden surfaces as well as fallen cedar house structural members.

The BC sites also may contain many remnants of fallen totem poles, mortuary poles, and collapsed red cedar house structural members.

Indigenous groups such as the Marquesan's on the island Nuku Hiva are vividly described by Herman Melville in the memoir adventure novel Typhee, which is a very thought-provoking book as well as providing several mental images of pre-European village life and customs of indigenous Marquesan's.

A present-day visitor to the Marquesas is still able to find many overgrown examples of similar village sites, stone paved access pathways, and stone house support structures that Melville describes.

Near the end of my 1995/1996 twelve-month first offshore training voyage which took Alcidae III from Victoria to the Marquesas, west to Bora Bora, and then back to the northern Marquesas, I had occasion to be anchored in Anaho Bay just before setting off on my direct passage back to Victoria.

As serendipity would have it, also anchored in the bay was a well-known French pair of nautical sisters.

I was to experience the pleasure of a day hike to a nearby unoccupied bay on the east side of Nuku Hiva called Hatuatua and was accompanied by one of the sister mariners.

Jacqueline was working at this time as a mathematics teacher and lived and worked in the tiny village on the isthmus between the islands of Tahiti Nui and Tahiti and was on a truncated Marquesas sailing adventure with her equally famous and competent mariner sister, Christiane.

The action in the Melville's novel Typhee took place on the same portion of the island of Nuku Hiva as our hiking destination of Hatuatua bay.

Hatuatua Bay is arguably the most beautiful beach I have ever seen, one can sit in the shade beneath what is certainly the exact same several hundred-year-old Tamanu (Calophyllum inophyllum) tree which would have been similarly used by the original Marquesian Hatuatua Bay inhabitants.

The original inhabitants would have likely experienced the same species of stinging jelly fish as I, while walking in the surf along the white sand beach but not the European introduced biting flies called no no's.

The tropical forest begins just off the beach and a short distance along a partially overgrown stone paved walkway are several overgrown original house platforms.

Our accessing them via this original stone paved trail would have been identical to several hundred years of Marquesian indigenous bare feet.

Reflection along such overgrown as well as purposefully and meticulously built stone paved trails, or upon the stone remains of the house platforms themselves, provides the same opportunity regarding spiritual sharing of the many previous critical life events which would have taken place on these exact sites throughout prior centuries.

ALEUTIANS 2001

Adak Island in both foreground and background.

The Aleut people reside at the pinnacle of my awe for their ability to adapt in a sophisticated, pragmatic, and technical manner to a harsh and rigorous set of physical, climatic, and oceanic conditions.
Specific adaptations span subjects and skills such as

clothing, transportation, fishing, hunting, spirituality, knowledge of human anatomy, and a functional understanding of botany including nutritional, medicinal, and as botanical toxins.

Approaching the end of my second training voyage I found I carried the idea that I should arrive in Aleutians when the snow was still at the shoreline, at about the time when the whalers and sealers used to arrive, however unlike the whalers and sealers my interest was living in the company of the annual sequence of appearance of the abundant herbaceous plant diversity which commences with an increasing tempo in sequence with the retreating snow.

I left Likiep Atoll in the Marshall Island Group at the end of the first week in March 2001 in company with my precious Minou and was probably a bit naive concerning the abrupt voyage that was in store for us both, although throughout the early and middle part of my life this naivete in combination with my sense of adventure may have been a critical component of my intellectual and nautical development.

I was driven to continually explore and approach the boundaries which demarcated the limits of my nautical and related abilities.

I had determined that if one does not on occasion exceed one's actual abilities, the knowledge of where the always expanding abilities reside, is not known.

In this period of my life, I had the attitude that whatever occurred weather wise, I would make the adjustments, however I always maintained and honoured the ship's basic rule that I would not enter or remain in a hurricane, cyclone, nor typhoon area during the active season, whereas relatively fast moving and occasionally intense lows along with their attendant cold fronts, I viewed almost with affection and certainly with anticipation.

On this passage from the Marshall Islands to the Aleutian Islands all was to be quite routine weather wise until one reaches the vicinity of 30 degrees north latitude - the same occurs in the opposite hemisphere in the vicinity of 30 S -.

On this voyage, once 30 degrees north has been reached the vessel would begin to experience exposure to lows generated in the area south of Japan.

Such lows normally track to the north northeast passing close to Japan, track more north easterly and end up in the Gulf of Alaska, or track just a bit north of east and end up off the British Columbia or the United States coast.

The second and third categories are the type of depressions that were to affect my vessel on this passage, and I was to leave Japan about twelve hundred nautical miles to port.

Prior to reaching the Aleutians I was to experience five closely passing low pressure centres and their associated cold fronts.

Two of these depressions were somewhat on the strong side however due to their speed I was usually only forced to heave-to for periods of fifteen hours or less.

This is in strong contrast to my third voyage in the Southern Indian Ocean when I was routinely forced to take defensive action for two to three days and one occasion for five days.

This first voyage to the Aleutians occurred before the Jordan Series Drogue was known to me, thus I had only a well used sail inventory, no spare sails, and a six-metre diameter Paratech sea anchor.

My first opportunity for an Aleutian landfall found me thirty miles off the Islands of Four Mountains with four hours of remaining daylight, the wind from the north-east was abrupt, very cold, and contained moderate snow.

I had consulted the pilot concerning anchorages on the Pacific Ocean side of the Islands of Four Mountains and had found none, rather the pilot recommended moderate tonnage and smaller vessels stay clear in such weather as I was experiencing, both because of the lack of a safe anchorage and the dangerous seas generated by the wind in opposition to the strong inter island tidal currents.

The vessel was presently hove-to on a starboard tack under the backed storm jib and triple reefed main, on this tack I could expect to run ashore in approximately five hours.

I recall I was very eager to end the voyage, anchor the boat, and start my wood burning stove because heat is not provided at sea.

I was also eager to have my traditional lip and leg numbing strength hot rum, however my inner voice instructed me to put the vessel onto a port tack which took me again further from land and into relative safety.

Two days later I recall an arctic front passing in the late afternoon of what turned out to be my last day at sea before my first Aleutian landfall, which was to be through Udagak Pass on Unalaska Island.

The arctic front was intense and as usual upon the actual passage contained a skiff of snow followed directly by a strong flow of dense clear cold air, direct from the

Bering Sea.

The vessels servo steering gear worked passably until this gusty northwest wind attained velocities above forty knots, at which time I would have to heave-to or hand steer.

I was reluctant to heave-to because on such a port tack I would be blown further than I wished to the southeast, thus when necessary I stood hand steering in the cold and spray.

On this second attempt to achieve landfall, which was to be my first visit to the Aleutians, I wanted to arrive off Udagak Pass during daylight early the following day at which time the present northwest winds were forecast to turn back into the northeast, thus I was motivated to keep the vessel moving and on course.

Such a luxury of accurate and timely weather forecasting that I and all modern mariners enjoy, was not available to Captain Cook nor the whalers and sealers.

What refused to leave my recollection during this somewhat trying cockpit duty was the almost completely clear blue sky except for the most impressive and distinctive rapidly passing black anvil shaped clouds.

The black clouds brought squalls containing strong and gusty cold wind, temporarily rougher seas, spray, and hail, the hail was somewhat painful to the facial skin when one chose to peek to windward.

I continued to hand steer until well after dark at which time the squalls ceased and I then plodded along for the night sailing a bit too close to the wind using a very inefficient and under powered sail selection, but now controlled by the steering gear.

Just before daylight my radar alarm sounded and there on the screen was my first 'glimpse' of the Aleutians, to be followed shortly by the actual sighting just after sunrise of the snow-covered mountains and coastline.

Throughout a mariner's nautical experiences, such proximity to the culmination of a difficult passage is always very memorable, satisfying, and a tiny bit emotional.

In this case I had indeed arrived in accordance with my goal, which was to see snow still at the tide line.

Upon entering protected waters after a difficult and turbulent passage one will witness one of the most satisfying and enduring experiences of high latitudes sailing, entering Udagak Pass which is less than two hundred meters wide will always remain one of my three most precious such experiences.

Another was many years later sheltering in the lee of Isle de Ouest on the west coast of Kerguelen, and third was placing the southeast cape of Tasmania between myself and the South Indian Ocean.

At this time in my sailing lifestyle, I had no spare sails and clearly recollect the experience of sitting in the company of wind driven snowflakes on the foredeck along with regularly boarding seas, while stitching chaffed and opening seams as the vessel slowly plodded to windward under solely a reefed mainsail.

Also, during this period of my life, I was fortunate that I seldom experienced fear or apprehension and was somewhat impervious to cold, I was not to notice the unwelcome visitors of fear and apprehension until my sixty-fifth year, I experienced a Wagnerian operatic flash back of when Siegfried first experienced fear when he met Brunhilda.

I had the view that fear was something to be considered a challenge and its boundaries were not to be avoided but rather probed.

Fear and seasickness appear to be bunk mates; however, it is imperative to recognize the symptoms so that these conditions are not permitted to deteriorate into vomiting and subsequent mental and physical resignation.

If a single-handed sailor is ever unlucky enough to experience full blown seasickness, this malady is best experienced well offshore where the vessel can be placed into an effective defensive mode.

I have indeed experienced the diagnostic early seasickness symptoms such as dry mouth, loose bowel sensation, and nausea.

Full blown seasickness was suffered on two occasions during my coastal training phase, I was able to place the vessel in a defensive position, however I was happy that luck was also a shipmate.

The north Pacific is unlike the southern oceans, in the north Pacific the lows tend to travel relatively quickly and on relatively widely varying tracks, thus they do not generate the sustained large seas from a constant direction as in the southern oceans.

The open ocean north Pacific winds and thus seas generated by depressions that pass to the south of the vessel's position, tend to follow the pattern of initially southeast, then back through the east and finally northeast, whereas depressions that pass to the north of the vessels position veer from southwest through northwest.

In late March and early April such a passage of a depression is normally followed by an interval of a few days before the approach of another depression.

Captain Cook is the historical sailing person that I admire the most and I have purposely anchored in the exact same anchorages as he on all three of my offshore voyages, these include anchorages in the Aleutians, Staten Island, Polynesia, Tasmania, New Caledonia, and Kerguelen, as well during earlier onshore voyages in Barkley Sound on the west coast of Vancouver Island.

During this visit to the Aleutian Islands, I was storm bound for four days in Dutch Harbor on Unalaska island, I remember the wind blew so hard that I futilely double moored my vessel, I was concerned the government dock may come apart.

This was my first experience of hurricane force winds which have nothing to do with a tropical hurricane, but indeed winds were more than one hundred knots.

While in Dutch Harbor I met the director the Museum of the Aleutians who informed me exactly where Captain Cook had set up his astrological instrument on top of a hill in the vicinity of English Bay.

As per his directions I attended the exact site and clearly visible was the still existing outline of the rectangular opening cut into the slow growing tundra ground cover where his crew had set up the telescopic instrument, as well the outlines of the actual trail from tide water that the crew and Captain Cook would have used to access this observation site.

While at the observation site, I sat on an obvious large rock approximately two meters from the spaded out rectangular shape which had been cut into indigenous ground cover made up of three species of moss, two species of heather, as well as several species lichens of which I was then unable to identify.

I sat on the rock and had the distinct feeling that Captain Cook had himself sat on this exact rock looking at the exact same spot as well as panoramic view to the north and east.

I have also visited the attic where Captain Cook slept during his coal ship apprenticeship training in Whitby, England, and there looked through the original leaded glass windows down onto the protected bay in Whitby where the coal carriers would certainly have been moored.

Within English Bay there also exists a pathway travelling from tidewater over the height of land to Deep Bay which is open to Beaver Inlet and Unalga Pass.

Unalga Pass must have been a wonderfully productive seafood supply for an Aleut village site, the relatively well-preserved remains of which are still obvious at Deep Bay.

It is apparent that this village was occupied in late June 1778, because this trail is referenced in Cook's journals and was used by Cook's crew as well as the inhabitants to access the village from Cook's anchorage in English Bay, the village inhabitants would have used the same trail to access English Bay and areas to the west and north.

The Cook journals also references specific trading activities practised with the inhabitants of the Deep Bay village which are presently not considered acceptable.

The anchorage of English Bay is also special because the physical setting, including all aspects of the surrounding countryside at both the English Bay anchorage and the village site on Deep Bay can be essentially identical now as when Cook would have seen them in 1778.

As well the edible berries, medicinal plants and other edible herbs observed adjacent to the village access trail, would also have been identical to those observed and utilized by the Aleut inhabitants of Deep Bay.

Near the Deep Bay village site and the adjoining trails, one almost feels the presence of the original Aleut inhabitants, principally since the surrounding countryside has not been altered.

Other than a few blinking navigation lights in Unalga Passage even the nighttime panorama would be essentially identical.

A similar claim of site originality cannot be made for most of Cook's worldwide anchorages that I have visited, nor most aboriginal village sites visited due to practices such as logging, cattle and sheep ranching, urban sprawl, and the other myriad examples of environmental degradation and change.

On the Pacific Ocean side of Unalaska Island, one finds a very well protected Raven Bay within which I visited a cove on the north side of Ogangen Island where there was an obvious previously inhabited Aleut site, and as usual one could easily follow the still existing original trail from the actual habitation site - termed yurts and barabaras by the Russians - in the order of one hundred meters to a pond of freshwater which was apparently used as a fresh water source and washing location.

At the edge of this slightly inland freshwater pond, I found the depth to be in the order of one meter and the water clear and cold.

There on the bottom, almost as if someone had just dropped it while cleaning was a broken stone dish with dimensions of 55cm long X 25cm wide X 5cm thick.

I classify the rock material as an andesitic type volcanic rock which is found in abundance in the area and often contained in geologic structures referred to as dykes.

I would guess that this dish was used to serve cold food, maintain food in a warm condition near or in a rare open fire, or possibly used as a wick dish for barabara interior lighting, it is also reported that Aleut women would stand over such an operating wick dish to warm themselves.

The oil consumed in such a wick dish would originate from whale, sea lion, or possibly seal blubber.

One must recall that in this routinely harsh environment, due to the total lack of trees an open fire whether to be used for cooking or personal warming would probably have been a rare event.

Therefore, most food would have been eaten raw as well as cold, and hot washing water other than from widely separated naturally occurring hot springs would have been almost unknown.

I am allowing myself to speculate that the stone dish that I observed was brought to the waterline possibly to be washed while it was still hot, during washing the dish cracked and was abandoned where it fell and thus there it was, sitting where it had been abandoned sitting with two perfectly matching pieces.

While on Ogangen I also saw what I identified to be a Great Grey owl flying around fifty meters overhead, this was unusual as it was daytime and Great Grey owls cannot be common on the Aleutians, although I suspected this one was hunting during daylight hours to provide young within a nearby nest with adequate nutrition.

I must also relate an experience in Raven Bay which caused an occurrence of one of the four scenarios that I wanted never to experience.

These experiences are being struck by lightning, which unfortunately I did experience in El Salvador resulting in a stainless-steel mast head mounted VHF antenna melting and vapourized circuit board tracing within my

HF antenna tuner.

The other items on my never to experience list were vessel roll over, the vessel being swept ashore on an open coast, and waking up at sea inside my bunk due to a flooded hull.

Although I was not awakened at sea by seawater entering my bunk, this did occur while I was purposely beached to clean the hull in a tiny cove at the head of Raven Bay.

This hull cleaning action was instigated due to a goose neck barnacle fouled hull to which I had not applied sufficient effort prior to leaving Likiep, as well as incorrectly determining that the water in the Aleutians was too cold for my wet suit.

Raven Bay contains a very protected and shallow cove at its head, where is also found a low angle soft sand beach, perfect for beaching one's boat and cleaning the bottom.

I had planned the boat beaching project meticulously so that I had yet several days remaining of rising high tides within the present two-week lunar tidal cycle.

All went very well until it came time to re-float the vessel, I was to find that I had made my landfall too high on the beach and high tide would allow the vessel to stand upright on the keel but would not lift the vessel clear.

I remained on this beach under the same rising and falling circumstances for two days, the daily tidal cycles gradually increased the height of high tide, however there were also two cycles of low tide per day when the boat repeatedly attained an angle of greater than forty - five degrees while lying sideways on the beach.

Minou and I became accustomed to this new routine as we had for all other temporary uncomfortable motions and angles experienced while at sea, however the low side of the beached vessel was on the port side which also contained two below waterline through hull valves, and these I must remember to shut off before the arriving flood tide would start to lift the vessel.

The second night I remembered to close galley sink however I forgot to close the head sink/toilet through hull, the vessel flooded through the head sink drain.

The situation would have become critical because as the vessel flooded while lying at forty-five degrees, the additional weight of the onboard seawater would not then permit the vessel to rise, thus I remained asleep until the cold seawater entered my bunk.

It was to become obvious that the vessel would not lift with rising tide due to the constantly increasing weight of the incoming seawater, thus in the darkness the immediate dual actions of closing the offending open through hull valve and the laborious manual bailing of the vessel through the amidships deck hatch were required.

When the point was reached where a sufficient weight of port side seawater had been removed, the vessel lifted to the upright position.

Subsequently for several days, the immediate adjacent shoreline rocks as well as the deck were observed to be encumbered with drying clothes and books.

My precious French pharmacist botany book by Paul Petard still bears the marks of this episode, however I would not then nor now part with this now seawater-stained book.

I never did attempt such a procedure a second time but rather opted for being cold inside of the wet suit, however the beaching process is sound and in case of a mishap involving a holed hull, propeller shaft or propeller issue, or a rudder problem, I would have no hesitation to repeat the beaching process however I would beach the vessel no higher than three quarters of the high-water range point.

This beaching location at the head of Raven Bay is a very sheltered and attractive beach and it was graciously shared by a mother and a large and young brood of Green Winged Teal.

I completed this second offshore training voyage with a 1265 nautical mile crossing from Akutan Pass in the northeast Aleutians to the mouth of Dixon Entrance located at the north end of Haida Guaii, which are all located on the north coast of British Columbia.

I had constantly been on the lookout for the Short-Tailed Albatross and had literally seen hundreds of Laysan and a smaller number of Black Footed Albatross.

I was about twenty miles offshore from Akutan Pass and there to landward was my first Short Tailed Albatross.

After observing hundreds of Laysan and Black Footed Albatross, it was obvious that this Akutan pass albatross was of a species I had not yet observed.

Peter Harrison writer of Seabirds utilizes a term 'jizz', it was this albatross's jizz which immediately clinched the identity of this rare oceanic pelagic bird, specifically it is manner of flight, size, and distinctive colour pattern.

During this relatively short passage when there remained greater than five hundred nautical miles to sail before entry into Dixon Entrance, I was bounding along in the darkness shortly after midnight, continuing to take full advantage of a moderate following wind which permitted a starboard tack powered by a poled out one hundred percent jib and a single reefed mainsail.

I was in my bunk asleep, and due to the moderate weather and seas the companionway door had been left secured in the wide-open position.

I had gone to sleep with the typical sounds of the following wind in company with the sloshing and gurgling of the passing seawater which are typical during the relatively heavy rolling motion of such a point of sail.

I was awakened by a deep reverberating respiratory sound which could almost be felt, and a distinctively fishy odour.

I decided that the sounds and odour were produced during the exhalation and inspiration of air from a large and nearby sea mammal which was apparently keeping station with my vessel.

After making my way in darkness of the cockpit, it appeared that the

visitor was probably closer than a boat length and was indeed keeping station with the vessel directly adjacent to the starboard side of the cockpit.

The following wind not only had permitted the deep rushing sounds of the respiration to enter the cabin but also the humid and distinctive odour of the whale's breath.

I had in mind this was a humpback which are relatively common in these waters, however it may well have been another large bodied species.

The sense I still recall is of the immediate proximity, power, and size of the producer of this deep and rich sound.

As well, since my nighttime visitor was keeping station with my surging and rolling vessel, it also must have been aware of my presence, course, and speed, which I interpreted as it intended me no harm.

As noted elsewhere, I would routinely proceed during darkness as near as possible to hull speed and would also not intentionally produce sounds such as an operating depth sounder that would be perceptible to the whale.

Therefore, the whale most likely became aware of the moving vessel from nothing other than the sound of water on my hull, followed by visual contact.

Our mutual darkness cockpit encounter probably had a duration of just over a few minutes, however those few minutes were filled with darkness, the flash of inflorescence within the wash from the speeding and rolling vessel and swimming whale, the whale's physical presence, and the humid and fragrant respiratory plume.

I retain the sense of having been in the presence of a benevolent and gentle soul, which was in total control within its element, whereas I was totally out of my element and would survive only several minutes without the boat.

CHILEAN PATAGONIA

Picking Calafate berries (Gaultheria buxifolia) near the Beagle Channel, to be made into jam or dried.

In the southern hemisphere spring of 2008, I arrived off

the south end of Isla Quehui, which is situated between Gulfo Corcovado and the south Pacific Ocean.

I was to spend a year and half in Chile, unexpectedly upon arrival I experienced an inexplicable sense that I had arrived home.

This concept of home undoubtedly related to several intellectual and possibly emotional factors, the first was my apparently deep seated and previously unacknowledged attraction to homemade clinker style rowing skiffs, larger commercial wooden working vessels, and wood smoke.

Coastal Chilean woodworking shipwrights and other woodworking tradesmen constructed heavy duty wooden rowing skiffs, entire commercial fishing vessels, spacious wooden Catholic churches, and large wooden houses.

The houses nor churches were provided with heat retentive insulation nor central heating; therefore, the interior humidity was relatively low which has resulted in sound structural wooden members even though the wooden structures may have been more than a hundred years of age.

In southern Chile there is a widespread use of wood as the primary source of cooking stove fuel as well as interior space heating, upcoming coastal villages would always be announced prior to arrival by what I interpreted as a welcoming pall of wood smoke.

It is typical in isolated Chilean village houses that the kitchen is the only room that is routinely heated.

This is accomplished by the high-quality Chilean made wood burning kitchen cooking stoves, elsewhere in the house sleeping warmth is provided by the local Chilote style traditional wool blankets.

The southern third of Chile may be described as moist and cold, not that dissimilar to many coastal areas on the British Columbia coast.

Like British Columbia as well, the local Chilean coastal village residents often exhibit truly little sensitivity to the cold and humid conditions.

A large percentage of the present day Chilean commercial fisherman were remarkably like my recollection's of 1950 era British Columbia fisherman, in that the Chileans remain robust, work with relatively simple and strong materials, and are a physically hard-working group of people.

Characteristics of such early British Columbia fisherman include the ability to repair the inevitable structural and mechanical fishing vessel and equipment damage.

Such repairs would often be required in very isolated locations and would also often entail partially dismantling the vessel until the issue of concern is exposed, completion of the necessary repairs, and reassembly of the vessel.

In Chile, most of such repair work takes place while the vessel is purposely beached high on a gently sloping shoreline in a well protected bay.

Such work on the coast of British Columbia would have occurred most often on a tidal grid, essentially all coastal communities and fish processing facilities were provided with one or several tidal grids.

The traditional selection of fishing vessel structural woods available in British Columbia are limited to Douglas Fir, Western Red cedar, and Yellow cedar.

These three species are valuable and effective, however must be considered paltry when compared to the variety and quality of indigenous woods available to Chilean shipwrights.

Southern Chilean forests provided different species of Nothofagaceae - Southern Beech - , Alerce and Cipres - both in the same family as British Columbia's western red and yellow cedars - , five different species of southern yew trees in the family Podocarpaceae, very hard and dense tool making wood found in several species of the family Myrtaceae, a species of small tree which provided a naturally dense and lubricated wood suitable for use in a propeller stuffing box, as well as selections from several other Chilean botanical tree families which provided interior finishing woods.

Heavy displacement type working vessel hulls like the British Columbia fishing industry packer fleet perform the same function on the Chilean coast, however this class of privately owned and operated public walk-on vessels also provide daily or bi-weekly transportation for dozens of isolated Patagonian island and coastal villages into regional supply and service locations.

In British Columbia, such vessels typically land at a government provided and operated driven pile supported wharf as well as floating docks.

Tidal ranges in British Columbia in some locations are occasionally slightly higher than in southern Chile, however the more cost-effective Chilean dock construction method is often to provide a concrete step like quay which extend into the water.

The vessel simply moors to whichever step is most appropriate to the level of tide, although the crew must be prepared to re moor or adjust the mooring lines as made necessary by the changing tide.

I will present two botanical and anchoring memories

from my one-and-a-half-year visit to Chilean Patagonia, the first my month long stay within Estero Quintupeu. This estero is not far from Puerto Montt and is the anchorage where the German pocket battleship Dresden hid from the British for a month or two in 1915 during World War I.

The Italian cruising guide -reference # 14 -, accurately states that this is a difficult anchorage due to williwaws and limited potential anchoring possibilities.

I decided to stay a month within this spectacular inlet which is exceptional both in terms of botany and topography.

At this anchorage I was to see my first Andean Condors who performed daily patrols along the estero's south side bordering range of mountains, often silhouetted against the magnificent Alerce (Fitzroya cupressoides), which is an especially useful tree to the Chilean coastal people,

The genus Fitzroya appears to be named after the captain of the sailing vessel 'Beagle' of Darwinian fame.

Darwin spent a significant amount of time during the voyage of the Beagle on Isla Chiloe which is located on the opposite side of Golfo de Corcovado from Estero Quintupeu.

Alerce is within the same botanical family as Western Red Cedar which can grow to equally large proportions on the west coast of British Columbia, both species were of great significance to both indigenous peoples and Europeans.

Reviewing my Estero Quintupeu list of birds and plants observed, I see botanical families such as Aralaciaea, Myrtaceae, Proteaceae, Winteraceae, Cunoniaceae, Escaloniaceae, Berberidaceae, Croiariaceaea, Ericaceae,

Onagraceae, Poaceae, Araliaceae, Grosulariaceae, Eleocaraceae, Eucritiaceae, Monimiaceae, Fagaceae, and Cupressaceae.

Only five of these lists of families have any significant indigenous presence in the northern hemisphere, which helps to illustrate the special stature held by Chilean southern hemisphere botany.

As well, several Quintupeu plant genera often contain greater than one species, thus the botanical biodiversity in this estero is both impressive and numerous.

Myrtaceae is a large, diverse, and successful southern hemisphere family and in Chile contains several especially useful species such as Arryan, (Luma apiculata) and Luma (Amomyrtus luma), the latter used for army rifle butts by the modern Chileans and tool handles and weapons by the indigenous peoples.

Patricia standing behind the vertical threaded Luma arbor on a chicha press on Isla Quehui in Golfo Corcovado.

A fermented alcoholic drink called chicha which is

made from pressed apples is almost universally consumed on all islands in Golfo de Corocovado.

The extremely hard and dense wood of Luma is critical in the creation of chicha, because it was an indispensable part of the wooden chicha press.

The original chicha presses contained a handmade work of art threaded wooden vertical arbor, which is approximately 300 mm in diameter and 1.5 metres in length.

There are numerous inhabited islands in Gulfo de Corcovado and essentially all are replete with apple trees, these trees seem to thrive in the cool maritime climate and the apples are left to fall onto the ground prior to collection.

No pesticides of any kind are employed; thus, the fallers almost certainly contain many insect and other biological protein additions.

The apples are simply picked up from ground complete with the internal creatures, attached bits of grass, leaves, and soil remnants, all of which immediately go into the large diameter wooden barrel to which the manually operated chicha press is applied.

Hundreds of litres of juice are expressed into fermenting containers which can naturally commence fermentation at ambient temperatures.

After what may be only a few days the locals start to consume fresh chicha, which is very desirable, sweet, and slightly alcoholic.

Upon the completion of fermentation, the cleared chicha is siphoned into glass containers and consumed throughout the year until the next the chicha season.

On my way south to the Beagle Channel I returned to Isla Quehui - where we had anchored for four months earlier in the visit to Chile - and stowed away more than one hundred litres of chicha which was to provide my post mid day meal glass of health tonic.

This modest supply of chicha stored in the bilge area of the hull provided my noon libation for several months, although equally available at very modest prices in Chile is Merlot wine which is also agreeable.

Land surrounding Quintupeu, like several other Chilean Patagonian inlets had been purchased by the late American millionaire Douglas Tomkins who endeavoured to rehabilitate and return the ecological condition of such locations to that present prior to European arrival.

This often involved purchasing houses and structures along with the land and requiring the previous Chilean owners to vacate, prior to demolition of the structures.

My memories of Quintupeu however always quickly return to the wind and anchorage issues.

I found this anchorage too deep for the use of shorelines, although one could so moor immediately adjacent to vertical rock cliffs and rely on an outboard anchor to hold the vessel clear of the cliff face.

I chose the steeply shoaling head of the bay where two boat lengths from shore the depth was found to be five fathoms, four boat lengths from shore depth were fifty fathoms.

The bottom turned out to be sandy mud which I always consider to be one of the best holding bottoms and thus I proceeded to develop a site-specific anchoring plan.

Upon entering a new anchorage, one does not know with confidence the actual wind direction nor strength before and after frontal passage, however useful guesses can be made.

I noticed patches of trees blown down on the south side of the inlet -this certainly indicated strong gusty winds-, thus I placed an anchor in five fathoms depth within a two-boat length band from shore and set the anchor rode parallel to the shore until a scope of greater than fifty to one was provided.

My second anchor as placed into the deep water ninety degrees with respect to the shoreline and set with a similar scope, however this second anchor was lowered into water with a depth of fifty fathoms and only five or six boat lengths offshore.

This second anchor was therefore set on a very steep underwater slope which would have resulted in a significant portion of the anchor rode digging into the steeply sloping sandy mud bottom.

Therefore, this portion of the rode was all chain because chafe may have been an issue, however nylon anchor rode containing only a twenty-meter section of chain is my first choice due to nylon ropes williwaw and wave shock absorbing characteristics.

A shoreline was also taken ashore which would prevent the vessel from moving out into the bay or further up or down the shoreline, thus holding the vessel approximately three boat lengths from shore and as described elsewhere the three lines were attached to an underwater swivel.

It turned out that pre-frontal passage winds were very violent and gusty and were responsible for the patches of blown down trees that I had observed on the south shore.

These violent winds, upon reaching the end of the bay where I was anchored would deflect off the south mountainous shoreline, change direction ninety degrees, and approach the vessel in a direction parallel to the same shoreline from which the vessels position was fixed at three boat lengths.

The roar created by an approaching williwaw is a sound not soon forgotten, not dissimilar to the sound of approaching williwaws in the Aleutian Islands.

After frontal passage the wind backed to the west and no longer deflected from the south shore, thus placing the full load on my offshore fifty fathom deep anchor, the stern would then approach very closely to the shoreline.

I tend to add nylon anchor rode lengths in multiples of one hundred meters and historically had used a double sheet bend for rode-to-rode connections.

Upon hauling anchors, I was habitually able to untie such tied connections, but on occasion may be required to use hand tools.

I was later in my voyage - Kerguelen to Tasmania - to find extreme strain on the nylon rode caused by the Jordan series drogue would sever the rode at the double sheet bend knot due a severing action caused by the sheet bends bight; thus, I now recommend a Carrick's bend be used to connect nylon rope anchor rode extensions.

The selection of knots available to mariners are examples of important human creativity, and the Carrick's bend, used for joining two ropes must be considered a high-level example of such creativity.

Several months after leaving Estero Quitupeu and descending the Chilean Patagonian coast, I was about to enter Golfo de Penas and had determined to spend a few weeks to a month within Caleta Suarez, which is a tiny bay off Estero Cono.

In the forest area accessible from this magnificently protected caleta I had an experience like Darwin, who mentions an encounter with the bird Huet-Huet (Tapaculo) which he reports alighted onto his boot.

Along the coast of Chilean Patagonia there are three different species of Tapaculos, all have an exceptionally loud and distinctive voice and all live in the often-dense rich coastal forest which contains many examples of both indigenous and endemic botanical species.

While botanizing one day in the region of Estero Cono I had the experience of having two different species of Tapaculo approach to within two meters of my boots.

On the coastal voyage south, this estero also contained the last small areas of high botanical biodiversity forest which was like larger areas found further to north.

After one pass to the south of the Golfo de Penas this type of forest abruptly gives way to a ground cover which is much less bio-diverse and one that has been more heavily and recently glaciated.

The portion of my descent of Chilean Patagonia from Golfo de Corovaodo to Gulfo de Penas contained three 'adventures', as per the quote which begins the coastal sailing chapter must be considered indications of my incompetence.

The third and what was to prove the final of these transgressions found me again trying to make use of a cold front while underway, this one involved entering Caleta Cono at 3 AM placing almost total reliance on the radar.

Passing cold fronts along with their usual characteristics such as violent wind gusts, changing wind direction and often severely reduced visibility, are a manageable issue in the open ocean however within narrow coastal channels or close to an open ocean lee shore, cold front passage can create critical situations.

Upon leaving Bahia Anna Pink I did have sufficient time to complete the transit into Estero Cono before gale force northwest winds were predicted, however shortly after leaving the protection of Bahia Anna Pink the Chilean Navy ordered all small vessels immediately into harbour, they had just upgraded the approaching weather system's severity and now expected an earlier arrival time, however I was already clear of land and on my way.

In hindsight I had two opportunities to make alternate decisions, either to return to Bahia Pink or complete a daylight entrance into a less but still adequately protected bay prior to Estero Cono, unfortunately I chose neither of these options.

I found shortly after midnight that the wind was quickly strengthening and now the entire shoreline had become a hazardous lee shore, both due to the arrival of the predicted gale force northwest winds.

I arrived off the entrance to Estero Cono at 3 AM and made an additional mistake in judgment which was not to-heave to and wait a few hours for daylight.

The wind was now gusting over fifty knots and I did not want to heave-to for two hours and forfeit a large portion of my remaining sea room, my reasoning included the fact the wind and seas were rapidly building.

I thus established the location of the one-hundred-metre-wide Estero opening using radar, gps, and my plotted paper chart positions, then immediately made for this long and very narrow bay in total darkness with complete reliance on radar hoping that once within the estero I would see the tiny Caleta on my radar screen opening on my port side in sufficient time to turn in.

I coasted in at essentially hull speed due to the strong and gusting following wind as well as following breaking seas, reserve power to manoeuvre was provided by the pole-less luffing storm jib hanked onto the forestay. This sail was permitted to luff due to the already sufficient vessel speed under bare poles, however I wanted the option of it is uses upon turning to port when I must expect to be briefly beam to the wind and waves to enter the tiny port-side cove.

Within this narrow estero it was indeed now possible to turn the vessel beam to the wind and waves because there were no longer open ocean breaking seas, but rather locally generated wind waves and only the heaving of the open ocean.

As well, and in accordance with ship's rules the motor was idling with the transmission in neutral in preparation for possible service in conjunction with the storm jib during the final cove entrance.

Unfortunately, even though I approached to within twenty meters of the port side estero coastline, I did not see in time the narrow opening on my radar screen and thus was quickly blown past the tiny entrance, at this time the radar screen began to indicate the end of the estero quickly approaching.

Prior to entering the estero's narrow entrance I had prepared my main bow anchor for release and thus in only a few minutes after being blown by the entrance to safety, the radar indicated that I had approached to within a quarter of a nautical mile from the end of the estero.

I had manoeuvred into the centre of the estero, turned into the wind hoping to slow the boat prior to releasing the anchor however the motor did not have sufficient power to even turn the vessel into the wind, thus I released the anchor while the vessel was broadside to the waves and wind, the vessel still possessed excessive velocity to leeward.

Quickly at least a one hundred meters of chain and double braid nylon rode were deployed, the anchor held but having concern about anchor dragging in the strong and gusty wind I let out too much additional rode before releasing my second anchor, and thus was now too close to the breaking waves on the rocky beach to deploy adequate scope on the second prepared anchor.

I now found myself exposed to the storm force winds, a two-mile fetch, no local knowledge of the anchor holding properties of this anchorage with only one well set anchor.

I then committed an impulsive action which to this day I am ashamed, and I am now convinced that cats can accurately gauge human emotions such as fear.

Immediately upon anchoring, Florito in very abnormal behaviour commenced his Siamese howling which was something he had not done since the first twelve hours of his unsolicited abduction from Isla Floriana in the Galapagos Islands.

I now experienced fear symptoms such as very dry mouth and a loose bowel and physically brushed him from his perch on cold box.

He immediately left the cabin and very uncharacteristically spent the remainder of this turbulent darkness sheltering under the deck mounted upended skiff, rather than in the bunk with myself, emotionally I do not think he ever recovered from this experience and in hindsight -although I do not really understand the thought process-, I think this episode was significant in what was to follow.

It became light in just under two hours and I could then see the protected caleta opening that I had missed, however due to wind and waves there was no way I could motor to windward to now achieve the entrance, thus I rode at anchor with one properly set anchor and my stern less than one hundred metres from the lee shoreline.

Throughout the day it became apparent that both anchors were dragging and since the actual cold front and expected relief providing wind shift were still several hours offshore, I was expecting to be pushed ashore during the oncoming darkness.

I note elsewhere that rowing the skiff into strong winds and wind generated waves to set an additional anchor is normally an option, due to the present wind strength it was not an option.

I was in my bunk around 11 PM and it was just getting dark when I heard a Spanish speaking voice on my vhf radio, he was calling me!

It turned out there were four Chilean long-line fishing vessels sheltering in the protected caleta that I had tried to enter and due to the darkness, I had not seen them nor they me, but during the afternoon crew members had been for a walk and observed my precarious position.

The voice belonged to Alberto the captain of the Chilean fishing vessel Rio Pelluhue and he immediately advised me that the cold front was still some hours off that I was in a very insecure position, further that I should immediately come into the caleta.

It must be noted that the captain nor any of the other approximately thirty Chileans who made up the crew members of all the anchored fishing vessels spoke any English, and thus without an ability to communicate effectively in Spanish, my rescue may not have occurred.

Chile was my eighth Spanish speaking country over a period of just over four years since the start of my nine-year third voyage, -over the entire nine-year duration third voyage I was to spend six years in ten different Spanish speaking countries-, and my policy of preferring not to associate with English speaking people now provided one of its rewards.

I quickly explained my situation, that I had missed the entrance in the dark, had released two anchors however both were dragging, and I soon expected to be on the beach, however under the present circumstances I was unable to retrieve either anchor or motor into the wind. He immediately offered to come and tow me in, thus we quickly organized a plan, I would go up and cast off my second and poorly set anchor and attach a buoy onto the rode, prepare the remaining anchor to be cast off also with a buoyed rode.

This I did, on the radio he explained he would come by my starboard side and as he passed his crew would throw me a towing line, he would then hold station with me just off my starboard bow while I made secure the tow line and cast off my last anchor.

This understanding had to be communicated on the radio as the wind and sea noise on the foredeck rendered shouting useless.

Shortly, I found myself standing on the foredeck, it was rapidly getting dark and there appears an eighty-ton displacement wooden Chilean fishing vessel close by and takes up position with his stern just off my starboard bow.

The towing line is thrown and caught, this line is made fast and strain is taken so that my vessel is held in position while I free and cast overboard the rode of my first deployed anchor, then the wonderful always to be relived feeling of the strain being applied to the tow line and I am being hauled to windward, away from the breaking waves now just meters aft of my stern.

Alberto was skilfully holding my vessel against waves and wind while ensuring my jettisoned anchor rodes, nor tow line, fouled his ships propeller nor rudder.

As well, he refrained from applying excessive power which would create the potential hazard of breaking the tow line or pulling a deck cleat, I was now without a prepared anchor.

It must be recalled that I and the rescuing fishing vessel are now close to shore, Alberto's present hazardous position was a direct result of my previous bad decisions.

In less than ten minutes we were entering the caleta and almost immediately I and my vessel entered perfect calm.

I will probably never part with the feeling of protection, calm, and well being that I experienced when the crew pulled and moored my vessel alongside the Rio Pelluhue.

On the second day after my arrival into the protected caleta, I rowed out in the skiff and successfully pulled and retrieved both anchors, chains, rodes, and buoys.

The weather improved, the fishermen left, and I was not to see them again even though I stayed in this botanical gem of a caleta for three weeks.

I was to spend many days with my Polynesian machete, rock hammer, binoculars, and notebook wandering through the indigenous forest.

Two days before leaving, sardine sized fish entered the bay and, in the past, I had scooped them up with the deck bucket and obtained ample supplies to feed Minou, thus I did the same for Florito and these he devoured.

There must have been something in those sardines that did not suit Florito because before leaving he developed incontinence involving both urine and feces.

Thinking back, I was again less than gracious with him when this occurred on my bunk, and in hindsight I believe I am responsible a second time for grievously wounding his emotional sensitivities.

The next morning, we left on an overnight passage across Golfo de Penas, Florito had already successfully experienced much rougher seas than we were to experience but was not to be found onboard once anchored at the south end of Golfo de Penas.

I had communicated via vhf radio with a Chilean Navy watch post at the south end of Golfo de Penas as I left it to starboard, but this was prior to my knowledge that I had lost Florito.

I could not accept he would have mistakenly gone overboard in the less than moderately rough conditions that we had just experienced, thus I took apart the boat to a point whereby his absence was confirmed.

It was no small task to unpack and then repack the vessel, however, I harboured the hope that he was upset with me or possibly still sick from the sardines and thus was hiding.

After my search, and to this day, even though I have tried to convince myself of more easily digested conclusions, I cannot escape the possibility that he purposely went overboard because his was of a very emotionally sensitive nature and had again been emotionally wounded.

I have tried to part with the sense of guilt and remorse but have found similar success as I have had in escaping the recollections of grief experienced upon losing Minou between Panama and the Galapagos.

I made a bit of a nuisance of myself with the Chilean Navy because I called them and explained that possibly my Siamese cat had fallen overboard while I was passing their station and would they please keep a lookout for the possibility of such an appearance.

I endured the anchorage without Florito for three more days and called the Chilean station twice per day, they were polite and considerate concerning my very unlikely presumption, however I am quite confident they were not overly impressed with this single-handed gringo.

I found I was becoming depressed and despondent, conditions which I have been lucky in life essentially to have never experienced, thus I recognized that something concerning my mental outlook was abnormal.

I moved to another anchorage however I found the same emotional situation, and even though I was ready to move after a period of just over a week, I found I had little incentive to pull the anchors and retrieve the shorelines.

Pureto Eden was less than forty nautical miles to the south and the possibility of finding a kitten in this most remote of Chilean Patagonian villages, was the impetus that finally got me underway.

I arrived, anchored in front of the village and rowed ashore, there leaning over the guardrail on the dock

where the two stationed Chilean Carabinieros.
They were aware of my identity and likelihood of arrival probably due to the particularly good communication between the Chilean Navy and Carabinieros.
The younger officer was completely out of uniform and the older officer was only partially in uniform, something which is completely unknown in larger towns to the north.
My intention of acquiring a kitten was broached almost immediately and the older officer accompanied me to a house where I could make an inquiry.
Together we marched down the boardwalk as roads nor vehicles exist in Puerto Eden and stopped at house which had a detached woodworking shop.
The lady was not home so we looked in the workshop where the officer advised me, he had the day before seen the single kitten, although at this time it was not to be seen.
I returned the next day to find the lady owner at home and more than willing to part with the sole kitten.
We attended the workshop and the lady advised me to lift an almost one-meter diameter and heavy circular saw blade.
I remember it was so heavy that I could just mange to tilt up one side, and there was the kitten who was to become Ede, she was tiny and four weeks old.
I carefully captured her with one hand as the other supported the saw blade, then placed her inside my Canadian iconic Stanfield grey sweater.
I had brought a two-litre box of Chilean white wine which the lady was very content to receive, the bargain completed, Ede and I made our way back to the skiff along the boardwalk.

I stopped along the way to fill a plastic bag with wood chips and sawdust, I had thought correctly that she may be familiar with such material to perform her bodily functions.

She rode the entire trip back to the boat, including the skiff ride to the anchored sailing vessel without a single meow or attempt to escape her Stanfield enclosed chest transportation nest.

In high latitude locations such as Chile it was my practice to habitually maintain three onion sacks hanging submerged aft on the sailboat, which would usually contain clams, mussels, and crabs, respectively.

This was the case upon Ede's arrival, I put her on the cabin sole and the communication I think I received was "ok, so this is my new home, what do you have for me to play with and I am hungry as well".

I threw her a rolled-up paper ball that Florito used to retrieve, which she immediately commenced batting.

I then retrieved two cooked clams from my cold box and threw them on the floor, Ede obviously knew immediately what she was to do with the clams and started eating and growling.

The habit of growling while dining soon ceased, however the zest for clams, mussels, fish, and crabs persisted.

I have had four separate cats throughout all three of my offshore voyages as well as most of my coastal training period.

I realize I may not be an ideal cat owner; however, I cannot imagine my accomplishments at sea would have been possible without these shipmates.

It was to be another month before Patricia joined Ede and I in Ushuaia, Argentina, we were all three to find

ourselves temporarily tied to a grounded wooden float in an isolated bay on Argentinian Tierre Del Fuego.
Patricia and I had just stepped ashore and had proceeded about one hundred meters on our daily walk and there were Ede, thus was born her daily multi kilometre walks.
Subsequently, she has been ashore with me, often daily on often lengthy joint rambles more than three kilometres in other Argentinian Patagonian anchorages, as well as Uruguay, the Brazil rain forest, South Africa, Kerguelen, New Caledonia, Aleutian Islands, and of course British Columbia.
I have now relinquished the sea for a recreational vehicle and Ede, and I spend six months per year in the mountains of the British Columbia interior whereby she has almost continuous access to the outdoors.
She is now not up to more than half a kilometre walks, however the tradition continues.

ARGENTINIAN PATAGONIA

Note the tiny sailing vessel at the bottom of the near vertical cliff on the left which is in Bahia Capitan Canepa on the south coast of Staten Island.

Staten Island for me holds mythical status, I had read accounts of its presence for more than five decades before it inevitably hove into view.

Botanically, leaving Beagle Channel bound for Staten Island is equally dramatic as when entering the Beagle Channel from the north, Beagle Channel is indeed a microclimate and the indigenous botany when compared to immediately north and south must be considered lush.

My comparison will be illustrated if one botanically compares their list of plants observed at Brecknock to the north of the Beagle, the list of plants within the Beagle, and the list obtained at Bahia Aguirre to the south of the Beagle Channel.

The most recent retreat of southern Patagonian glaciers left this entire area almost completely free of topsoil and therefore plants.

Botanically speaking, even though the biodiversity is substantially less than the Galapagos, New Caledonia, and the Aleutian Islands the Beagle Channel is precious.

I have been fortunate to visit Charles Darwin's house in Downe, England, including sitting under his surviving seven-hundred-year-old Yew tree, walk on his thought ruminating daily walking pathway, and visited his actual study/laboratory.

In view of my previous research and my visit to Downe, it was not possible for me to botanize in any of the forests surrounding Golfo de Corocovado, Beagle Channel, nor the Galapagos without thinking I was sensing Darwin's spirit.

Not dissimilar to Darwin before me, I was in his previous locals also with my pocket notebook, hand lens, rock hammer, and curious documenting nature.

The insightful brilliance, however, is not comparable.

I first sighted the southwest corner of Staten island while experiencing a rare northeast wind and thus was not quite able to point the vessel into the west entrance of La Maire Strait without being forced to tack, although I did not need much of an excuse to proceed to the fully exposed southern coast of Staten Island.

I arrived a mile off the entrance to Bahia Capitan Canepa and found myself in the temporary lee of this very infamous island, experiencing relatively calm seas along with that magnificent Southern Ocean southwest swell. The northeast wind was only in the order of twenty-five knots; however, it was already creating williwaws on the lee side of the Staten island, such williwaws contained energy sufficient to hoist an occasional seawater mist, my inner voice murmured the question as to the williwaw strength when the wind reached gale and storm force, thankfully I was to discover the answer.

I started the motor and made for the entrance to Bahia Capitan Canepa, loosing steerage during the short-lived williwaws but managing to make steady progress into the large open bay.

The Italian guide speaks of two anchorages, I chose the first on the port side which in my voyaging experience is quite singular because it is in the order of a quarter of a mile long and not wide enough to turn the boat without jogging back and forth.

On the south side of this narrow anchorage is a sheer two-hundred-meter-high cliff, thus when anchored one can look up at this cliff whose base is less than a boat length off the port side.

I proceeded to set three anchors and six shorelines, two shorelines to be doubled up once the unexpected ocean surge arrived.

Upon entering this long and very narrow opening I utilized my method of releasing a stern anchor during the entrance so that it would physically arrest the forward motion of the vessel once enough scope had been released, thus ensuring that this critical stern anchor was well set.

The set stern anchor rode would then be released, and the vessel permitted to power forward to approach as closely as possible the head of the bay.

This is necessary to achieve the maximum scope for both the bow and stern anchors.

Once the forward progress of the vessel is arrested at the head of the bay, the sole occupant must proceed forward and release the bow anchor, then immediately return to the stern, and commence the exercise of pulling the vessel backwards until sufficient scope fore and aft is achieved.

The bow anchor may be set either using a large sheet winch, the anchor winch, or reversing the motor although I prefer a winch due to the possibility of fouling the stern anchor rode in the ship's propeller.

I used the maximum scope possible for both anchors due to the shallow anchorage depth, the likely potential of violent williwaws and the potential of ocean surge.

Regardless of anchorage water depth I have always preferred deploying greater than one hundred meters of nylon and at least fifteen to twenty meters of chain which is attached to the anchor.

I am aware all chain rode proponents will adhere to the view that the weight and therefore the resulting catenary characteristics of chain will provide the necessary anti shock and jerking performance necessary, however such is not my experience.

As noted elsewhere I do not take an abundance of photos, however I do have a photo in this anchorage, this photo illustrates the narrowness of the bay, the height of the cliff and the proximity of this port side cliff with respect to the vessel.

Once both bow and stern anchors have been set, single-handed mariners must then leave the vessel and commence attaching shorelines as well as rowing out additional anchors if necessary.

It is ship's practice to put the skiff alongside just prior to entering such an anchorage and place the first shoreline into the skiff in a manner so that it is immediately available for rowing ashore and deployment.

This anchorage was like many others in Chilean and Argentinian Patagonia in the requirement for both multiple anchors and shorelines, however somewhat more challenging due to the requirement to scramble up vertical rock faces to attach shorelines as well as installation of piton type shoreline anchors.

My one-meter-long stainless-steel angle iron rock pitons are a necessity in such instances because they can be installed in the optimum location, all that is required is a suitable crack or opening in the rocks, as well, one requires agility, a four-kilogram hammer, and the where with all to use it.

As previously noted, I entered Bahia Capitan Canepa and anchored during northeast winds, winds from this direction in this region are not to be expected to persist for lengthy periods of time.

The wind changed the same afternoon that I anchored

back into the more common direction of northwest, later to back to west and later still backing to southwest. The entrance to the large Bahia Capitan Canepa system is open to the southwest, thus I chose this very narrow anchorage which would hopefully be protected from anchorage entering southwest winds, seas, and surge, however I was mistaken concerning the surge and wind.

Strong and gusty northwest gale force winds arrived the first night and immediately created williwaws which descended the face of the two-hundred-meter-high cliff on my port side, then striking the vessel broad side.

These gusts contained such force that the vessel heeled in the order of forty-five degrees to leeward, recall I was anchored less than a boat length from both port and starboard shorelines.

The port side shore is the base of the cliff and the starboard shoreline is a combination of rock faces and boulders.

At 2 AM the first storm force williwaws commenced blowing, the keel almost immediately grounded on the starboard side of the anchorage and I was forced to increase the shoreline tension using the sheet winch on the windward port side.

Due to the violence of the newly arrived williwaws, I feared the existing shorelines may part, therefore two trips ashore in the dark where required to place two additional windward shorelines.

Shorelines must be arranged so that they can be adjusted with respect to length and tension from the vessel with aid of either the largest jib sheet winch or the capstan portion of the anchor winch.

It is almost inevitable that slips and falls will occur during such shoreline emplacements of lines along with their anchoring sections of chain, such an accident occurred in this anchorage resulting in a very painful and swollen sprained ankle.

When one is alone, there is little use complaining or calling for help, thus the work continues until the vessel is secure however one must always be mindful that one is alone.

Such awareness however has never precluded me from voyaging single-handed.

Subsequently, I found that a deck bucket full of frigid Southern Ocean seawater was a reasonable replacement for ice during frequent swollen ankle soakings, fortunately this was one of the very few physical injury issues I experienced during my nine-year third voyage.

This anchorage during storm force williwaws created wood stove smokestack down drafting and was to be the only anchorage I have visited where my wood and coal burning steel and fire brick stove was unable to operate without smoking.

As expected, following the strong northwest winds, stronger and longer lasting southwest winds began to blow.

I recall gazing towards the entrance of my narrow anchorage and seeing the quickly moving clouds of dense seawater spray which were lifted by the williwaws.

They would form on the south side of the anchorage entrance, proceed up the anchorage to my location and then sweep up the cliff face on my starboard side, this magnitude of natural violence was also experienced during my second visit to the Aleutian Islands.

In conjunction with the williwaws came the surge

which I had endeavoured to escape by anchoring within this east west oriented, very narrow, and long anchorage.

The Southern Ocean surge began entering my narrow anchorage to break on the beach which was now located approximately one hundred meters forward of my bow. The vessel would alternately be thrust forward on the incoming surge and do exactly the opposite on the outgoing surge, thus a frequency of forward and aft vessel motion with approximately one cycle every two minutes was initiated.

These conditions were to persist for longer than twenty-four hours and is the only event which I have experienced which puts almost equal strain on the vessel restraining lines as was to be experienced using the Jordan series drogue in the Indian Ocean.

It was difficult to conceive of how the three-nylon anchor rodes could resist such extreme shock loading, however none of my anchors dragged nor were any rodes nor shorelines broken.

It bears repeating that line chafe is a major issue and must not be permitted!

Other than wind, williwaws, and surge, this anchorage will also be remembered for the twenty-seven different species of plants identified, five not personally previously observed.

Mat forming specimens of severely wind pruned and shaped Azorella selago created large areas of ground cover.

Though these specimens on Staten Island were magnificent, I was to see more impressive specimens on Ile d'Ouest in the south Indian ocean somewhat later in my voyage to Kerguelen.

One must be careful not to walk on such growth forms of Azorella selago because this supremely well wind adapted, and the slow growing plant will be damaged.

This Staten Island long and narrow anchorage is also the site of my sole encounter with a Leopard seal.

I was on deck obtaining a fresh cold bucket of sea water to soak my swollen ankle and there not two meters from the side of the vessel looking me directly in the eye, was a magnificent leopard seal, with head and long neck completely clear of the water.

I will always recall the proximity, size, and sleekness of this animal, but especially it is eyes, for there, I saw a tiny bit of surprise, curiosity, and interest, but they were devoid of fear.

I will use this very brief and intense wildlife sighting to further justify a possible reason that I gave up taking photos many years before, if I had been fiddling for a camera, focus, angle, depth of field, and zoom, I am not likely to have had burnt into my memory the long lasting vivid mental image of this magnificent animal, created during an approximately one-minute duration sighting.

When my ankle and the weather cooperated, I made my way around to Puerto San Juan Del Salvamento which in the past functioned initially as a lifeboat base aiding nineteenth century sailing vessel crews in crisis plying the Cape Horn area and later as a penal colony.

The penal colony site is immediately evident on the starboard side as one enters a J-shaped bay where the anchorage is located.

Entering this anchorage, I inexplicably experienced emotional sensations such as gloom, sadness, suffering, loneliness, and despair, which I had not experienced during entrance to any other anchorage, the usual anchorage arrival sensations are those of security, welcome, friendliness, discovery, and adventure.

Upon going ashore at the head of the inner J-shaped bay I found several totally unkempt, overgrown, disordered, and apparently indifferently arranged graves, this was the cemetery of the penal colony.

My sense was that human mortal remains had been essentially discarded, rather than respectfully laid to rest.

I now suspected the source of my previously experienced sense of almost dread and foreboding upon entering this anchorage.

It is not my practice to spend less than a week at an isolated anchorage nor give credence to non-objective phenomena, however I left the next day, writing this several years later the dark emotions remain profound.

I have never visited a site such as Auschwitz and the penal site on Staten Island is by no means quantitatively similar, however qualitatively I believe I may have sensed a similar manifestation of human evil.

Subsequent references indicated that this penal colony had held political prisoners, which possibly relates to a reason why Beethoven's only opera Fidelio, continues to generate powerful emotions.

In contrast to the dark emotions encountered entering this anchorage, one also passes a disused nineteenth century lifeboat station where Argentinian crews rowing open boats braved some of the most challenging tidal and sea conditions in the world to assist unknown and foreign mariners in distress.

My final port of call on Staten Island was to be Puerto Cook.

I have visited many of Cooks exact anchorages and none

including such anchorages as English Bay in the Aleutians, Papeete, and Venus point on the island of Tahiti, Cook's Bay on Moorea, Kealakekua Bay in Hawaii, Kerguelen, or his apprenticeship period residence in Whitby, England contained an equal strength of Cook's spirit as did Puerto Cook on Staten Island.

Within Puerto Cook there are few options for potential anchoring locations thus I suspect that the Argentinian navy steel mooring buoy in the centre of the bay must be close to location that Cook would have chosen, thus during the period I was moored to this mooring buoy I would have had the same view of the essentially identical surroundings that Cook would have experienced two hundred and fifty years previous.

Of the many Cook anchorages that I have visited it is only Staten Island, Kerguelen, and English Bay in the Aleutian Islands that are essentially the same as when Cook visited.

When Cook visited the Beagle Channel it was inhabited by the Yaghan, further south by the Onas, whereas Staten Island had its own indigenous people who Cook also visited and described.

I waited for a fair wind southwest wind to leave Puerto Cook on my passage seven hundred and fifty nautical miles up the Argentine Patagonian coast to the settlement of Puerto Deseado.

Prior to sailing through the narrow entrance which connects Puerto Cook directly into the Straits of La Maire, my vessel was prepared for the sea, including carefully stowed anchor, sealed chain locker, raised storm jib and triple reefed mainsail.

The fair southwest wind was generated just after the passing of a cold front, thus would likely persist in a robust manner for at least a few days.

Caleta Horno, Argentina
Maihuenia patagonica in full bloom

At Puerto Deseado I spent a month ascended into the lengthy and challenging tidal estuary, another month at Caleta Horno a further one hundred and fifty nautical miles to the north, the entire time improving my understanding of the local geology, Argentine Patagonian botany, and that Latino outlook on life which contains an appropriate mixture of food, wine, smiles, and laughter.

I remained four months in isolated locations in Argentine Patagonia and maintained an essentially daily SSB schedule with the Prefectura, mostly conversing with the station at Ushuaia but on occasion also Mar del Plata.

I welcomed this daily verbal contact as well as their apparent concern for my well-being and thus their interest in my safety, I have not elsewhere found such a level of interest.

Specifically, I found interesting the very dry Andean rain shadow botany of southern Argentinian Patagonia, as well as the pyroclastic volcanic deposits containing free standing volcanic vent remnants and other dramatic volcanic flow structures observed in the vicinity of both Puerto Deseado and Caleta Horno.

It was at Caleta Horno where I also shared almost daily company with a small group of guanacos.

In Puerto Deseado I was fortunate to view a collection of local indigenous stone projectile tips, as usual aboriginal skills in adapting materials at hand continued to be impressive.

This area geologically contains predominantly pyroclastic volcanic rocks however it was a silicified sedimentary rock termed chert that appeared to be the preferred material for projectile tips, although specimens containing a local volcanic glass, not dissimilar to obsidian were also in evidence.

In the southern British Columbia interior, indigenous peoples favoured a small list of specific obsidian sites for projectile tip material and I suspect the indigenous people of the Puerto Deseado area also had favoured preferred sites for chert projectile material.

In Puerto Deseado I was not able to touch the projectile tips physically, however many appeared to be made of chert and that must have come from outside this area, on my almost daily rambles I had not yet seen any sedimentary rocks; however, it is very possible that sedimentary layers including chert were present underneath the pervasive surface layer of volcanic pyroclastics.

I still slightly shudder when I think of the occasional rivers of extreme wind which descend from the lee side of the Andes mountains to cross the coastline of Argentinian Patagonian and then off into the south Atlantic Ocean, fortunately I did not experience firsthand any of such winds.

The coast of Argentina is a challenging part of world to sail in a small boat, as well the River Plate contains numerous not insignificant difficulties and hazards for the single-handed mariner.

Throughout my travels I have visited very few yacht clubs, probably for quite a host of reasons, however it is likely I preferred isolated anchorages and nearby small villages.

It was not necessary to find a marina to physically leave my vessel because during the nine-year third voyage I returned only once for a four-month period to Victoria. As well, possibly I have never felt overly comfortable in the company of most yacht club members nor Yachties from English speaking countries who are often found in such marinas.

Argentina is somewhat of an exception to this quirk in my personality because although I did not leave the vessel to return to Canada, I did haul out for the better part of two months in San Fernando – a suburb of greater Buenos Aires- and performed extensive steel work on the hull.

I recall sitting in Puerto William at the chart table just

off the elbow of Isabelle Autissier -a famous French single-handed sailor- who graciously described the complicated route to follow in the River Plate to safely arrive in San Fernando.

It was made clear to me that yacht club rules forbade an owner from living aboard while the vessel was in the yard, however this was never enforced, and I readily adopted the concept of the unseeing Latino eye.

The English speakers were fortunately rare, and I was completely accepted as almost just another worker by the two dozen boatyard day workers.

I found the work ethic and skill level of the workers and most contractors for whom they worked to be very commendable.

I would get invited daily for the Argentinian chai breaks, where everyone shares the same tea drinking pot and straw.

I suspect this sharing resulted in the respiratory infection I contacted while in the yard, which consigned me to my bunk for a period of almost one week.

Though I was alone and a single hander, the workers and contractors would knock on my hull throughout those days to inquire if I needed assistance.

I also attended, in company with yard workers several Argentinian asados, which are singular in the quality and quantity of meat barbecued over wooden coals as well as the quantities of Argentinian red wine consumed.

The only other countries where I have observed similar traditions in terms of quantity and quality of meat and wine are Chile and South Africa.

A significant percentage of the actual sailing yacht club members in the River Plate area I also found to be very impressive day sailors.

Most sailing vessels were not fitted with any form of motor, yet voyages are routinely made to all anchorages in the outer one hundred miles of the River Plate estuary on both Argentinian and Uruguayan sides.

Numerous observations revealed sailing vessels returning to their docks, mooring to buoys and most impressive mooring bow first to a stone quay, all done with no motor and usually in the absence of a dinghy.

One must also understand that this area of the River Plate estuary is replete with tidal and river currents which can reach more than seven knots, as well as the presence of ubiquitous and changing mud banks.

Therefore motor-less sailing vessels must first successfully navigate the numerous side channels, river branches, currents, and unmarked sunken wrecks finally to be presented with the opportunity to finally be challenged by the often intricate and difficult harbour entrances on both the Argentinian and Uruguayan coasts.

It is mostly indigenous and endemic plants which arouse my botanical interests, but greater Buenos Aires contains a rich assortment of naturalized street trees many of which attain sizes and structures which are not often seen.

Of note are members of the botanical family Rutaceae which contains that gift to humans, the genus Citrus, however, there also exist world class specimens from several dozen different botanical families.

Seville oranges are a common street tree in some areas in greater Buenos Aires and it was from such street trees that I collected sufficient Seville oranges to make three dozen litres of marmalade which was suitably canned, stowed away, and taken to sea.

My lengthy stay at the yacht club in San Fernando permitted ample time for visiting central Buenos Aires by train.

I do not have an explanation why Buenos Aires is now one of my favourite cities, however such an explanation may include the Opera House.

I would often walk by the front and one side of this structure and I could almost hear Maria Callas, Giuseppe Di Stefano, and Tito Gobbi singing Verdi and Puccini, all three performed famous roles in this exact venue during the 1950's and 1960's.

A memorable sense of relief was experienced upon again entering the open ocean after seven months in Argentinian and Uruguayan River Plate waters when my vessel finally passed into mud free open ocean water, the reflected depth sounder signal disappeared, and I was again out of the influence of the River Plate and into the open ocean.

KERGUELEN

Anchored in the lee of Ilse de Ouest (background) using three anchors and three shorelines.

After a fifty-seven-day passage from Brazil, complete with six quite abrupt days caused by five rapidly moving cold fronts off Cape Agulhas which is the most southern point of land on the African continent, I decided I would modify my planned passage from Brazil to Madagascar and thus looked on the chart for a likely candidate in South Africa.

There was East London and its protected Buffalo River, the only remaining challenge, to cross the Agulhas current.

After completing the necessary official paperwork, I soon discovered that my bank cash card had been cancelled during my fifty-seven-day passage, as well, both my VISA cards had expired.

The cash card cancellation I still do not understand however the two expired VISA cards must be considered an indication of poor planning, although I had not used either credit card during the past couple of years.

I carried several thousand dollars onboard in US funds however I was unable to find a bank in East London which would convert these dollars to Rand.

I treasure an enduring mental image of Graham, a member of the Buffalo River Yacht Club whom I had just met, reaching into his pocket, and lending me two hundred Rand to buy needed fresh supplies.

The South African amateur radio net is the most useful net I have had the pleasure of contacting anywhere during my travels, they kept an ear on me as I was bobbing off Cape Agulhas and later the west coast of Kerguelen.

As per my custom, once I put down the anchor I tend to stay in the same location for extended periods, I left the Buffalo River in East London after a stay of just over seven months.

I found South Africa to be a complicated country, however I found the indigenous South Africans as well as South Africans of English, Dutch, and Indian ancestry to be very friendly and supportive.

Concerning vessel repair facilities and vessel re provisioning supplies, East London is excellent.

Just prior to arriving in East London during the fourth of a series of six passing cold fronts that I experienced off Cape Agullas, my sailing vessel, while hove-to, suffered it is first ever knock down, the mast struck the ocean surface.

Had the vessel not been equipped with an essentially unbreakable sealed companionway door, I am confident that the combination of the boarding wave and the ensuing seawater momentarily flooding the cockpit would have inundated the vessel.

Immediately after this knock down it became apparent that my well used practice of heaving-to was not going to be adequate for certain areas and conditions found in the southern oceans.

Thus, it was also at East London where I ordered two hundred Jordan Series Drogue cones and assembled my first series drogue made completely from different lengths and diameters of double braid nylon and chain that I found onboard, double braid nylon was not available in South Africa.

Without this addition, I nor my vessel are likely to have survived the upcoming passage from Kerguelen which would terminate in Tasmania.

Upon leaving the Buffalo River breakwater one is immediately in the southwest flowing Agulhas current, which flows in the order of three to five knots and provides a rapid trip down the east coast of South Africa.

An operatic metaphor is apt at this point in my life.

Before leaving South Africa bound for Kerguelen, throughout my entire sailing experience, I had endured and learned from multiple nautical hardship's and hard lessons.

This is not dissimilar to Siegmund in Wagner's "Die Walkure" who has led an exceedingly difficult and violent teenage and early adulthood.

In Act 1 of this opera, Siegmund has just met, fallen in passionate love with, and rescued his twin sister Sieglinde who has also led an exceedingly difficult and violent teenage and early adulthood.

In the first three scenes of this opera, Wagner captures the essence of a metaphorical springtime period in one's life.

Which is to say when one is looking forward with unbounded optimism and strength, the pinnacle of which is exemplified with the triumphant music as Siegmund draws the sword, which has been impaled into an ash tree by Siegmund's and Sieglinde's father, Wotan.

It was with this sense of past training, endurance, and forbearing -as related to perseverance at sea-, along with the almost guarantee of future exhilaration, anticipation, and the soon to be experienced, 'adventure of my lifetime', that I, Alcidae III and Ede departed East London bound for the west coast of Kerguelen.

I had a relatively easy passage to Kerguelen which lasted just over two weeks and produced only four rather gentle passing cold fronts.

My plan was to sight and skirt the Crozet Islands, I did not plan to visit fearful that the Crozet French authorities would report my position and course to the authorities at the base on the east coast of Kerguelen.

I was aware the French on Kerguelen required all visitors to land first at the east coast base, which then placed the entire Kerguelen west coast to windward.

As well, permission to visit the west coast was very unlikely to granted, possibly the necessity to pay cruising fees may also have been a factor.

I was about to implement a concept that the French mariners referred to as “Systeme D”.

I was aware that if discovered, the French were not likely to display a sense of humour, however I also knew that the French respect such moderately daring nautical exploits and several of their fellow countrymen are well known regarding such exploits.

I also recalled the reception that the French authorities had given one of the early small sailboat English mariners, Bill Tillman, on the east coast of Crozet and did not want to experience a repeat of such a welcome.

The desired sighting of the north coast of Crozet accomplished from twenty nautical miles, I made for my preselected arrival point, approximately three degrees longitude west of Ile d'Ouest.

I set this as my arrival point because if the weather were inappropriate for a landfall, I could still easily adjust course to pass either south or north of Kerguelen, the whole time maintaining the apparent wind aft of the beam thus theoretically maintaining the ability to sail out of the zone made potentially hazardous by the lee shore on the entire Kerguelen exposed west coast.

Upon arrival at this predetermined point, I found a low-pressure system along with an active cold front approaching from the west, however I decided I should be able to achieve sheltered water before its arrival, I must admit, at this stage of a passage when the goal is a high latitude sailors’ lifelong treasure, such as Kerguelen, there is an immensely powerful motivation to proceed.

In another section of this book, I write of miss calculations and the necessity of carrying a Paratech type sea anchor, which can be used to provide the mariner with a possible option if such a miscalculation has been made and one finds oneself too close to a lee shore to use the Jordan series drogue and the wind too violent to permit sailing off the lee shore.

Desperation is not an excessive word to use in this case because one would require to be very desperate to attempt to deploy, ride, and retrieve a bow deployed sea anchor off a lee shore of the stature of the west coast of Kerguelen.

The last thirty miles before reaching the coast presented fog and snow along with westerly wind in the order of forty knots and building.

Thus, I was a bit late, however now fully committed because the entire west coast of Kerguelen was now essentially an open lee shore, my destination in the lee of Ile d'Ouest was the only known to me - shelter, on Kerguelen's entire west coast.

Situations such as these require complete focus on the present and I have never felt more alive, aware, and even fulfilled, than during this approach.

Similar conditions and circumstances were successfully faced by Captain Cook as well as the sealers and whalers; however, they did not have the benefit of a chart, professional weather forecasting, the global positioning system, nor radar,

I, however, did not have the benefit of a robust and well drilled crew.

I found myself barrelling along in strong westerly winds under solely a poled-out storm jib into the fog and snow with visibility in the order of one mile.

I first briefly 'saw' Kerguelen on the radar screen at just over ten miles, then again out of the snow and mist Ile d'Ouest appeared briefly at four miles distance, visibility did not again return until I was in the lee on the north side of Ile d'Ouest.

As I approached closer to the coast the wind became more southwesterly -possibly due to my proximity to Kerguelen- which is the reason that I chose the north side of Ile d'Ouest. I had left myself in a position so that I would be able to choose either side of the island, depending on where I found the actual wind direction upon arrival.

When I had just arrived at the lee of the north side of Ile d'Ouest I experienced the immediate satisfaction and relief which always arrives in conjunction with the reduced vessel motion due to the diminished seas found in the proximity and lee of an offshore island.

I was now 1.5 nautical miles off the north coast of Ile d'Ouest and noticed radar images of what appeared to be solid objects located to the north and east of my position, where there should have been no radar reflections. The only relevant nautical chart onboard was French, with a nineteenth century date, this chart indicated that the radar echoes could not be land and upon closer examination of the radar screen the returning echoes had the fuzzy look previously proven to be sea spray or heavy rain.

Such sea spray generated radar echoes can be generated by williwaw gusts, which should have been expected under the present conditions on the lee side of Ile d'Ouest.

The williwaw generating wind was now gusting in the order of fifty knots, thus indicating the source of the small and moving areas of spray reflecting radar images.

In situations such as this, one is encouraged to have complete confidence in the radar images because, due to mist and snow it was not actually possible to see the actual williwaw generated clouds of mist.

The vessel was now in the lee of Ile d'Ouest and I found myself in typical lee conditions such as intermittent wind velocities from near calm to fifty knots, along with up to six-meter-high confused seas.

Upon reaching the lee at the west end of Ile d'Ouest I started the motor having already raised a triple reefed mainsail.

I then sailed the short distance to the east end of the island and motored through the narrows to anchor just before darkness within the kelp filled mostly landlocked opening between the east end of Ile d'Ouest and Kerguelen.

The anchorage was somewhat lumpy as I now had a full view through the southwest entrance where the arriving wind driven ocean seas were breaking across the entrance, thus my selection of the north entrance was warranted.

To say I was very content to get the anchor down and my arrival hot rum in hand, may be somewhat understated.

Writing this several years subsequent, the actual emotional sensations such as accomplishment, pride, and relief remain powerful.

Reliving such experiences through writing was the first motivation which has morphed into this book.

During first night at anchorage, I heard my first exposure to the sound of Elephant seals, of which I was to see and hear many.

As noted, I chose the west coast of Kerguelen due to its

exposure and isolation, I was aware of the French prohibition on ocean mariners such as myself, they would have forced me to stay in the open bay where their base is located on the east coast, which is unsuitable for small under powered sailing vessels, as well as charge me several hundreds of euros for the privilege.

My rational for choosing the fully exposed west side of Kerguelen was to be justified. After I had been in the shelter of Ile de Ouest for just over two months the French sent a patrol vessel which came as far as the north west corner of Kerguelen, -which was the site of Cook's anchorage during his visit -, and then decided – probably due to gale force southwest winds -, that the west coast was a bit too aggressive now and returned to base.

I was aware -through a means I choose not to divulge -, they were on their way, but I was resigned to be discovered, because I was anchored in plain view of any vessel passing between Ile d'Ouest and the main island. I would have begged forgiveness, but I was under no illusions that I would most probably be arrested, and the boat impounded.

On the one hand, I would rather the French behave in a more lenient manner but on the other Kerguelen and especially Ile d'Ouest is a botanist's gem and is well worthy of such protection.

I stayed in the south east corner of this anchorage for just over three months where I employed the main bow anchor forward with greater than 50 to 1 scope, a stern anchor taken ashore and buried behind boulders, as well as five shorelines.

To say the wind was somewhat abrupt on occasions during that three-month period would be understated, at times I imagined that I could almost feel the land vibrate as the magnificent Southern Ocean southwest seas collided with the Kerguelen west coast cliffs, upon impact creating a roaring thud.

Kerguelen is just within the Antarctic convergence and thus one encounters very cold seawater as well as cold ambient air temperatures.

My magnificent wood and coal burning heater was not to be used more than one evening per week as there was essentially no driftwood to be found on shore, I had brought only one hundred kilograms of coal from South Africa.

Young Elephant seals which weighed approximately 500 kg would routinely come alongside my steel hull and run their teeth along the hull, typically from the keel to the waterline.

This sounded horrendous inside the vessel, as well as potentially damaging my anti fouling paint, thus not wanting to injure but rather only dissuade this activity, I brought a twenty-litre bucket of grapefruit sized rocks from shore and when the offending animal reached the waterline I would as gently as possible drop not throw the rock onto its head.

They did not seem to like this, and the offending activity was not completely stopped but was greatly reduced.

When I finally reached water of suitable temperature for snorkelling in New Caledonia many sea miles later, I found no sign of any paint damage.

I have several recollections of wildlife on Kerguelen, most notable would be the nine Antarctic Skuas sitting within a meter of myself and Ede during one of our shore trips, Ede was later to stop demanding to go ashore after being chased down a rabbit hole by Skuas.

The other incident I will mention concerned a group of Southern Giant Petrels which observed, harassed, and finally killed in a very rapid and violent manner a Royal Penguin which must have been somewhat compromised in terms of health, because it was alone and would not leave the shoreline over a period of two days.

Identical to all the locations that I anchored, I came away with my notebook containing my amateur geological impressions, list of all birds and mammals observed, and my list of the plants which shared my locale. The botanical biodiversity on Kerguelen is sparse and limited due to its isolation and the introduced rabbits, however Ile d'Ouest where the rabbits could not reach was in the same pristine botanical state as when Cook and the first sealers arrived on Kerguelen.

At the north end of the anchorage there is a very tidally active narrows between Ile d'Ouest and Kerguelen which is only in the order of twenty meters wide, however it is this narrow strip of water which has saved the botany on Ile d'Ouest from the ravages of the introduced rabbits.

The experience of visiting such pristine sites throughout my nine-year voyage will be my enduring gift to myself.

Upon leaving the shelter of Ile d'Ouest one is immediately in the full fetch of the southern oceans and immediately encounters a thirty mile stretch of lee shore before rounding the southwest corner of Kerguelen.

I did try to wait for a favourable departure weather forecast however there appeared to be a continuous series of passing low pressure centres and associated cold fronts, most of which bring gale force northwest winds before the front which immediately back to stronger southwesterly winds after the frontal passage.

Thus, I chose to leave the protection generously offered by Ile d'Ouest shortly after the commencement of north west winds related to the next approaching cold front, thus my passage through the southwest anchorage passage into the southern Indian ocean was be relatively straight forward.

As per ship's rules, just after leaving the southwest entrance the motor was turned off and exhaust pipe as well as engine raw water-cooling water line valves were closed, not to be opened until I found myself forty-nine days later entering an anchorage on the east coast of Tasmania.

What I will recall from that thirty mile stretch to the southwest cape of Kerguelen, is Peter Harrison's "Seabirds of the World" where he illustrates seven distinct plumage stages concerning the Wandering Albatross.

To this point throughout all my Southern Ocean passages I had kept written records of bird species observed, numbers, and if relevant plumage stage.

This data included the plumage stage of all sited Wandering Albatross, as per Harrison's drawings.

This initial thirty-mile west coast Kerguelen leg put me on a course to pass among a small group of surface paddling adult Wandering Albatross which were taking a break from nesting duties and who took little notice of my passage through the middle of their casually separating group.

They were almost pure white, thus examples of what must truly be Harrison's plumage stage seven, I now must alter my written records so that each Wandering Albatross plumage stage be reduced by one stage, thus previously I had not actually seen one true stage seven plumage Wandering Albatross at sea.

I had hoped to enter an anchorage on the south coast of Kerguelen's big island for the first night after leaving Ile d'Ouest and possibly spend another week or so, however due to strong adverse tidal currents in the vicinity of the southwest headland and me pitifully under powered motor I arrived at the uncharted bay entrance after dark and thus thought it prudent to cancel this plan.

This change in my plan did not alter the pending arrival of the approaching low-pressure system along with it is associated cold front, I thus hove-to off the south coast of Kerguelen and accepted my treatment, which was to be delivered by the expected cold front due to arrive during darkness hours.

Just after midnight now of actual cold front passage the wind and accompanying snow became so violent, I was forced to preclude potentially destructive sail luffing damage, to hastily lower and furl my triple reefed mainsail, this turned out to be a prelude to the conditions I was about to endure for almost the complete voyage to Tasmania.

When daylight returned, I was approximately fifty miles offshore, thanks to the pre-cold front northwest winds which blew all night along with powerful williwaws generated as the cold air descended from the Kerguelen ice cap of which I was now in the lee, thus my forty-nine-day passage to Tasmania had begun.

This route is essentially identical to that plied in the 1700 and 1800's by vessels such as the Cutty Sark which was involved in the tea and wool trade.

My vessel and crew are not comparable, however the wind, seas, albatross, the constantly following group of

Spectacled Petrels and gale force wind acrobatics of the Prions would have been identical.

Yound elephant seal just finishing rubbing it's teeth along the hull from keel to water line.

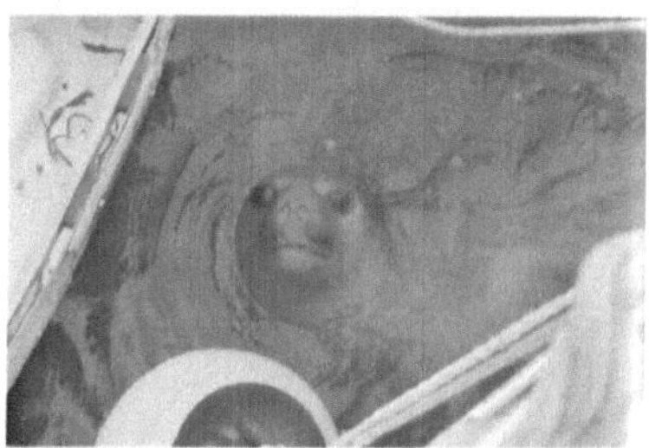

BOTANY

Patricia eating Llao Llao (Cyttaria darwinii) in the southern Beagle Channel on Tierra Del Fuego.

"If one does not know the name, one's knowledge of things perishes"
Carl Linnaeus (1707-1778)

Typically, anchorages would retain my company for an interval between a few weeks to one month, during which time I kept a running list in my ever-present pocket notebook containing all the plants that I was able to identify.

Along with the notebook, I was not usually to be found onshore without also the rock hammer, binoculars, and hand lens.

If I was anchored in a country where the local people spoke a language other than English, this notebook was also used to note words that I did not understand, speech patterns, and expressions.

I spent relatively little time during my third nine-year voyage in French speaking countries, however I spent six of those nine years in ten different Spanish speaking countries, thus my notebook entries of Spanish words, phrases, and people's names is extensive.

Late during this six-year period of almost exclusively Spanish speaking countries I noticed that I had essentially stopped making notes of new Spanish words and phrases, I had apparently finally arrived at a linguistic level where I intuitively felt comfortable and had achieved a reasonable functional fluency.

Botany in the southern hemisphere holds an equally high level of my esteem as does Southern Ocean seabirds.

Upon completion of my third offshore voyage the vessel contained approximately fifty kilos of southern hemisphere botanical books, mostly in Spanish however also French, English, and Portuguese.

Fortunately, botanical identification and plant classification terms are quite easily identifiable in the above languages, thus the importance of obtaining a basic botanical vocabulary.

It is critical to learn the internationally accepted botanical nomenclature concerning plant parts as well as plant classification, thus my many field notebooks contain numerous pages of lists commencing with botanical family, followed by genera, and species, if I was sufficiently fortunate to be able to provide such detail.

I always kept in mind a quotation written by that Swedish gift to the world, Carl Linnaeus, who invented and extensively contributed to our present botanical nomenclature and classification system.

I found Linnaeus's inscription, "If one does not know the name, one's knowledge of things perishes" in the dedication page of Eric Hulten's Aleutian botany reference book.

Common names are quite suitable for birds but not plants because the same plant often will have different common names in different countries and sometimes different common names in the same country but on separate islands.

Furthermore, a large percentage of plants have not been given a common name.

In French Polynesia one may sequentially find themselves in the Marquesas, Tuamotus, Gambiers, and Society Islands and may find that there will be a different local name for the same species of plant, examples would include Callophyllum innophyluum and Casurina equistetifolia.

However, this is not to discourage the ardent mariner from the opportunity of also learning and noting the common plant names in each location, because without the knowledge of the common names it is difficult to discuss the specific plant and it is uses, lore, myth, and taboos with local people, as well as ask the location of an actual specimen.

On my second visit to French Polynesia, I had the opportunity to spend my entire ninety-day visa anchored in the Gambier Group of islands, at Mangereava.

This anchorage rests in a small band of latitudes which occur in both hemispheres which I consider the most pleasant climate known to mankind.

Almost everyday of my stay at Mangareva I could be found ashore botanizing and socializing with local people, thus I learned and noted as well, several Mangaravan names for plants.

Prior to leaving I presented the Mayor of the island with a list of seventy-three different species of plants, adjacent to each I attempted to list the Mangarevan, Polynesian, French, English, and of course the botanical names.

The Mayor presented me with a necklace made from shells found nowhere other than the Gambiers.

Decidedly non botanical was Luciano Pavarotti's passing, which I learned while anchored at Mangareva on a daily early morning BBC world service news broadcast.

I was first introduced to Pavarotti by Clyde Gilmour during his weekly Canadian Broadcasting Corporation radio program aptly called Gilmour's Albums.

I was grieved to hear of Pavarotti's death and immediately planned an afternoon wake.

In addition to my eighty or so onboard complete operas I also carried a significant amount of orchestral music and of operatic soloist recordings.

My wake started with Pavarotti in recital, this combination of only piano and the human voice is both intimate and exceptionally beautiful.

My selections covered the years from 1961 until the late 1990's and although it was clear that Pavarotti's voice had darkened, his voice still retained the ability to speak directly to one's soul.

The wake performance began with selected arias from operas and recitals followed by selections from the first Three Tenors performance, where those three world class tenors on occasion humbly sing harmony for each other, my wake closed with Pavarotti and Joan Sutherland singing the love duet from Verdi's Othello.

I remember arising with Patricia at 4 AM in 1997 well before the beginning of my third voyage, to watch Princess Diana's funeral.

Pavarotti was in attendance and had been asked to sing, he was one of the Princess's close acquaintances, however it was reported that he declined possibly because emotionally he would not be able to complete his performance to the necessary standard, such latent emotion was a critical component of the emotional impact of his selected arias to which I had just listened.

Sir Elton John, of whom I also had an onboard selection of cassette recorded music, did agree to perform in Princess Diana's honour.

I have seen a previous photo of the Princess sitting on the piano bench beside Sir Elton while he performed what was one of her favoured Elton John songs.

During the funeral, Sir Elton sat at the piano and played the first chords of the Princess's favourite song, adapted in her honour “Candle in the Wind 1997”.

I am confident he felt Diana's presence beside him, I have not before nor since witnessed such artistic professionalism under such intense emotional stress.

Throughout the course of my Pavarotti wake, I knew I would almost certainly imbibe an excessive amount of gin and beer; thus, I prepared my evening meal before the wake, however I became so overly emotional and inebriated I was unable to eat and I did not fully recover for thirty-six hours, however during this exact afternoon of his passing, anchored at Mangareva in the Gambier Group, I held Pavarotti's wake.

Botanically, successful also refers to invasive species. Many species of northern hemisphere plants in families such as Asteraceae and Fabaceae have been found vastly out compete many southern hemisphere families and once introduced by mariners, settlers, and locals, have become botanical plagues, whereas similar problematic transplantations of southern hemisphere plants to the northern hemisphere are not as common.

Various southern hemisphere botanical families do contain species which are naturally occurring in the northern hemisphere; however, these often present as small in stature herbaceous plants whereas many of the southern hemisphere species are immense, abundantly useful, and magnificent trees, Euphorbaceae and Rubiacea are examples of such families.

Naturally occurring populations of southern hemisphere botanical families such as Eleagnacacea, Rutaceae, Rubiaceae, Euphorbaceae, Auraucariace, Podocarpaceae, Nothophagaceae, Dioscoreaceae, Araceae, Convolvulaceae, Pandanaceae, and Aracaceae, are not naturally found in the northern hemisphere, thus the personal opportunity to view and study never personally observed plants in their natural environment is precious.

I usually resist the urge to elevate a group to the favourite category, as this practice is a difficult and possibly meaningless intellectual pursuit, however the family Rutaceae which has provided humans with the seven species within the genus Citrus, would be my favourite. Tropical botany I found exceedingly difficult due to factors such as the immense diversity and the often-encountered difficulty of close observation of the leaves, fruits, and flowers of tall tropical trees.

The Swiss botanist Roland Keller (reference # 17) provided an eminently useful and creative reference book designed to overcome this issue; however tropical tree identification remains a challenge.

Joseph Konrad describes the terrestrial fragrances which almost certainly originated from tropical plants, which he sensed upon his first and seminal arrival in total darkness off what was most likely at a present-day Indonesian or Malaysian island.

Arriving off and downwind, with respect to any offshore island in total darkness, one is often presented with odours and if one is fortunate, fragrances.

Atolls which are not usually considered highly botanically diverse, under such lee side darkness conditions often provide the unmistakable and pleasant fragrance of Scaevola.

As well as the fragrant experiences, such arrivals are made more alluring because since one is downwind of the island one is also in the lee of the island and thus experiences the welcome offered by the noticeably calmer seas which in darkness can be felt rather than seen.

Such a total darkness leeward combination of fragrance and much reduced vessel motion is one of the special experiences of sailing within the world's tropical latitudes.

As noted, such a similar nighttime experience occurred early in Konrad's nautical and literary lifetime and remained in sharp focus during the entire remainder of his life.

I read Konrad's description several decades before my

first arrival off a tropical island, which was in the bay of Taihoae on the Marquesian island of Nuku Hiva.

My arrival occurred not in darkness but rather at dusk, however the fragrant scents of Frangipani and cooking firewood smoke immediately returned my mind to Konrad's written words.

After my first tropical arrival, which terminated my first offshore passage, I was to learn to identify and describe a few hundred tropical plants in addition to several hundred higher latitude southern hemisphere plants.

At this time in my life, I believe I subconsciously understood the metaphorical gate through which I was passing, that being on the verge of entering into a wide world of new physical and intellectual experiences which would endure during the remainder of this first voyage and then be continued during the remaining two offshore voyages.

These periods of personal discovery which concerned both natural and nautical components was to persist for approximately fifteen percent of my life.

Throughout my travels, the ability of aboriginal peoples to recognize and utilize the useful characteristics of plants such as bananas, yams, sweet potatoes, mangoes, coconuts, and even pandanus continues to be very impressive.

The foregoing are only a few botanical examples from a long list which include, in addition to nutritional, also medicinal, structural, nautical, tools, warfare, and food acquisition.

Personal favourite botanical locations to which I have had the opportunity to visit include Chilean Patagonia in the vicinity of Golfo Corcovado, Argentian Patagonia, the east lagoon on Palmyra Atoll, New Caledonia, Tasmania, South Africa, the Atlantic Rain Forest in coastal Brazil and the Aleutian Islands.

The accumulated botanical lists to be found within my notebooks which were generated during visits to these sites is not overwhelming, but rather may be considered merely a botanical introduction regarding this subject and as only a small portion within the process of lifelong learning.

Aboriginal peoples also utilized toxic compounds produced by plants for the purpose of protecting stored foods and themselves against insects, reptiles, rodents, and other groups of humans.

My second offshore training voyage which entailed 15,000 nautical miles and was fifteen months duration included a two week stay on Palmyra Atoll.

Concerning botanical and birding possibilities the eastern lagoon of this double lagoon atoll is a natural and rare treasure.

Rare in botanical terms because the eastern lagoon portion of the atoll has not been stripped of its natural vegetation to facilitate the production of copra, within the western atoll can be found the location of the anchorage, air strip, and small resort as well as a myriad of world war II ruins, abandoned equipment, and the remnants of a past copra plantation.

The eastern atoll appears essentially untouched concerning the original indigenous botanical flora and contains the most impressive specimens of Pisonia grandis that I have been fortunate enough so see, some of which also contained hundreds of active Black Noddy nests.

I have visited many atolls in the north and south Pacific oceans and essentially all these atolls have had their indigenous botany destroyed to facilitate the production of copra, this is the major reason the east lagoon of Palmyra is precious.

Botanically, a visit to the east lagoon is an experience that is life enduring, however if the visit occurs in seabird breeding season, it would be hard to find a suitable comparison throughout my travels.

Seabirds can be found nesting within most of the botanical communities at Palmyra.

Within the more diminutive botanical structures such as Scaevola and Guettarda, one may find nesting Red-Footed and Brown Boobies, on the coral sand nests containing Masked Boobies, White-Tailed and Red-Tailed Tropic Birds, and Lesser and Great Frigate Birds may be seen nesting in the upper reaches of coconut palms along with that harbinger of world peace, simplicity, and purity, the White Tern, balancing her single precious egg on the upper surface of a coconut palm frond. Other Palmyra nesting birds include the Sooty Tern, and four species of non nesting but rather visiting shore birds which include the Bristle Thigh Curlew, Wandering Tattler, Ruddy Turnstone, and Golden Plover.

All to be seen, experienced, and processed, while walking bare foot along coral sand shorelines, the whole time embraced by the nurturing and life-giving combination of tropical warmth and humidity.

Within this often very narrow strip of atoll forest - found between the open ocean exposed atoll beach and the inner lagoon atoll beach- one also finds in addition to Pisonia grandis, coconut palms, varieties of pandanus, and of course magnificent specimens of the nocturnal flowering bat and moth pollinated Barringtonia asiatica whose seeds also provided indigenous people with a source of a powerful and useful fish toxin.

Other indigenous atoll plants such as Hernandia, Calophyllum, Morinda, Artocarpus, Hibiscus, Terminalia, Cordia, Neisosperma, Ficus, Guettarda, Cassytha, Tournefortia, Pemphis, Vigna, Ipomoea, Suriana, Scaevola, and several more are readily apparent.

I have used Palmyra as an example, however similar lists of bird and botanical species

were created for most anchorages encountered during my four decades of voyaging under sail.

GEOLOGY

Caleta Horno, Argentina
Example of thunder egg tuff

Volcanic island geology in the south and north Pacific oceans is both consistent and interesting.

Island chains such as the Marquesas, Society islands, and Hawaiian Islands are still being formed within the portion of the earth's outer crust termed the Pacific Plate, which is moving in a northwest direction above numerous hotspots.

Each of the three above noted island chains has its own hot spot, in all cases located to the southeast of the youngest island, thus the active hot spot for the Hawaiian Island chain is located just southeast of the island of Hawaii.

The Hawaiian Islands are currently being built by a supply of magma -basalt- through an opening in the Pacific

Plate which is termed a hot spot.

The Pacific Plate is moving towards the northwest at a rate of approximately 20 mm per year, thus in a thousand years each island will move about twenty meters with respect to the fixed hot spot.

Thus, as the islands become older, they move farther from the hot spot and are each consecutively cut off from a supply of magma, thus the youngest island of Hawaii is in the order of 0.7 million years old, followed by Oahu which is 2.2 to 3.4 million years old, which in turn is followed by Kauai which is much further to the northwest and is in the order of 5.1 million years old.

This is to say that 5.1 million years ago Kauai was located at the same longitude and latitude as Hawaii is today.

On my second voyage I had planned to enter Midway Atoll which was over the same hot spot as Hawaii is presently, in the order of 35 million years ago, however the sea gods had other ideas because once I was released by the north east trade winds on a voyage from the Marshall's to the Aleutian Islands, I was not motivated to beat back to Midway, as well during this second training voyage I had undoubtedly already visited enough atolls.

The same concept of a moving lithospheric plate with respect to a fixed hot spot also applies to the Marquesas and Society Islands.

Tahiti Nui is younger than Tahiti, which is much younger than Bora Bora, the ages of these two islands being like Hawaii and Kauai

The ages I list for Hawaii, Oahu, and Kauai commence when the islands first start building from the very deep-sea bottom, which in the case of Hawaii is greater than five thousand meters below sea level and the ages previously listed relate to the time the lava reached sea level and started erupting not into seawater but into the atmosphere.

The Marquesas, Society, and Hawaiian Islands all move and age towards the northwest, they also are eroded by the sea, wind, and rain so that as they age, they also dramatically become lower and finally are eroded to sea level, hence, to become atolls if they still happen to remain in the warm tropical waters otherwise, they will become submerged banks and guyots.

Thus, a long line of Hawaiian volcanic islands all originating from the same hot spot are of decreasing elevation and finally reduced to a similar oriented line of atolls such as Midway, which are then replaced by a similar northwest heading line of submerged banks and guyots. In the Hawaiian chain example, atolls like Midway are replaced by submerged banks and guyots, in this case because the water becomes too cold for coral to grow, thus the growth of coral can no longer keep up with the rate at which the atoll is sinking due to ongoing cooling and the resulting contraction of the oceanic basaltic floor.

This continuous train of now submerged former atolls in the form of submerged banks and guyots ultimately arrives at the Aleutian Trench subduction zone, where the original basaltic -now cooled and substantially contracted- sea floor layer -which was possibly created more than 100 million years ago off the Mexican coast- now slides under the Aleutian Islands.

The subducting Pacific Plate does not subduct in a graceful manner, thus the numerous earthquakes experienced in this area, earthquakes are also initiated due to volcanic activity which is also related to the subducting Pacific Plate.

It is somewhat humbling to consider that this moving Pacific Plate basaltic sea floor is only in the order of six kilometres thick.

The attached chain of past atolls, submerged banks and guyots along with sediments such as accumulated limestone and siliceous sedimentary rocks – often to become chert, which is a preferred material for arrow and harpoon heads- do not pass down and rejoin the mantle along with the basalt sea floor but are mostly scrapped off and form an accretionary wedge, which I sail over just before arriving in the Aleutian Islands.

Such accretionary wedges are a distinctive rock type and contain a convoluted, tumbled, and often severely broken mixture of all the above noted scrapings, and when observed far inland from the coast within continental crust indicate the site of an ancient subduction zone.

Relatively recent accretionary wedge rocks which have been naturally bulldozed onto dry land may be observed on the coast of southern Vancouver Island and the Olympic Peninsula.

When one is sailing over top of this jumble of past atolls and their remains, one is close to the Aleutians and has just passed over the Aleutian Trench and usually has other things in mind, such as making a safe landfall within this dangerous, isolated, and ethnographic and ecologic rich chain of islands.

New Caledonia and the Loyalty islands, which are both situated upon the Indian-Australian Plate, are both moving to the northeast and subducting under Vanuatu, which is relatively fixed, although essentially represents an identical process to that occurring at the Aleutian Trench.

The subducting material beneath New Caledonia and the Loyalty islands, like the oceanic crust subducting under the Aleutians Islands also creates a chain of active and potentially explosive volcanoes.

I have sailed over the Vanuatu subduction zone once and the Aleutian trench twice, both times my imagination of what is occurring beneath was temporarily well entertained.

The French have dredged newly erupted basaltic vesicular and pillow lavas from this trench and the lava originated from underwater volcanic vents on the west side of Vanuatu, such underwater photos as well as other impressive tectonic and geological information is presented on the walls in a hallway in a public building nearby the public aquarium in Noumea, New Caledonia. The same building on the ground floor also houses an impressive herbarium which contains thousands of dried botanical samples of indigenous and often endemic New Caledonia plants.

New Caledonia itself is an excellent example of tectonic obduction which is the opposite of subduction, when the ocean plate which usually goes under the obstructing plate is pushed out on top.

It is in this manner that New Caledonia received its ultra mafic rocks which also contain the chromium and nickel which have been economically mined from their 19th century discovery until the present.

I collected ultra mafic rock and mineral souvenirs on New Caledonia which include reasonable examples of peridotite, pyroxenite, olivine, harzburgite, and dunite.

Tectonically, New Caledonia is a broken off portion of the northeast corner of Australia and is on its way to the subduction trench just to the east.

This physical separation of part of Australia occurred in the Cretaceous period and thus New Caledonian botany, as is New Zealand botany has been isolated from the Australia for the past approximately eighty-five million years.

It is this relatively recent tectonic separation and its relative isolation which is the source the extensive numbers of endemic plants that are found on both New Caledonia and New Zealand.

The endemic plants have survived on these two isolated groups of islands probably due the lack of botanical competition, which is not the situation in northeast Australia.

New Caledonia contains at least thirteen species in the family Arauacariacea, which are naturally occurring nowhere else in the world.

I was fortunate to find seven of these species growing naturally during my three months in New Caledonia.

This family also contains the so-called Chilean Monkey puzzle tree from the Chilean province of Araucaria, for which this entire southern hemisphere family is named, however this species does not naturally occur on New Caledonia.

Possibly the most famous member of this family may be the one Captain James Cook termed Norfolk Pine.

Volcanic islands such as the Hawaiian, Marquesian, and Society chains are constructed of a mixture of several thousand individual volcanic flows interspersed with pyroclastic layers.

Volcanic island structure is complicated and often is not to be observed as obvious layer upon layer of consecutive lava flows because volcanoes regularly become dormant for several decades to several centuries, therefore the newly created volcanic crater continually moves with respect to the hotspot and suffers from constant erosion, thus a classically shaped crater is seldom observed.

Exceptions include the very impressive volcanic crater, which is Mehetia Island, located approximately sixty nautical miles to the southeast of the island of Tahiti.

Mehetia remains volcanically active and is still supplied with lava from probably the same hot spot that formed the entire Society Island chain.

Further complicating the issue many volcanic layers are often composed of very poorly cemented volcanic rock due to the explosive nature of the material erupted, this class of lava is termed pyroclastic and erodes quickly and relatively easily.

The increased susceptibility to erosion, results in the present day rapidly changing structures such as the fantastic sea cliffs, razor back ridges, interior valley cliff walls and hanging valleys often replete with impressive waterfalls which are observed in all parts of these types of island chains, however, are most dramatic on the windward coasts.

As tropical islands age, they are subjected to constant erosion as well as submerging into the sea, which is due to sea floor contraction.

Such contraction and island sinking are one of the causes which results in the creation of a natural underwater shelf which completely encircles the island and upon which coral reefs can grow.

Such barrier reefs can only occur however if the conditions are correct for coral growth, and thus are not observed surrounding volcanic islands located outside of the tropics.

As the tropical volcanic islands age and subside into the sea we would expect the coral reefs to become wider, thicker, and more extensive which is exactly what is observed in locations such as Bora Bora, whereas surrounding the much younger Tahiti Nui and Tahiti, coral reefs are relatively young and therefore narrow in width and thickness.

Coral prefers more protected waters thus more extensive reefs are usually found on the leeward sides of such islands.

The Marquesas, where conventional coral reefs are rare to non-existent is an exceptional case which is probably due to the turbid water found around most of this group of islands.

The Marquesian turbid seawater may be a result of the rapid erosion of poorly consolidated pyroclastic volcanic rock, which is easily eroded by the numerous and frequent passing heavy rain showers, referred to by Jacques Brel as "la pluie torrentialle qui passe grain sur grain", heard in his emotional farewell to life and the Marquesas in the song Les Marquises.

Most French sailing vessels which arrive from Panama first stop at Fatu Hiva, and many will often listen to Brel singing "Aux Marquises" when they first sight the island, Brel does indeed capture the essence of the Marquesas in this song.

It has become apparent to me that Europeans, especially the French, have much culturally and spiritually to offer North Americans such as myself.

It is not far from Fatu Hiva to Jacque Brel's grave on Hiva Oa, where a fragrant Frangiopani unofficially seconds as a head stone.

Volcanic craters on tropical islands viewed from above may ideally be visualized as a doughnut shaped structure, whereby the original lava vent is represented by the doughnut hole and the surrounding doughnut represents the top of the multilayered consecutive lava flows.

The foregoing is an unforgivably simplistic representation because the vent position constantly changes over time and the cone sides are continually eroding and collapsing, only to be rebuilt in a nonconforming manner during subsequent eruptions.

The doughnut metaphor is useful in that it helps visualize the presence of numerous radial cracks which take the form of spokes inside of a wagon wheel and are a common geologic structure on volcanic islands, formed because the most recent layer of hot lava heats the lower layers of the island as well and then the radial cracks are formed upon lava cooling and contraction.

Over multiple eruption cycles a complicated system of such near vertical cracks are formed and the cracks are often filled with an andesitic type of volcanic rock, structures geologists refer to as dykes.

The combination of erosion, collapse, and radial cracking all contribute to the creation of highly variable and fantastic rock structures.

The entire period whereby the tropical volcanic island sinks beneath the oceans waves to become an atoll, is in the order of five million years.

If such islands remain in tropical waters such as the entire Tuamotu Group, coral continues to grow in step with the subsiding island and therefore the coral thickness continues to increase.

Climate change which results in coral death may possibly result in existing atolls sinking beneath the sea because contraction of the ocean floor lithosphere will not cease.

The Tuamotu Group in French Polynesia have been atolls for approximately forty million years and thus the coral thickness between sea level and the supporting submerged basaltic volcanic rock is substantial.

The foregoing structure and formation of an atoll were first theorized by Charles Darwin in the 1830's and along with many other of Darwin's theories have morphed into facts.

There are environmental and political issues concerning Mururoa Atoll which appear not as severe as Christmas Atoll in the Line Island Group nor issues in the Bikini Atoll in the Marshall Island group, however the French decision to share Mururoa drilling data has advanced geological atoll understanding and has helped to solve many questions concerning atolls.

Volumes I, II, & III of "The Atolls of Mururoa And Fangataufa" (reference # 3) should be part of the onboard reference library of any sailing vessel visiting atolls anywhere in the world.

The hot spot that created the volcanic islands that were to become Pitcairn, Gambier Group, and Mururoa began to erupt about ten million years ago.

French drilling data from Mururoa indicates that the present coral thickness between sea level and the original supporting volcanic island basaltic rock which originally erupted to the southeast of Pitcairn's present position, is in the order of four hundred meters thick.

This would correlate with a coral growth of about 0.1 mm per year which logically must correlate with a similar 0.1 mm per year loss due to lithospheric contraction, and thus balance is preserved, and the coral remains at sea level from one millennium through the next, the entire period constantly growing thicker.

Thus, when compared to cold water higher latitude islands, atolls at the top layer are living and growing ocean structures, whereas submerged islands outside of warm coral growing waters constantly increase in depth due to shrinkage of the earth's crust, until they reach a subduction zone.

Travelling into southern Chilean Patagonia, one will enter areas such as the Beagle Channel which were covered by glaciers as recently as seven thousand years ago.

Throughout this area one can observe relatively freshly made glacial rock scratches, very impressive examples of glacial scaling, rock glacial plucking, and botanical succession which has taken place over the past seven thousand years since the continental glaciers retreated.

Brecknoct, -which is just south of the Straits of Magellan- is an excellent example containing examples of all the above noted glacial structures.

At sites such as Brecknoct it is possible to follow the above noted glacial structures from approximately seven thousand years ago to the present, by simply hiking from the shoreline to the toe of an existing glacier.

The world contains many fine examples of lines of volcanoes referred to as continental arc volcanoes, which are found above existing subduction zones such as the Aleutian Islands, Japan, Indonesia, and Chile.

These types of volcanoes produce lava which is viscous and thus somewhat reluctant to flow, and therefore explosive eruptions of pyroclastics and volcanic ash result.

This type of molten lava generates high and impressive volcanic cones such as can be seen in several locations within the Aleutian Island chain, I will choose Kanaga Island as my type location.

Kanaga Island weather, like the entire Aleutian Chain is changeable and potentially violent, therefore only rare, and short periods exist during which one may be sufficiently fortunate to see a clear view of this crater.

It was during one such short clear weather interval that I was fortunate to have a clear view of the volcanic cone on Kanaga Island.

After a low-pressure system cold front passage, which is often followed immediately by clear and cold arctic air, opportunities for viewing peaks such as on Kanaga Island are most successful.

As noted, concerning tropical volcanic islands, poor volcanic rock consolidation also often applies to the Aleutian Islands and results in equally impressive windward sea cliffs but with the addition of numerous Pacific Ocean side sea caves.

I previously mentioned the radial wagon wheel like cracks that develop within tropical volcanic craters, such radial cracks also develop on Aleutian craters.

Such cracks can coincide with geological jointing and shearing which can grind and shatter rocks on both sides of the radial cracks which creates areas of weakness very susceptible to erosive forces.

When such cracks align with the direction of arriving Pacific Ocean seas, long sea caves can be the result. I have bobbed just outside of several such sea cave mouths in my skiff and taken care to remain just outside the suction zone while gently holding position using the oars as the Pacific side seas and resulting surge arrive, enter, and exit the cave mouth. When the wave cycle timing is synchronous with the length of the sea cave, the arriving sea enters the cave mouth just as the previous outgoing wave generated surge which has ricocheted of the caves interior terminal wall has just exited the cave mouth. At this moment one can measure the time taken for the incoming surge to collide with the terminal end of the cave -the incoming wave impact at the end of the cave can be clearly heard-, the resulting time interval for the incoming wave taken to reach the end of the cave will indicate the cave length.

I will estimate the arriving sea to be travelling at twenty knots, thus if one waits one minute after it has entered the cave before hearing it strike the end of the cave, the wave has travelled in the order of just over six hundred meters. The Aleuts would routinely enter such caves in their kayaks and safely exit after conducting their necessary business, necessary business would include depositing and visiting mummified human remains along with transporting all the necessary accoutrements.

This is just one more example of the Aleut maritime skill and confidence concerning kayaks.

BIRDING

Martins roosting on clothes lines while anchored in Rio Chorcha on the west coast of Panama.

I have been interested in birds for as long as I have been interested in nature, which is to say all my life.

Raptors received much early attention, I was a member of the British Columbia Falconry Association between 13 and 16 years of age during which time I had sequentially in my possession a Marsh Hawk, Barn Owl, Long Eared Owl, Red Tailed Hawk, Great Horned Owl, and an immature female Goshawk.

Birding in combination with navigating the worlds oceans provides the opportunity to observe both land and seabirds but is distinctive in the unique opportunity it provides to observe seabirds in their natural and pelagic habitat.

I carried onboard multiple bird reference books, however for pelagic birds one need only one reference, that is Peter Harrison's 'Seabirds'.

This book is remarkable in that it is useful at any combination of oceanic longitude and latitude that the world may provide.

Botanically it is essential to use scientific names, however the use of common names is quite useful for birds.

During all my ocean passages whether they lasted one week or just short of two months, I kept a running list of all birds observed at sea and next to each species was an indication of the number observed.

Concerning albatross, Harrison lists three species in the northern hemisphere and thirteen in the southern hemisphere.

Albatross have different plumage patterns depending on the age of the bird, thus in my written notes I also noted the plumage stage, the Wandering Albatross has seven different plumage stages.

As noted in the Kerguelen chapter, I had also recorded albatross plumage stage notes, however when I was leaving Kerguelen, I was obliged to alter my previous passage notes concerning this species because I had misjudged stages six and seven and thus other plumage stages of this species were also likely to be miss identified.

When in the company of the stage seven Wandering Albatross off the west coast of Kerguelen, I had the sense that I was in the presence of a combination of intelligence and wisdom, these almost entirely pure white birds were almost certainly close to my then age of sixty-three years old.

I also remember the location in another ocean where I saw a Wandering Albatross for the first time, an experience which for a reason not entirely understood, does not leave my active memory.

I can remember where I was and what I was doing when men first landed on the moon, as I can remember the details of when I saw my first Wandering Albatross, several hundred miles southeast of the Gambier group in French Polynesia.

Observing seabirds in their natural element can be somewhat challenging because both the viewing platform and the birds are moving simultaneously in three dimensions.

Prior to leaving Victoria on my third offshore voyage in 2004 I purchased two sets of Swarovski 10 X 25B binoculars, it was imperative that if something happened to one set, I would never be without this critical piece of equipment.

It was also essential that I did not venture anywhere outside of the vessel's cabin or on shore without these binoculars suspended from my neck and underneath my shirt.

This model of binoculars does indeed have a relatively small range of vision; however, one soon becomes habituated to this restriction.

Larger binoculars have a larger range of vision and are therefore somewhat easier to use when locating a flying bird, however I found such wide visual range binoculars to be excessively weighty and thus I would not habitually, or for long periods of time carry them ready for immediate use.

After my nine-year duration third voyage, I only then retired my first pair of binoculars, switching to the second set which was still in its original box.

The nine-year-old pair had been doused on several occasions by rain, snow, hail, spray, and boarding seas as well as surviving a limited number of whole-body submersions.

Such unplanned whole-body immersions occurred entering and exiting the skiff in the tropics, after enjoying the company of local inhabitants and possibly the consumption of slightly excessive quantities of local beer.

After a suitable amount of practice with such small range of vision binoculars, one becomes skilful concerning locating and holding in view seabirds who are often following very unpredictable flight paths, among the most challenging are prions, storm petrels, and phalaropes.

At sea it is possible to observe a range of pelagic seabirds which includes large numbers of different species included within groups such as petrels, storm petrels, albatross, prions, diving petrels, many members of the order Pelecaniformes, terns, phalaropes, and shearwaters.

Some species of boobies and most species of frigate birds may be seen several hundred miles from land, however they along with gulls and cormorants usually indicate that land is within one hundred miles.

Red Footed Booby which became tangled in my trailing fishing line, showed it's gratitude for an injury free release by numerous bites.

I always welcomed the site of a booby or two landing on my spreaders and spending the night, although I did not much care for the mess they left on my mainsail and deck, thus I would try and nudge them off the mast, hoping they would roost on the transom arch where they could roost on the aft edge of a solar panel, although for their security I would then be obliged to lash the transom arch mounted wind generator's propeller.
I have never fitted an anemometer onboard, however nature has provided species such as the albatross who will begin to flex their carpal/wrist joint when the wind approaches forty knots, to reduce their aerodynamic lift.
These sea birds begin to flex this wing joint when the wind speed approaches forty knots, and further increase the flex angle and thus further reduce lift as the wind increases.
Another form of natural anemometer also presents itself when the vessel is sailing hard on the wind, I have

observed that if the wind was more than forty knots the bow generated spray will begin to sweep to leeward before it reaches the cockpit, although this does not preclude the prudent use of rain gear.

Some species of pelagic seabirds will spend violent gales on the ocean surface, however other species such as some albatross, all storm petrels, and some terns can be observed performing very impressive aerial manoeuvres, however the opportunity to watch prions when the average wind is greater than fifty knots, I consider one of natures natural wonders.

Storm petrels also possess intricate and delicate aerial control, apparently aware of the wind as well as the breaking seas and flying ocean sea spray, among both they dart and hover while feeding on momentarily exposed zooplankton.

The wind is of such strength at such times that a fastened but not lashed rain gear jacket may be stripped from one's body.

Within tropical latitudes, equally impressive are boobies holding station at the mast head, they are on watch for flying fish which are put to flight by the vessel's bow wash, followed by their pursuit and often airborne capture.

Boobies are very tempted to land on the masthead, where I had placed a perch for their use – which I termed 'PP' for Pelecaniformes Perch -, however the nearness of my large and homemade stainless steel wind indicator, always dissuaded the perches use.

I did not bring myself to remove this homemade wind indicator because two previous models of commercially available mast head wind indicators had both broken when the wind exceeded fifty knots, my homemade stainless-steel version arrived back in Canada after my nine-year circumnavigation having endured many exposures to winds well more than fifty knots, as well as Patagonian and Aleutian williwaws.

If the vessel is charging along off the wind, the resulting rolling creates a great deal of lateral as well as the ever present up and down motion at the masthead, however the boobies can anticipate such movement and thus able to maintain station usually to within a meter.

In the northern hemisphere, the family of seabirds termed Alcidae can be found within both the north Pacific and north Atlantic oceans, their feeding and underwater locomotion is identical to the Diving Petrels of the southern oceans who are found in the classification family Pelecanoididae as well as in a separate classification order.

This similarity in behaviour is a classic example of convergent evolution whereby two unrelated and geographically separated species develop similar behaviour, to adapt to identical natural conditions.

Nine different breeding species within the family Alcidae can be found on the west coast of British Columbia and six additional species may be added if one visits the Aleutian Islands.

I had the notion at the beginning of my sailing obsession, that this family which spent only the breeding portion of their annual life cycle immediately adjacent to the coast, and the remainder offshore, would signify a naturally occurring example of my mariner goal, which was to become equally competent within both coastal and offshore oceanic environments, thus my first sailing vessel in 1978 became ALCIDAE.

Individual species in this family such as the Tufted

and Horned Puffins vacate the coastal areas outside of breeding season and probably become pelagic but their exact whereabouts during this period are not known.

During all times on deck while north of 30 degrees north latitude in the Pacific Ocean, I would be on watch for the Short-Tailed Albatross.

Throughout most of all three voyages while traversing the north Pacific Ocean I saw several hundred Laysan and several dozen Black-Footed Albatross, but not a Short-Tailed Albatross.

During my second trip to the Aleutian Islands in 2013 I did sight Torishima Island where most of this rare species are reported to breed, however I did not - due to head winds - pass closer than twenty nautical miles offshore and again was not able to see a Short-Tailed Albatross.

It was to be always only during both visits to the Aleutian Islands and within proximity to shore that I made my three Short Tailed Albatross sightings.

During both Aleutian occasions I was able to observe an immature and two adult Short Tailed Albatross.

The actual species identification during these sightings was to be easy because after having seen so many Laysan and Black-Footed albatross, it was immediately obvious that here were birds of a larger size, different feather colour patterns and style of flight.

A very pleasant birding experience occurs in total darkness, often when one is sitting on the aft weather side transom box.

This experience entails storm petrels -which are almost within arms reach- becoming silhouetted against the star filled sky while feeding on the zooplankton disturbed due the turbulence created by the rudder and

steering gear.
They are usually silent, however occasionally they will make sounds, especially when they perceive a watcher's presence.

ALEUTIANS 2013

Three Arm Bay, Adak Island, williwaws severe during gale and storm force southerly winds.

During my previous three months visit to the Aleutians in 2001, I had departed Likiep Atoll in the Marshal Islands in mid March.

Now in 2013, late in my nautical adventures, I still possessed the idea that I wished to spend the maximum amount of time in the higher latitudes.

My intention was to again be anchored in the Aleutians just before the shoreline snow had melted, so that again I could witness the plants in the order as they appeared in their annual sequence.

This however again subjected me, as it did the whalers and sealers, to probable weather on the severe side, although like the past such a prognosis was not found to be dissuading.

I left Saipan in the Northern Marianas on the third of April on a course to the central Aleutian Island chain, the Andreanoff Group.

I had spent my whole sailing career looking for a sperm whale, -some of which exist on the open coast of British Columbia-, however I have never been sufficiently fortunate to observe such a whale.

During a coastal trip, many years previous from Victoria to Cape St. James, -the most southern cape on Haida Guaii- aboard Alcidae II, I had just arrived off Cape St. James, still in the clutches of a southeast gale only to learn from a recently anchored black cod fishing vessel which was sheltering from the gale, that they had just finished feeding a sperm whale ground fish that they were not legally permitted to keep.

However, on this my final voyage to the Aleutian Islands, shortly before reaching the tropic of cancer I was finally to have my first and only Sperm whale sighting.

I was sailing to leeward and the sun was close to setting

and was in that seemingly ever-present few degrees of cloud band on the western horizon, about two hundred meters off my port beam was the obvious square snout of a sperm whale heading south, contrary to wind and seas.

It was one of those numerous examples of immediate identification based on years of previously studied photos and written descriptions.

It is square snout, long head, and narrow lower jaw were all immediately visually apparent and thus the identity was certain.

Then, at half the distance towards the vessel and directly between myself and the first whale appeared a second, this second animal was much larger than the first.

I determined that it must be a protective male which was making the statement "maintain your speed and heading", which I did.

The much larger male was also heading directly to windward and into the approaching seas, his large square snout creating a large and impressive sea spray as the seas were deflected directly to windward.

Sailors such as I who operate a very mechanically under powered sailing vessel are always impressed by the raw brute force of a powerful motor vessel powering directly to windward against strong winds and rough seas, these two whales commanded the same admiration.

I clearly recall the raw power as well as the protective demeanour of the male who had likely purposefully inserted himself between my vessel and the female.

My sense of satisfaction at this sighting was immediately somewhat tempered with a modicum of sadness, I thought of the many certain encounters in the past between whalers and wounded females who must almost certainly have been also attended by such a protective male.

I realized that my anthropomorphism concerning the male's sentiments was undoubtedly just that, I am normally opposed to such use of anthropomorphism's however I have accepted that higher mammals such as whales are essentially the same as humans, except for three items.

First, they cannot deal with history, for example over a decade and certainly not over a century, second, they cannot imagine the future beyond a few years and certainly not over a century or millennium, and finally they have no comprehensive, descriptive, and technical spoken language capable of verbal images and abstractions.

Most of the remaining attributes that humans possess including sadness, happiness, grief, anger, aggression, love, and hate are likely similar or even identical as those experienced by most other mammals.

I had expected to spend just over a month at sea therefore I was not surprised to find myself anchored in West Cove on the west end Agattu Island on the tenth of May. At first light on the tenth I found myself within sight of both Agattu and Attu islands, and it was immediately apparent that I had not arrived late because snow appeared to approach the shoreline.

I found myself much further to the west than initially hoped during before voyage planning due entirely to the seemingly interminable northeast headwinds which would not permit the vessel to point towards the Andreanoff Group.

During such passages when the wind does not permit me to point where I plan to go, I often simply change my plans, however if I were not to be able to point high enough to attain the west coast of Attu, I would soon have found myself off the Commander Islands in Russian waters.

The weather that morning was mixed cloud and quite cold, by cold I mean gloves were needed to change head sails, otherwise finger control would quickly be lost due to numbness, such conditions I would usually start to experience in the vicinity of zero degrees Celsius.

During the morning hours I had the intention of laying the southeast corner of Agattu Island and anchoring in Karab Cove, a depression and associated cold front were forecast to arrive during the coming night and winds would be expected to shift to the southeast followed by east and of course be quite strong.

Shortly after noon it became apparent that I would not be able to achieve these intentions because the wind continued to back to the northeast and thus, I altered course to an alternate anchorage on the west side of the Agattu, appropriately named West Cove.

The tidal currents in the vicinity of the Aleutians are very impressive and can easily reach 4-6 knots through inter island passages, such passes can attain a width of sixty nautical miles.

When such inter-island tidal current is in opposition to either wind, seas, or both, from the Pacific Ocean or Bering Sea sides, the result is breaking, triangular, and collapsing seas, which are like a fine Burgundy red wine, they must be experienced to be genuinely appreciated.

It is just such seas which are referred to in the official US coast pilot which cautions vessels smaller than the approximate two hundred tons displacement, -medium tonnage vessels- from approaching during such inclement conditions.

It is such contrary tidal currents, as well as the potential of local contrary winds which makes beating in vicinity of major Aleutian passes a potentially futile endeavour, my normal options are either to change course or remain at sea, however remaining at sea usually results in a substantial loss of position.

The reader will be aware of my limited diesel power situation thus the ability to sail to the lee side of Agattu and then motor a few hundred meters into a lee anchorage was clearly my most agreeable option.

The forecast depression was predicted to pass less than fifty nautical miles to the east of my position and once it was past my latitude on its northerly course the depression would be expected to generate strong north winds which would continue to back into northwest, which would then enter directly into West Cove.

This combination of a partially open anchorage, rapid depression passage and proximity, illustrates challenges concerning anchoring in the Aleutians.

My landfall successfully completed just before dark, I anchored in a somewhat bumpy and northwest exposed anchorage, upon arrival as expected the wind was from the land.

I now clearly saw that my goal of arriving with snow down to the high-water mark had been achieved.

A partially open and therefore quite rally anchorage such as West Cove may appear a poor choice to a mariner who has lost sea legs, however immediately after a lengthy and often turbulent passage as I had just completed such an anchorage appeared tranquil and even almost calm.

Wood stove: indicating roaring fire, wood box, stainless steel smoke pipe and fiddles, along with a bucket of mussels and a sauce pan.

As per ships rules, the immediate high latitudes routine after anchoring includes installing the wood stove chimney, starting a roaring fire with maximum draft until the bottom of the stainless-steel chimney starts to become cherry red, preparation of my lip and leg numbing strength hot rum, followed by its cherished consumption while sitting along with Ede in the shelter of the stainless-steel cockpit dodger, both admiring our new surroundings.

Ede may have been admiring the Kittliz's Murrelets, however considering the name of her sailing vessel this was certainly an understandable pass time.

I had fitted an expanded metal stainless steel screen enclosure on two sides of the wood stove, this storage structure carried approximately a one-week supply of firewood, thus there was never to be a cold high latitudes anchorage arrival without an immediate and dry source of firewood.

Such arrivals are always accompanied with a genuine sense of accomplishment, as well as that elusive and brief sense of enjoying living in the present, the enjoyment of both is made more precious after a particularly rough and cold passage.

Continuing to adhere to ship's rules, after the welcoming hot rum I disappeared into the now toasty warm and dry cabin, removed layers of underclothes that had probably not been removed in quite some time, scooped from my cold box a moderately sized pot of at sea beans, and cooked a suitable amount of rice.

All to be placed onto a warm holding area on the wood stove.

Tradition then dictates that I assume my music listening position with a generous supply of suitable alcoholic libations, all placed immediately accessible and commence listening to my arrival opera, Cavalleria Rusticana by Pietro Mascagni.

I had onboard three different recordings of this opera, however my favourite is the 1953 recording conducted by Tullio Serafin with Maria Callas, Giuseppe Di Stefano, and Rolando Panerai.

This recording evokes powerful and endearing emotions which are generated from the mixture of such vibrant lyrical music and singing, alcoholic refreshments, warm cabin, crackling wood fire, relatively safe and stable anchorage, and possibly the immediate proximity to ancient Aleut village sites where possibly Aleut spirits continue to reside.

The forecast cold front arrived and passed as expected during darkness hours and as expected I was well protected from any direct wind generated seas.

The anchorage remained swelly however the sea legs developed during the past month at sea were still fully intact, therefore neither I nor Ede seemed to notice the boat rolling and pitching throughout the night.

In the morning, no sooner had the skiff been launched and moored beside the sailing vessel, Ede was first aboard the skiff and impatiently running up and down the skiff's very narrow port and starboard wooden gunnels, vocally giving instructions.

Once underway shore-ward, she would habitually assume her position perched on the tiny piece of wood where the two skiff wooden gunnels met at the bow.

We landed on a very rocky, slippery, steep, and swelly coastline, as usual Ede sitting perched on the most forward point of the skiff's bow would again be first ashore, with an appropriately timed leap, usually taken when the skiff had just approached to within two meters of shore.

This landing must have been special for Ede because she had not been permitted ashore due to local legal requirements during our three months stop at Siapan in the Northern Marianas, nor our previous three months stop at Kosrae in Micronesia.

On occasion, she would miss-time or slip, however a dunking was of no concern as she would quickly scramble out of the surf and be bounding up the beach taking no notice of whether it be composed of sand, pebbles, cobbles, or slippery boulders, she understood the next incoming wave would be closely lapping at her heels.

I would be fully occupied either safely mooring the skiff offshore or landing and hauling the skiff up the beach, in this case I moored the skiff offshore.

So, I had arrived onshore in the Aleutian Islands for the second time in my life!

I normally had two possibilities regarding the skiff, one was to push it back towards the sea and once it was out of the breaking surf zone, I would trip an anchor which would hold the skiff within this offshore safe zone until I hauled on the shoreline.

The second alternative was for me to throw a meter-long section of rigid plastic pipe under the heavy grounded skiff's bow and then roll the skiff multiple lengths up the beach until an appropriate distance had been achieved.

When returning the skiff into the surf another procedure was necessary concerning Ede, for safety reasons she would often be left to her own volition because open coastal beaches require complete concentration so that damage to the skiff or myself is avoided.

This translated into her being left ashore until she was ready to leap back into the skiff on her own volition.

Often, she was not agreeable to return to the sailboat at the same time as myself and thus she would be left ashore.

When she deemed it an appropriate time to return, she would return and sit remarkably close to where the skiff had been landed and look expectantly towards the anchored sailing vessel.

I would then obediently row to shore for the pickup, due to breaking surf usually a suitable boulder or rock ledge would be necessary.

Ede became aware of the drill, whereby I would row parallel to the shoreline until I was adjacent to such a suitable location for her embarkation.

I would then back the skiff within two meters of the of the appropriate boulder or rock ledge, when the sea lifted the skiff's stern as close as was likely, Ede without necessary verbal instructions from myself would leap onboard.

She would then walk up one of the narrow wooden skiff gunnels and take her position on the bow, the entire time giving me what sounded to be curt verbal admonitions or possibly instructions.

This practice was obligatory because Ede cannot be caught for skiff embarkation when she has contrary ideas and serious injuries can potentially result on an open beach if a poorly timed incoming sea upends the skiff onto the mariner.

The Aleutian Islands may be described as an acquired taste, and such tastes contain a singular combination of botanical, ornithological, geological, meteorological, and ethnological delights.

An ethnological incentive concerning an early springtime Aleutian arrival is the increased possibility of viewing the actual Aleut village house sites before the waist high herbs such as Conioselium, Ligusticum, Heraculum, Elymus, as well as several other genera of herbaceous plants start emerging from the ground.

Upon arrival at such an ancient house site, before such perennial herbs start to emerge, one can walk inside and around the well preserved and obvious depressions -some greater than one meter deep- and feel the sense that one is standing with the Aleuts.

To appreciate the efficacy of the barabaras, -Aleut partially underground habitation structures- one must appreciate the extreme violence of the wind and spray encountered on the Aleutian Islands.

The Aleut habitation sites were most commonly within one hundred meters of the shoreline and were certain to receive copious amounts of ocean spray generated from storm force winds associated with passing intense low-pressure systems.

Aleut habitation sites often contain between one and twenty habitation sites, some of which may be large multiple or extended family structures.

Excavations at Nikolsky have been dated to just over eight thousand years before the present, the further west one goes the habitation age decreases because this volcanic arc of islands are thought to have been initially colonized from east to west.

Therefore, during the period of the most recent maximum glacial ice advance approximately nineteen thousand years ago, the Aleut ancestors had probably crossed the exposed Bering land bridge and had stopped at what is now Unalaska Island and decided to settle.

The Aleuts appeared to locate their village sites governed by priorities such as a freshwater source, kayak landing beach access, ability to see maximum distances in all directions and close to sea lion rookeries, seabird colonies, and productive fishing grounds.

All three of these criteria are usually concentrated near passes between the islands, because it is there that the richest food resources are usually located.

The passes are also very agitated locations due to strong tidal currents, arriving open ocean seas, and frequent periods of strong winds.

The actual village site locations indicate the Aleut facility with kayaks, and this crafts intrinsic sea handling characteristics which are profound examples of successful human adaptation to the natural world.

The Aleutians typically requires that one anchor on either the Bering Seaside, Pacific Ocean side, or within the inter island passes where an anchored vessel may be subject to swell from both north and south.

Walking inside the habitation sites before the herbs have grown, one may see numerous artifacts such as arrow and harpoon heads, flattened rocks used for bowls, stone plates, and carved out flat rocks used to hold blubber and burning wicks.

It is my policy as well as the law to refrain from digging into an existing site or collecting any artifacts from Aleut house sites, however some sites have had their contents opened and spread onto the beach surf zone by way of changing locations of creek beds which have washed away one side of a habitation site, in which case one may find examples of the above noted artifacts spread along the stream beds and the adjacent beach.

I have often sat beside or within these abandoned habitation sites with closed eyes knowing that the physical surroundings as well as sounds, are the same as when a long deceased village resident may have been present in this exact location.

Most village sites visited have not suffered site degradation due to human activity since the moment the village was abandoned.

Specifically, one can hear and see the same nearby freshwater stream, the surf on the kayak landing beach, the seemingly constant wind rustling the same species of grasses and other herbaceous plants which are identical to those present during ancient Aleut habitation, as well as the same actual odours of the sea, inter-tidal zone, beach, and early springtime fragrance of flourishing plants such as are contained within the botanical families Apiaceae -carrot, celery, parsley family- and Brassicaceae -mustards and cabbage family-.

When anchored at Agattu Island, I visited West Bay, Karab, and Okriti.

Agattu contained at least thirty-seven village sites, this entire island is less than twenty miles long and at most a mile wide.

It is the changeable wind direction on the Aleutian Islands which usually necessitates the requirement of frequent anchorage changes, it is possible to remain in some anchorages with onshore wind, however I always rest easier if a dragging anchor will result in the vessel being carried offshore rather than the opposite.

The site in Karab Cove found me moored Chilean Patagonian style, a boat length from the cliff face on the west shoreline using three anchors and two shorelines.

Thus, anchored I soon found that the overhead cliffs contained thousands of nesting Tufted Puffins along with several dozen pairs of Horned Puffins.

Karab cove and West Cove anchorages both contain several well-preserved habitation sites, all as expected, located less than one hundred meters from tidewater.

The villages within Karab cove were located on the west side of a wide and very tidally active inter island passage, this major passage contains the well-known bird colony on Buldir Island, thus the two tiny villages in Karab and the nearby Okriti cove must have been on the edge of a very productive foraging area throughout the possibly several thousand years during which they were inhabited.

After a week I moved to another anchorage called Okriti approximately one quarter of a mile to the east because another low-pressure system was going to track to the south of my position and pass again on the east side of Agattu island.

This again was predicted to produce strong southerly and then easterly winds when the depression was passing to the south and then east.

The anchorage move was necessary because the easterly winds had the potential to pin me against the cliff to which I was attached on the west side of Karab Cove.

One of the issues when cruising in uninhabited isolated locations, one does not have local knowledge which could be helpful regarding predicting wind direction and strength with respect to very closely passing intense low-pressure systems.

I suspect the Aleuts used a combination of wind strength and the predictable sequence of wind direction changes as well as the changing direction of arriving seas, to track the progress of passing depressions.

Such local knowledge would have been critical for launching and retrieving kayaks and such local knowledge would have been preserved and passed via oral traditions from generation to generation.

The passing depression followed the predicted route and affected my vessel as expected within the new anchorage in Okriti Cove, although as is common in the Aleutian Chain, Okriti itself is also somewhat exposed.

My purpose for moving anchorages from Karab Cove was to receive the strong easterly winds in Okriti on the bow, and with the shortest possible fetch.

The strong passing depression as expected generated

wind from the southeast and then continued to back into the east as the low tracked by the island.

This all unfolded as per the plan; however, the unplanned component concerned the seas generated while the low was passing to the southwest during the previous 24 hours.

They now entered my new anchorage which as noted was open to the southwest.

The vessel was lying at anchor facing the east and thus my stern was now facing the five- to seven-meter-high incoming swell which was entering from the open southwest.

I was anchored in sufficiently deep water so that the large southwest seas entering the anchorage were not an issue regarding potentially breaking over the stern, however just one hundred and fifty meters forward of the bow these seas were breaking on the kayak beach with full open coast violence.

The way the ancient resident Aleuts managed such conditions during kayak landing and launching is difficult to surmise, although one can be sure that they had a workable and repeatable plan, probably involving alternate landing beaches.

I particularly remember a rocky island about thirty meters wide by two hundred meters long and reaching thirty meters above higher high-water level and which is located just off the southwest entrance to my anchorage and fully exposed to the north Pacific Ocean.

My attention was drawn to this island because the previously noted southwest seas were occasionally completely engulfing and breaking over the top of this thirty-meter-high island.

These apparently thirty-meter-high shoaling and

breaking southwest seas must have been partially generated due to the contrary tidal current ebbing from the adjacent inter island passage.

This illustrates what must have been a major nautical danger for the Aleuts, completely secure and protected kayak beaches are not common, thus they must have always attempted to have an alternate kayak landing beach even though it may have been in an adjacent village.

In Okriti, once the wind had shifted to the southeast and then into the east synchronous with the low centres passage, I always maintained the option to haul anchor and safely coast downwind in a westerly direction back to the lee of Agattu and thus the option to return to West Cove.

It is such potential escape routes and strategies which the mariner can accomplish without use of the motor, that one is inclined to keep in mind when cruising the Aleutians as well as other isolated open coast high latitude locations.

After leaving Okriti, I was then off across to Amchitka island which was infamous for nuclear testing performed when I was in my teenage years growing up in Vancouver, British Columbia, Amchitka protests also led to the birth of the Green Peace organization.

Possibly, if countries such as the US had been willing to share nuclear technical details learned in the Aleutian Islands, and the United Kingdom similar data learned from nuclear testing on Christmas Atoll in the Line Islands, the French would not have found it necessary to perform their testing many decades later Mururoa Atoll.

Amchitka has more than seventy known past habitation sites, many of which are still clearly visible because of the presence of what Captain Cook referred as Lyme grass (Elymus maritima), which grows abundantly directly on and around past habitation sites, probably due to the increased nitrogen, calcium, and phosphorous content in the surrounding soil resulting from Aleut seafood and other refuse.

When one sees the distinctive green of Lyme grass, it is not always, but often marking the location a past habitation site.

The Stellar's sea lion was a particularly important animal to the Aleuts concerning clothing, thread and leather, food, oil, and kayak hull construction materials.

This sea mammal prefers open offshore rookeries, preferably located in a strong tidal current therefore the hunting prowess, nautical abilities, and courage of the Aleut hunters must have been formidable.

The Stellar's sea lions are mammals, however their level of adaptation to such extreme conditions of tidal current and breaking ocean seas is most impressive to behold.

The Aleuts would not have been hunting these mammals during such extreme conditions, however, rarely can sea conditions among the Aleutian Islands be described as tranquil.

As well, the Aleuts did not shoot these mammals with a high-powered rifle from the safety of a passing motor vessel, rather they harpooned the up to four-hundred-kilogram animals at close range from a kayak.

It is not difficult to imagine that the sea lion would not be overly content with such behaviour, and it must have been not unknown for the hunter to be overturned and thrown from his kayak.

Sea lion rookeries are usually located in tidally active passes between the islands, thus rescue of the hunter would have been a constant and challenging consideration.

As well as dead sea lions the Aleuts would also bring dead whales through the surf to village sites.

The seawater temperature is like the air temperature in the Aleutian Islands and must be considered very cold because these islands straddle the junction between the north Pacific Ocean and the Bering Sea, thus the Aleut hunters and their shoreline assistants must have often been soaked from frequent rain, ocean spray, and surf during what must have been lengthy periods spent in the seawater butchering sea mammals.

Frequent whole body seawater soakings must also have been routine during beaching and launching kayaks.

To routinely endure wet clothing in such a cold and windy environment, without a ready source of heat nor hot food, indicates the environmental hardship that an acclimatized human constitution may successfully and over the long term withstand.

The Aleuts did not just endure such harsh conditions, they thrived for greater than eight thousand years.

Recall the Aleutian chain of islands is completely treeless, the only wood available for wood fires would have been driftwood, driftwood was almost certainly sparingly used for warming fires as it would have been too rare and therefore much too valuable for kayak ribs, tools, and house pit roof structures, thus their hardiness must have matched that observed within other indigenous groups such as the Yaghan and Kaweskar of Chilean Patagonia.

Presently, I had little problem collecting sufficient wood

stove destined dry wood, I was to find significant driftwood along the Pacific side of the Aleutians however this was probably was not the case prior to heavy coastal logging on both southeast Alaska and the west coast of British Columbia.

The Aleuts, unlike the Patagonian indigenous groups developed a very sophisticated wardrobe of clothing, actual examples of which may be seen in the museum in Dutch Harbor on Unalaska island.

The geology of the Aleutian Islands may be described as a volcanic island arc; however, the geology is more like Japan than for example Vanuatu because in the Aleutians the volcanic magma often passes first through a fragment of continental crust before appearing as cinder cones containing both volcanic flows and pyroclastic layers.

I have seen dozens if not hundreds of Orcas during my sailing lifestyle and never tire of seeing yet more of this member of the dolphin family.

These whales are typically a coastal species however I did see a small pod less than one hundred nautical miles northwest of the Crozet Islands in the southern Indian Ocean, thus they must certainly be pelagic as well.

Shortly before arriving off the Pacific Ocean side of Kanaga island in the Aleutian Group, I saw a pod of Orcas approaching the vessel from closer inshore and was astounded to see an enormous dorsal fin with the upper third distinctly curved and almost pointing back towards the fin's owner.

I would estimate this dorsal fin to be in the order of three meters or greater in height and much larger than any Orca dorsal fin that I had previously observed.

This whale approached the sailing vessel in a direct

manner and purposefully passed under the hull.

As it passed, I had a clear vision in the clear Aleutian water of this male whale's eye, which also appeared focused on myself, as he and I shared this moment in space and time.

He appeared fully aware of the height of his dorsal fin and its proximity to my keel, my intuition informed me there would be not collision.

Kanaga Bay on the south coast of Kanaga island requires caution when entering and exiting but is one of the most well protected anchorages in the Aleutians, containing a reasonably good sloppy mud holding bottom, negligible williwaws, and complete protection from wind from all directions.

Upon entering Kanaga Bay one leaves to starboard Kayak Cove which is one of the most dramatic Aleut village sites that I have seen on either of my voyages to the Aleutian Islands.

I visited this site later in the season and the Lyme grass, Brassica family, and carrot/parsley families were well represented and already grown to chest height, which greatly impeded my exploration of this very well-preserved habitation site at Kayak Bay.

There was no mistaking this long-term village site which contained greater than a dozen house pits, most in the order of 1.5 meters deep and immediately adjacent to each other as well as being surrounded by extensive middens.

Seated beside the house pit in closest proximity to the beach, one is almost able see the kayaks entering and exiting through tidal channels whose positions vary depending on the state of sea and tide.

This kayak beach and bay would have been identical to

that used for possibly several millennia by this village's past inhabitants.

Once the channels are transited a sandy pebbly beach appears, again it is not difficult to imagine waiting village and family members wading into the clear cold shallow seawater to assist returning hunters.

As well, village members would have been seen foraging within the bay collecting mussels, whelks, snails, crabs, clams, and octopus, the entire time probably showing little concern regarding the cold seawater nor habitually rainy windy weather.

Kayak bay is open to the southwest thus under heavy southwest sea conditions such as I experienced on Agattu Island, the returning and departing kayaks would probably enter and exit further into Kanaga Bay, gain shelter, and walk back to the village site, although alternatively many ancient village sites contain kayak access from two opposite sides of a small peninsula upon which they are often located.

Thus, kayak access would always be possible regardless of the wind and sea direction.

Due to the slow growing tundra type moss and lichen ground cover observed in the vicinity of most habitation sites, the pathways from the alternate kayak landing beaches, immediately adjacent villages, as well as freshwater supply locations remain clearly visible.

At Kanaga Bay the Aleuts had preferred the exposed entrance site at Kayak Bay as the long-term habitation site, even though a mile further up Kanaga Bay there are sources of freshwater as well as all-weather protection, thus it appears to have been especially important for a village site to have attributes such as a suitable lookout vantage point and located close to food resources.

Their semi underground turf covered habitations would have effectively protected the occupants against wind and spray which surely at this site would have arrived from both the southwest and southeast.

I left Kanaga Bay with the intention of entering the Bay of Waterfalls on the south side of Adak island, however the wind as well as tidal current opposed my progress as I approached Cape Yakak and the twenty-seven-horse-power motor which propelled my seventeen-ton displacement steel vessel again caused me to change plans due to insufficient power, thus I entered Adak Strait where the flood tide and wind were in my favour.

The Aleuts would have known well of such local vagaries of wind and tide and followed known close to shore back eddies, regardless of the main channel tidal current or wind direction, as well they would often have been towing heavy loads such as a dead sea lion or whale.

I anchored in the most southerly arm in Three Arm Bay and stayed for just over two weeks, during which time a gale arrived, and the low-pressure centre passed less than fifty miles to the west.

This weather feature created a twenty-four-hour period of high winds including williwaws which were equal in violence to anything I had experienced in Chilean and Argentinian Patagonia, although it is Staten Island that holds my recollection of the most powerful williwaws.

Due to the physical setting in Three Arm Bay, I could not find a suitable location to use the most secure arrangement, which is anchors and shorelines, this is because the wind direction would be expected to shift at least one hundred and eighty degrees throughout the course of the gales passage, thus I used my practice of setting three anchors all attached to a swivel, the details of which are described elsewhere in this book.

I also associate with this anchorage the herbaceous plant Monkshood (Aconitum delphinifolium), found in relative abundance and containing impressive floral specimens within nearby wind protected locations.

This is not to say that this beautiful plant, which is in the Rannunculaceae family, is only found in this locale because it is reasonably common throughout the Aleutian Islands but usually found only in similar damp protected locations.

It was mainly the phytotoxin from this plant with which Aleuts used to anoint their arrowheads, spears, and whale harpoons to add the highly effective neurotoxin which this plant contains within its flowers, leaves, stems, and roots.

After leaving Three Arm Bay I again went around to the Pacific side of Adak island to discover that Adak's southern coastline is somewhat atypical concerning the Aleutian Islands.

Specifically, there appears to be several potentially safe anchorages during storm force winds, however I did not fully explore.

The south coast of Adak island is very spectacular because the low angle southern dip of the volcanic flows has been eroded by the sea and a jagged cliff bound open coast has been created, along with many sea caves and narrow entrances into potentially well sheltered anchorages.

I turned into Boot Bay and then turned in again at the north end of Elf Island, set two anchors, two shorelines, and prepared for strong winds.

Williwaws do not often arrive on the windward side of

an island; however, I was now on the leeward side of Elf Island but unfortunately during my month long stay in this anchorage, gale force winds did not arrive.

There is a mysterious feeling of comfort and safety experienced when securely anchored within a well protected bay during extreme weather.

I habitually consider a well protected anchorage such as Elf Island as a possible entire winter anchorage.

This Elf island site contained all the necessary components of such a secure winter anchorage, which are isolation, potential for violent weather, all direction protection, freshwater, easy shore access with abundant walking routes and an abundant source of suitable firewood on nearby beaches.

The attractions of this anchorage during my visit also included tufted and horned puffins as well as sea otters.

Close on hand to this anchorage were two past Aleut habitation sites, one of which contained a wholly protected one hundred meter long by five-meter-wide access channel, which terminated at the habitation sites kayak beach.

I rowed my skiff using one of my several pairs of stout Chilean oars to the North Pacific open ocean side of Elf Island and approached closely the mouths of four separate sea caves.

The largest of this group of caves seemed to be formed along the shear zones of faults in the volcanic rock flows.

These cracks often contained sheared and shattered rock throughout their length which could often be physically traced from above approximately one hundred meters inland.

It is precisely this shattered rock which is the source

of weakness which is exploited by the ocean waves and over time results in long and narrow sea caves.

I estimated that the largest cave I observed on this Elf Island site was in the order of five meters in diameter and greater than one hundred meters long.

There is a period when the water either rushes into or out of the cave, if an Aleut in a kayak wanted to safely enter, one must not be caught in a narrow and dark cave without the ability to turn around, therefore complete entry on one surge was required, or alternatively, predetermined interior cave rest points would be required during the intermittent periods of contrary surge current.

Also, possibly the kayak paddler could simply back paddle in almost total darkness and thus hold station during periods of contrary cave surge current.

Aleut people made burial chambers within some of these caves and entered and exited in their kayaks, thus whatever their procedure, this is an impressive, skilful, and daring people.

Throughout this second visit to the Aleutians, I identified seventy-six species of plants and fifty-three species of birds.

One week into my passage from the Andreanof Group within the central Aleutian island chain on a course for the southern west coast of Vancouver Island, the vessel was coasting downwind at near hull speed on a far reach, I was sitting on the leeward transom box and was probably involved in my seemingly never-ending northern hemisphere vigil for the Short-Tailed Albatross.

I then became aware that I was being chaperoned by five almost vessel length Minke whales.

This species is quite common in this portion of the

north Pacific Ocean and this group of whales appeared to be keeping station with me at less than one boat length on both the port and starboard sides.

They accompanied me for about fifteen minutes and would periodically dart forward and circle away from the vessel's course, then again take up station at less than a single boat length distance on both my port and starboard sides.

As noted, the vessel was charging along and was controlled only by the servo pendulum steering gear, thus I was merely the spectator when the whale on the starboard side darted forward as usual however did not turn away from the vessel's course but rather directly into its course, and there, directly in front of the vessel's surging bow did the whale appear to linger.

I looped my arm around one of the twin backstays and braced for a jolt, but nothing, and as I passed directly over the whale, I peered down on the port side and there not far below the bottom of the keel was the whale, who appeared to be peering up at me.

These mammals are clearly in their element and appear keenly aware of space, speed, and distance.

SHIPMATES

Patricia in Anaho Bay on the Marquesian island of Nuku Hiva just before my return to Victoria in 1996

Patricia has tried valiantly to overcome her proneness to sea sickness; however, this has not been successful. Patricia would typically gain her sea legs after a few days if sea conditions were what I would describe as less than sea state six, however when more agitated seas returned so did the seasickness which would then persist until almost calm conditions returned.

Thus, for offshore voyages two and three, I would always pick up and deposit Patricia at an international airport closest to a secure anchorage.

It appears that most mariners acquire their sea legs in 24-48 hours, and after such time regardless of the passage length or sea conditions encountered, do not again suffer sea sickness.

There are exceptions concerning this observation, I can experience symptoms of seasickness when I experience fear regardless of how long I have been at sea, although it results in a feeling of nauseousness but not vomiting. Personally, fear also manifests symptoms such as loose bowels, dry mouth, difficulty making decisions, and dizziness.

Examples of such instances of fear have been induced by my vessel being physically pushed aside by the bow wave of a freighter, loss of visibility in narrow Chilean channels synchronous with cold front passage in the company of strong onshore wind.

As well as the fear generating circumstances during arrivals off an open coast, usually uncharted, poorly charted, when I am not one hundred percent certain of my exact position while off a lee shore, or occasionally while using a low detail nineteenth century chart in the company of poor visibility and strong onshore winds.

Throughout all three of my offshore voyages, I was not to be without one of four notable shipmates, they were all the four-legged variety: a cat.

My first was a part Siamese female named Wrangie which we first acquired in Terrace, British Columbia and at the age of four years she started accompanying me sailing out of Prince Rupert, during the second phase of my coastal sailing training, this phase I termed "serving as a journeyman seaman".

Extending this metaphor, my apprenticeship stage had been completed in Georgia Strait in my first sailboat which was a lightly built twenty-four-foot fibreglass sloop.

After moving to Terrace, I decided to buy my second sailing vessel which was a Spencer 31 fibreglass sloop.

It was this vessel upon which Wrangie would accompany me on my perpetual two-, three-, and four-day weekend trips as well as a two-month summer coastal voyage along with a one-month winter coastal voyage.

Sailing this vessel during this period of my training program, it was not uncommon for me to make mistakes in judgment which resulted in damaged equipment, damage to the vessel, and bumps, bruises, and muscle strains to my body.

Identical philosophy as described concerning the first sailing vessel in Georgia Strait, the philosophy of increasing the maximum wind velocity was also applied to Alcidae II while sailing out of Prince Rupert.

Once confidence had been achieved at a maximum wind velocity, Wrangie and I would search for a new and higher wind velocity, not with fear or trepidation but rather anticipation.

The Prince Rupert area of the British Columbia coast was ideal because there is not a shortage of strong winds.

The Alcidae II period witnessed in addition to the constantly increasing wind velocity, also ample experience regarding hank-on sail handling, anchoring, navigating, electronic communications, and all facets of vessel repair skills.

Wrangie also accompanied me on my first offshore voyage to French Polynesia in 1995 as well as the thirty-four-day return passage from Anaho Bay on the north coast of Nuku Hiva in the Marquesas to Victoria harbour, aboard Alcidae III, a thirty-nine-foot steel cutter.

Upon returning in 1996 we lived on the vessel and I am left with the memory of Wrangie on my lap listening to the obligatory Saturday afternoon opera, near the end of which she had a stroke and immediately suffered great pain and became paralyzed in her hind legs.

We took her to the veterinarian who advised us there was little recovery opportunity for our fourteen-year-old companion, thus she was euthanized, I remember carrying her still warm body wrapped in a blanket to our onshore Victoria home, where we buried her under a fifty-year-old apple tree.

Patricia soon found me a new shipmate, whom we named Minou.

The French mariners that we had met while in French Polynesia had a proclivity to the name Minou, used for felines as well as special friends of the female persuasion.

Minou was tiny and one hundred percent Siamese.

She took several days to habituate herself to us and the vessel, but once habituated she and I were essentially inseparable.

Minou accompanied me on my second fifteen-month duration, thirteen thousand nautical mile second training voyage in 2000/2001, which was to find us both in Hawaii, Palmyra Atoll, Christmas Atoll, Kanton, Butaritari, Majuro, Likiep, and the Aleutian Islands.

Upon returning to Victoria in the fall of 2001, we moved from the vessel into our house where Minou adored the free range of our garden and immediately claimed and commenced defending 'her' territory.

In October 2004 Minou and I left from Barkley Sound which is on the west coast of Vancouver Island on what I termed my "third voyage of discovery", whose purpose was to fulfill my dream, first conceived in my early twenties in southern Spain.

In the late spring of 2004, we had sold the house in Victoria and bought a nearby condo, Minou had been left in the sold but not yet possessed house, as pets were not permitted in the condo.

I stayed on the vessel during this period and would return everyday to the house to continue to transport nautical equipment and supplies to boat, usually loading the vehicle early each day.

It was my intention that Minou, who knew the house and yard would be comfortable even without my nightly presence.

Minou had always shown fear and refusal ever to enter my vehicle, however after the third night alone in the house, I found her sitting in the back of the vehicle which had been loaded and was ready for departure, thus our short nocturnal separation was terminated and Minou and I subsequently both lived on the boat from that spring until our fall departure.

In the order of three years later I remember sitting on my vessel's settee in Costa Rica with Minou on my lap and distinctly palpating an enlarged gland where the lower jawbone approaches the throat.

I had hoped that this may be a result of an infection such as tooth decay, however I could see no obviously damaged teeth.

It was then time to set sail for Panama, upon arrival off Chorcha - after several harmless mud and sand bank groundings in the uncharted shallow river-, the vessel was securely anchored on a swivel in a small tidal and muddy river containing crocodiles of similar size to the skiff.

After several weeks in Panama the lump had not receded but rather enlarged, with the addition of a matching lump on the other side of the throat.

We attended a veterinarian in a small city named David, who stated he could operate and remove the lumps.

I knew this was risky, but I was willing to try, however upon arriving at the clinic with Minou at the appointed time he had changed his mind and now stated that such an operation was too risky and estimated that Minou had no more than six months to live, I recall I did not emotionally handle this revelation in a stoic manner.

The veterinarian prescribed Prednisone and I bought a one-year supply.

The Prednisone immediately permitted Minou to again swallow both soft food and drink water without pain.

A few weeks later Patricia flew back to Canada and Minou and I headed for the Galapagos Islands.

This is a relatively short voyage; however, it is far from trivial due to contrary winds and currents, numerous Panama Canal inbound and outbound freighters, and hot and humid conditions.

I later was to look at a picture of Minou taken the day before her and I shoved off from Panama, and it must have been obvious to all but me that she was deteriorating at a rapid pace and would not likely live for the promised six months.

My seamanship skills rest upon principles such as planning for future courses of action based on what may occur, although these usually concerned only nautical or vessel maintenance issues.

I now applied this same pre-planning aforethought process to Minou's worsening condition and decided that I must physically end her suffering when the time arose that she was no longer able to eat or drink.

Less than a week after leaving Panama Minou stopped eating soft food due to excessive pain during swallowing.

I interpreted this as a disaster, because it was mixed with soft food that I provided the ground up Prednisone, her throat was just too painful for me to attempt forcing pills.

Less than twenty-four hours later I was in my sea bunk with the ever-present Minou lying beside me, just within the lee board, when she goes up to drink from her own special sea glass, from which she had been previously capable of drinking even during very violent sea conditions.

She would wrap her front paws around the top of the fixed in position English pub pint glass and on occasion her hind legs would swing back and forth with the motion of the ship while she drank.

On this occasion however, I listened intently to hear the anticipated lapping sound of successful drinking but heard nothing, upon observation I saw she was very thirsty and repeatably attempting to drink but it was just too painful.

My threshold for action concerning Minou's suffering had been reached.

I waited another hour but Minou now without Prednisone medication could not eat or drink.

With the assistance of a deck bucket of sea water, I put Minou out of her pain, and it seemed, as suddenly as her suffering had been terminated, mine intensified, I had not planned for such an emotional outcome.

With the vessel remaining hove-to, I placed her in a weighted sack and put her overboard, watching the sack spiral into the clear tropical ocean, saying my goodbyes to Minou.

When Minou had disappeared into the depths I turned

my head skyward, there was a magnificent Swallow-Tailed Gull hovering not four meters directly above my cockpit.

I inform myself I am not a spiritual person, however to this point in the voyage as well as subsequently, I had never seen a Swallow-Tailed Gull at sea, this seabird is arguably the most beautiful gull in the world, certainly the most beautiful member of the gull genus that I have had the opportunity to see.

The spiritual straw to which I may have been clutching, would be the interpretation that this exquisitely beautiful Swallow-Tailed gull represented Minou's departing spirit.

I immediately got underway as well as commencing having a bit too much scotch whisky, which did nothing to dull my emotional pain, writing this several years later I find the long-ago experienced emotions have not completely departed.

The nine-year duration third voyage was to witness me loosing two feline shipmates in a sudden manner, and the immediate as well as long term emotional distress is difficult to stow.

I arrived a week or so later at San Cristobal Island in the Galapagos, the Galapagos Islands must be considered one of the magnificent jewels in the world.

The Galapagos is one of the few locations in the world where one can view the large Waved Albatross, during my final approach I was fortunate to see several from a range of less than one hundred meters.

The Ecuadoran Navy gave me only two weeks to remain in the Galapagos, as well I was not to be permitted leave the harbour thus, I bicycled most of the island and was fortunate for the opportunity to mingle with a local Ecuadorian family who ran a local restaurant and owned an acreage in the island's interior.

One morning at 7 AM, I was bicycling through the village on my way to geologize and botanize when I saw a Siamese cat pass in front of me and enter a restaurant.

Cats are prohibited on the Galapagos; thus, this sight was both unexpected and demanded my immediate attention and action.

I immediately stopped, propped the bike against the restaurant wall and entered.

Little English is spoken on this island but by this time in my third voyage I had learned to speak Spanish in a very functional manner, I had essentially refused to speak English during the interval when Patricia was not onboard.

Upon entering the restaurant, I saw a lady who turned out to be the restaurant owner cradling the cat in her arms, I approached and asked if she knew of any kittens that may be available.

She was at first skeptical -probably because cats are illegal-, thus I poured out my story of my Minou at sea, her heart softened as I am sure I presented in Spanish quite an animated and possibly emotional description, most single-handed sailors when the opportunity presents itself tend to talk a bit too much.

She then told me that there were not kittens available on this island as they are illegal on the entire Galapagos, however there may be Siamese kittens available at her aunt's residence on Isla Floriana.

I inquired for the phone number and immediately called after thanking this lovely lady in a manner which was probably somewhat excessively effusive.

The lady who answered the phone on Isla Floriana

sounded younger than the retirement aged restaurant owner's aunt and was somewhat suspicious as again, cats are illegal.

I of course would have a strong Gringo accent and manner of speech, however I poured out me at sea story again to which she listened to in silence, afterwards she said her mother who was indeed the restaurant owner's aunt had died the previous week.

It was now my turn for silence, the deceased aunt's daughter surely sensed my awkwardness, probably utilizing that worldwide innate female ability to perceive the presence or absence of sincerity.

She stated that indeed they did have Siamese kittens and she would be pleased to give me one, or more than one if I so wished.

She explained what I was to say to the local Ecuadorian Navy harbour master to prevent my being arrested -Isla Floriana is a prohibited island for foreign vessels such as Alcidae III-, and provided directions concerning the location of her house.

I arrived off Isla Floriana, followed the daughter's instructions, and arrived chez elle with a plastic carry all bag.

My cat carrier might have been a bit too obvious for the Ecuadorian Navy representative, whom I advised that I had only stopped for an hour or two to change a non-functional alternator.

I was given a tiny Siamese male kitten which I wrapped in a t-shirt and put in the shopping bag, -there were more kittens available however they all disappeared under a building-, walking back to the beach and waiting skiff I decided his name must be Florito.

I returned to the anchored sailboat and within one hour

had the skiff loaded, anchor hauled and stowed for the sea, and was underway.

Florito was not to experience the sensation of coming to anchor again for forty-three days as we passed within sight of Easter Island but were unable to land, followed by a momentary anchorage at Ducie Atoll where I was to see my first Giant Petrel, and finally a mile offshore sail past off the south end of Henderson Atoll, before finally shaping a direct course for the south entrance of the Gambier Group in southern French Polynesia.

Just to leeward of Henderson Atoll

We passed intentionally within a mile of Henderson Atoll because it is one of only three raised atolls in the world, Makatea just east of Tahiti is also a raised atoll.

Raised atolls have been elevated above sea level due to a peripheral bulge in the earth's lithosphere, caused by something heavy which is located at just the right distance.

Henderson is raised due the deflection caused by the weight of Pitcairn Island -mutiny on the Bounty fame-, and Makatea is raised due the weight of the island of Tahiti.

The passage from the Galapagos to Gambier was a duration of forty-three days, which had included those few hours anchored at Ducie Atoll.

I found Gambier to be the most agreeable climate and tropical island that I have visited on any of my three off-shore voyages.

Florito and I left the magnificent Mangereva anchorage after using up our entire ninety day maximum permissible stay and set sail for Isla de Chiloe off the Chilean coast.

Florito was but four weeks old when he was shanghaied from Isla Floriana and had screamed seemingly continuously for the better part of the first thirty-six hours, then he accepted me without apparent reservation, and we were to be the best of friends until his untimely loss. I took him to a Puerto Montt Chilean veterinarian to be castrated, we were on the bus and he in his carrying case when a Chilean lady boarded the bus with a poodle under each arm.

Florito saw this and immediately started screaming at the dogs at a volume and with an aggressive tone which I had not previously heard.

The two dogs cowered under the lady's jacket, the bus full of occupants found humour and smiles such as I have only witnessed among Latinos.

When Patricia visited in Chilean Patagonia, Florito would not accept her and would continually threaten in a very physical manner.

I was too loose Florito overboard on my voyage south to the Beagle Channel, which is detailed in another chapter as well as my acquisition of Ede in Puerto Eden.

I have previously described many of Ede's singular habits both ashore and regarding the skiff.

Ede's preferred but precarious sitting position on the

skiff's tiny wooden bow plate would on occasion result in her being unexpectedly catapulted into the sea due to the skiff hitting an unexpected, submerged rock or log, however she proved to be a natural swimmer and would return immediately to the skiff, swim to the amidships lowest free board oarlock location, reach up and sink her ample meat hooks into a wooden gunnel strip and pull herself back onboard.

After an appropriate shake and curt verbal comment, she would regain her bow position.

Within an isolated anchorage on the west coast of Vancouver Island I awoke one morning to what sounded like Ede calling from shore, upon reaching the deck I found that indeed she was calling from shore, thus she had swum ashore after going overboard.

I habitually left a bumper amidships on either side of the anchored vessel with which she would usually haul herself back aboard, however they were not used on this one occasion.

The bumper system was routinely utilized because there were many instances while at anchor that she would enter through the open galley porthole and appear inside the cabin in a sopping wet condition.

Ede would routinely march with me through locations such as Chilean and Argentinian Patagonia, Brazilian coastal jungle, Kerguelen, New Caledonia, and the Aleutian Islands, whether we travelled a few hundred meters or three kilometres.

Often, she would get sidetracked, tired, or if in the tropics overheated and would stop, refusing to proceed.

I would then mentally record where she had stopped and upon returning, often a few hours later, whistle and emerging from dense vegetation, there she was.

Often during anchorage days when I remained onboard, she would 'ask' to go ashore, I would drop her off in the skiff, return to the anchored vessel and several hours later she would appear in the exact place where I had earlier dropped her and gaze and call in an expectant manner, which was my instructions to collect her.
I do not expect I will be sufficiently fortunate to have such a cat again!

Ede in her landing position once the skiff is within two meters of shore.

Partial view of Mathiew Hammond who was assisting in collecting firewood gathering tools from the sailing vessel.

AFTERWARD

My post nautical lifestyle seems not overly different in the five major areas of interest than had been my previous nautical lifestyle, although in the physical sense the nautical portion is no longer present.

These interests include the five major components, birds, botany, geology, any mammals I am sufficiently fortunate to see, and indigenous ethnological sites and practices.

Ede and I now spend six months per year in the mountains of British Columbia, preferably in isolation.

During June and July, I prefer to set up camp in the sub alpine with the option of making multiple trips on the motorbike, mountain bike, or hiking to the alpine, which normally takes me to an elevation of 2200 to 3200 meters above sea level.

During the last week of August when blooming wildflowers start to become scarce and the hummingbirds begin their southern migration which may take them as far as Central America, I return to spend the winter six-month period in Victoria.

Not dissimilar behaviour to the hummingbirds who are embarking on long voyages to climates which are less harsh.

I clearly recall numerous occasions where I left cold latitudes bound for warm, although I have also on several occasions untaken voyages in the opposite direction.

The comparison with hummingbirds is somewhat tenuous in that I would often leave with a fully stocked vessel containing an almost innumerable number of supplies, whereas the hummingbirds leave to travel a similar distance with nothing more than they can carry and must make do with what nature provides.

SHIP'S REFERENCE SECTION

1-Fueguinos
Fotografías siglos XIX y XX
Imágenes e imaginarios del fin del mundo
pehuén
Editores: Margarita Alavarado P., Carolina Odone C., Felipe Maturana D., Dánae Fiore
Santiago de Chile, 2007

2-Islands
H.W. Menard
Scientific American Library
A division of HPFLP
New York

3-The Atolls of Mururoa and Fangataufa (French Polynesia)
Volumes I, II, & III
Direction des Centres D'Experimentations Nucleaires

4-Keinikkan Im Melan Aelon Kein (Plants and Environments of the Marshall Islands)
by
Mark Merlin, Alfred Capelle, Thomas Keene, James Juvik and James Maragos

1st printing 1994
2nd printing 1997
Funding provided by the
John D. and Catherine T. MacArthur Foundation, Chicago, Illinois, USA

5-Manual of the FLOWERING PLANTS of HAWAI'I
Volumes 1 & 2
Warren L. Wagner
Derral R. Herbst
S. H. Sohmer
University of Hawai'i Press
Bishop Museum Press

6-Flora Silvestre De Chile
zona araucana
Quinta Edición
Adriana E. Hoffmann J.
ISBN 956-7743-01-0

7-Flora Patagonian
Claudia Guerrido & Damian Fernandez
Fantástico Sur
ISBN 978-956-8007-16-4

8-L'Archipel Des Marquises
Emmanuel Deschamps & Paule Laudon
Les éditions Le Motu
61 rue des Peupliers, 92100, Boulogne

9-Ethnobotany of Pohnpei
Michael J. Balick
University of Hawai'i Press, Honolulu
The New York Botanical Garden

10-Tropical & Subtropical Trees

by Margaret Barwick
Chief Editor: Anton van der Schans
Thames & Hudson
ISBN: 0-500-51181-0

11-Plantes Utiles De Poynésie
par Paul Pétard
Éditions Haere Po No Tahiti
ISBN 2-904 171-06-1

12- Aleuts: Survivors of the Bering Land Bridge
William S. Laughlin
Harcourt Brace College Publishers
ISBN 0-03-081269-0

13-Seabirds
by Peter Harrison
Houghton Mifflin Company, Boston
ISBN 0-395-60291-2

14-Patagonia & Tierra Del Fuego Nautical Guide
Mariolina Rolfo and Giorgio Ardizzi
Editrice Incontri Nautici
ISBN 88-85986-34-X

15- The Journals of Captain James Cook on His Voyage of Discovery
'The Voyage of The Resolution and Discovery'
1776-1780
Edited by J.C. Beaglehole
Cambridge at the University Press
1967

16- Mision Al Cabo De Hornos
Louis-Ferdinand Martial
Zagier & Urruty Publications

2005
ISBN 1-879568-99-3

17- Identification of tropical woody plants in the absence of flowers
A field guide (2nd edition)
Roland Keller
Birkhauser Verlag
ISBN 3-7643-6453-X18- Food Plants of The World

18-Ben-Erik van Wyk
2005
Briza Publications
ISBN 1 875093 56 7

19- Medicinal Plants of The World
Ben-Erik van Wyk
Michael Wink
2004
Briza Publications
ISBN 1 875093 44 3

20- Mind-Altering and Poisonous Plants of The World
Michael Wink
Ben-Erik van Wyk
2008
Briza Publications
ISBN 978-1-875093-71-7

ACKNOWLEDGEMENT

Thank you to Fran Hammond aboard MV Maia from New Zealand who kindly permitted me to use the cover photo as well as all photos depicting the Aleutians.

Thanks also to her young son Matthew Hammond for requesting to accompany me out to the anchored sailing vessel to collect my firewood gathering tools, otherwise I would have been without the photos of myself and Ede in the skiff.

Thank you to my cousin Jacquie Clair who photocopied and stored my 9 year supply of emails.

Finally thank you to Patricia who has supported my nautical endeavours since 1978.

ABOUT THE AUTHOR

Greg Soroka

Greg Soroka was born in Vancouver, British Columbia on Canada's west coast in June 1949.

He has spent his entire life interested in nature and determined in his early twenties that a sailboat could provide access to a lifestyle containing a suitable amount of solitude and to some of earth's isolated locations.

He presently resides with his spouse Patricia, in Victoria, BC.

www.ingramcontent.com/pod-product-compliance
Lightning Source LLC
LaVergne TN
LVHW050930080826
845145LV00001B/288

9781771369534